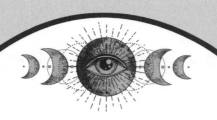

*The*

# MODERN WITCHCRAFT

## Book of

# Astrology

### YOUR COMPLETE GUIDE to EMPOWERING *Your Magick* with the *Energy* of the *Planets*

Julia Halina Hadas

Adams Media
New York London Toronto Sydney New Delhi

Adams Media
An Imprint of Simon & Schuster, Inc.
100 Technology Center Drive
Stoughton, Massachusetts 02072

First Adams Media hardcover edition January 2023

ADAMS MEDIA and colophon are trademarks of Simon & Schuster.

For information about special discounts for bulk purchases, please contact Simon & Schuster Special Sales at 1-866-506-1949 or business@simonandschuster.com.

The Simon & Schuster Speakers Bureau can bring authors to your live event. For more information or to book an event contact the Simon & Schuster Speakers Bureau at 1-866-248-3049 or visit our website at www.simonspeakers.com.

Interior design by Kellie Emery
Interior images © 123RF
Energy center image by Eric Andrews

Manufactured in the United States of America

1 2022

Library of Congress Cataloging-in-Publication Data has been applied for.

ISBN 978-1-5072-2015-3
ISBN 978-1-5072-2016-0 (ebook)

# Dedication

*For all the mystic dreamers,*
*staring up in wonder at the cosmic*
*blanket of the night sky.*

# Acknowledgments

To my amazing friends, colleagues, and teachers from The Mystic Dream (now known as Datura Trading Co.): Storm, Devin, Chas, Paul, Ana, Lia, and Jessica. The Mystic Dream was the perfect nebula to birth this cosmic witch. Learning from and working with all of you in that magickal space brought me to be the witch and healer I am today. Special thanks to Paul Bogle for guiding me on my astrological path and supporting my exploration of the stars as they pertain to my soul.

I want to thank all at Adams Media who have made this book possible, especially Rebecca and Laura for your guidance and insight. Writing this book has been a celestial dream, and thank you to all of Adams Media for the amazing work you do.

And most of all, thank you to the lucky stars in my life, Ryan and Baxter, who continue to mesmerize me and keep me centered in your steady gravitational pull.

# CONTENTS

# Introduction

Our vast night sky—which cradles the earth and the celestial gems that dance upon it—has guided humankind since the dawn of time. The practice of astrology is both an art and a science that has helped people all over the world find meaning and purpose. You can inform your witchcraft practice and supercharge your magick using these astrological energies with *The Modern Witchcraft Book of Astrology*.

Astrology and witchcraft are a natural pairing—they both promote self-discovery, celebrate the natural world, and empower you to fulfill your dreams. Whether you're well versed in witchcraft and astrology or just beginning to learn about these fascinating topics, *The Modern Witchcraft Book of Astrology* will help you combine the wonder of astrology and the magick of witchcraft. In Part 1, you will learn about the planets (plus comets and other celestial bodies) and houses; their meanings, myths, and associations; and how to use them to empower your magickal work. Then you will explore the hidden power of each zodiacal sign.

In Part 2, you will find spells of all kinds—potions, crystal grids, talismans, meditations, and more—that are infused with astrological principles. You'll take advantage of the timing of planetary movements, the traits of each sun sign, and the power of each element. Start the zodiacal year off on a strong foot with an Aries Celestial Spark Meditation, which can harness Aries's power to initiate new beginnings. Add some Leo Solar-Spiced Creativity Syrup to your morning caffeine during Leo's new moon to spark your creativity. Try the Gaia Grounding Meditation when the Sun passes through Taurus—there is no better time to focus on connecting to the earth and recentering yourself. You'll also uncover ways to be flexible with your astrological timing, and you'll even learn how to layer spells and rituals together to create the ultimate divine magick.

There are endless ways that astrology can honor and celebrate your unique position within the universe. Your witchcraft practice will thrive when you are in sync with the movements and insights of celestial bodies around our beloved planet. Tune in to that special power and discover how the meaning and magick in the night sky can support your healing, encourage your growth, and initiate the manifestation of your dreams.

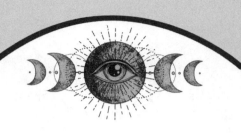

# PART I

# UNDERSTANDING ASTROLOGY AND MAGICK

# Chapter 1

# WITCHCRAFT AND ASTROLOGY

From ancient prophets mapping the planets' movements in the night sky to divine a god's will to the modern witch watching the lunar eclipse out her window as she lights a candle, the blending of witchcraft and astrology is a time-honored tradition. While their roles in society have certainly shifted over the centuries, astrology and witchcraft continue to provide valuable insight to anyone wishing to learn more about themselves and unravel and use the magick and power of the stars.

In this chapter, you will uncover astrology's ancient origins, not just as a spiritual practice and mystical art but also as an integral part of society that inspired the sciences and development of civilizations. You will also learn how you can begin to make astrology a powerful and integral part of your magickal practices in meaningful and accessible ways.

## THE ANCIENTS AND ASTROLOGY

Astrology combines the mathematical calculations of movements of the stars; the study of astronomy and deep-sky objects; and the spiritual art of myth, meaning, and determining why we are here. It was an integral, central part of ancient society. From calculating the seasons and when to plant or harvest crops, to forecasting the weather or interpreting the ideal day to celebrate a god, astrology was ingrained in every aspect of life. Even as far back as ten thousand to eighteen thousand years ago in the Lascaux caves of France, ancient peoples appear to have painted the bull of the Taurus constellation in hues of white, red, and brown, marking the importance of the stars to our earliest ancestors. Astrology helped people uncover the secrets of the galaxy and understand their place in the universe (spiritually and literally), and still does to this day.

In ancient times, the stars were not just symbols of the will of the gods; they were also the very calendar that marked the rhythm of life of ancient peoples. The ever-changing positions of stars in the night sky marked the coming and going of seasons. Key stars, like Regulus of the Leo constellation, once marked the coming of summer when it greeted the horizon just after sunset. To understand why the stars change position, you have to go back even further in time, to the conception of the solar system.

### *Earth, The Cosmos, and the Celestial Sphere*

Due to our unique position within the solar system and the universe, we experience a rotation of the night sky throughout the year. The earth orbits the sun on an axis that leans at an angle of 23.5 degrees. Even as the earth revolves around the sun, the earth's axis always points at the same direction in the night sky. And the earth itself spins as it makes the larger orbit.

To visualize this, you can hold an orange (a symbol of the sun not just in color but in energy too) in one hand. Then, tilt the index finger of your other hand at a slight angle. Rotate your index finger around the orange, always keeping the finger pointing in the same direction. Imagine that your finger is also rotating as it orbits the orange. Visualizing solar rays shining from the orange, you can see how different parts of the earth are exposed to more sunlight during different times of the year. We also experience different views of the night sky throughout the year as the earth makes its orbit around the sun. So, whichever stars were visible at different times of night and different times of year was linked to the coming and going of seasons.

To make matters slightly more complicated, the earth's axis has a very slight wobble to it (balanced in part by the moon), and so while it is mostly stable, the positions of the equinoxes and solstices, and therefore the start of the seasons, actually shift zodiac sign every 2,160 years, for a 26,000-year cycle.

# WORSHIP, WITCHCRAFT, AND THE STARS

In the modern era, people define witchcraft in different ways—some see it as worshipping the earth and her cycles and seasons; some call down the power of the gods to bless their endeavors, petitioning them with offerings and invoking them through sacred symbols or words; some combine herbs for their metaphysical properties to call in prosperity; and some do it all. How you define witchcraft is personal.

In ancient times, the concepts of astrology and witchcraft were inseparable. To ancient cultures, the gods were the stars and their religion. People petitioned gods with offerings and sacred symbols for healing or to get their blessing for different endeavors. Ancient worship and astrology were inseparable from magick.

The first record of the intermingling of astrology and worship comes from ancient Babylon, where the gods were the planets. Each god ruled various domains in which they could be petitioned for blessings. For example, the morning and evening star Venus became associated with Ishtar, goddess of growth, fertility, love, and sometimes war. The Babylonians devoted their cities to various planets that were synonymous with their gods. They also built multitiered towers, called "ziggurats," with a terrace for each of the seven planets that they knew of at the time. Thus, the unit of the week was developed—one day for each of the seven planets. The custom of assigning hours of the day to each of the seven planets was later adopted by the Romans.

## Religion, Culture, and Astrology

From the ancient priests atop temple ziggurats mapping the stars to understand the will of the gods, to the modern witch using the magick of the full moon, astrology and witchcraft have maintained importance throughout many cultures, religious practices, and times. Easter in Christianity, for example, is usually the Sunday after the first full moon following the vernal, or spring, equinox, and Ramadan starts with the new moon in Libra. All of the oldest major religions still use the celestial timing established in ancient times as the determining factor in their celebrations.

Even the names of the week are dedicated to the planets and gods, although some of the days' names have been adapted from Norse mythology: Sunday as the sun's day, Monday as the moon's, Tuesday from Tiw (a god of war similar to Mars), Wednesday from Woden/Odin (akin to Mercury), Thursday to Thor (Jupiter), Friday to goddess Freya (Venus), and Saturday as Saturn's Day.

# THE BIRTH OF WESTERN ASTROLOGY

Cultures from all over the world developed their own understanding of the stars, and with them, oral myths and tales that explained the power of these celestial objects. While many of the myths we associate with the constellations come from ancient Greece, some date even further back to Babylon and even Sumer (the earliest-known human civilization in Mesopotamia). The seed of modern Western astrology, in particular, was born from the prophets of ancient Babylon, who used the stars to determine the wills of the gods. Mixing these observations from Babylon with those of Egypt and the mathematical calculations of Greece, the foundation of Western astrology was created.

Even certain superstitions came forth from the Babylonian observation of the night sky, such as that a halo around the moon indicates an overcast month.

Babylonian ideas of astrology migrated to Egypt, merging with Egyptian practices of medical and occult astrology. And with Alexander the Great and his conquests, astrological concepts from Egypt, Babylon, and Greece melded to create a whole system of astrology. Today, Western astrology has branched into many different traditions—astro-psychology, vocational astrology, medical astrology, and even relocation astrology.

Astrology wasn't just a way to predict the seasons that guided ancient ways of life; its uses also extended to the personal sphere. Ancient peoples tried to understand more about themselves from their birth charts and orient their plans according to fortuitous astrological placements to gain the blessings of the gods. That's where its connection to witchcraft comes in.

# SUMMONING THE POWER OF THE STARS THROUGH WITCHCRAFT

Principles set forth by astrology can be used as celestial guidance to empower spells in witchcraft practice. For example, you can:

- Charge water with the energy of a particular astrological event.

- Rest and rethink during hectic Mercury retrograde.

- Meditate with the phases of the moon in various signs.

- Cast a spell in alignment with a certain day of the week, such as Wednesday, to call down the power of the god of communication and planet Mercury.

Witches continue to use and honor the magick of celestial alignments in modern times. Understanding and applying astrology as a witch doesn't have to be an elective tool to use only on occasion—it can be an everyday way to engage in an active relationship with your orientation in the cosmos. When you have an understanding of the astrological seasons, you can develop a potent relationship with the magick of each sign, planet, and star, and use this to amplify your spells.

Astrology can be an active partner in your practice that doesn't just help boost your magick. It can also help you dance to the rhythm of the universe and call upon the power of the stars as you recognize and celebrate your own cosmic identity.

## Chapter 2

# ASTROLOGICAL ELEMENTS

Since the dawn of time, fire, water, earth, and air have framed human experience on the earth. These elements (referred to as "classical elements" in astrology) were observable markers of the everyday experience of life—fire for heat and light, air for breath and communication, earth for the material form of all life and nourishment, water for liquids and sustenance. These elements defined ancient life, and from them, zodiac signs were born as an expression of that element's celestial power. While in modern science, the term "elements" means something completely different, the meaning, symbolism, and power of these core ancient elements remain a source of knowledge and power in both astrology and magick.

Understanding the elemental foundations of astrology can help you grasp and call on the specific powers of various signs, planets, and asteroids. The information in this chapter will help you understand the elemental building blocks of astrology so you can identify the challenges in your life and remedy them through magick by summoning the power of a given element through its zodiacal expression. Engaging with these elements in an active way can connect you to understanding, healing, and increased magickal potency. Let's look at the different elements, their modalities of expression, and what they can mean for your astrological spellcasting.

# ASTROLOGICAL MODALITIES/ELEMENTAL EXPRESSION: CARDINAL, FIXED, MUTABLE

In astrology, each element is given one of three modalities—cardinal, fixed, and mutable—to help further describe the way that element's energy might take form. These three modalities give way to the three zodiac signs for each element and will help you understand what aspect of air, fire, water, and earth to work with for your astrological magick.

## Cardinal Energy

Cardinal energy is the initiator—it sets things in motion. Like the spark that lights the fire, this type of energy can be used to start projects or even inspire personal drive relating to that element's energy. A lack of cardinal energy can indicate difficulty getting started, whereas too much energy might take the form of starting too many projects or being unable to focus on one thing at a time. To take advantage of cardinal energy, you can look at its respective zodiac signs—Aries (fire), Cancer (water), Libra (air), and Capricorn (earth).

## Fixed Energy

Fixed energy is centered energy—it sustains that element's energy. It is the type of energy to work with in magick to endure and stay true to a purpose. Stubbornness can be an indication of too much fixed energy, whereas a lack of stability in a given element's meaning might hint at a lack of fixed energy. The signs Aquarius (air), Taurus (earth), Leo (fire), and Scorpio (water) can help you work with fixed energy in astrological spells for matters that need persistence, stability, and focus.

## Mutable Energy

Whereas cardinal energy initiates, and fixed energy sustains, mutable energy adapts and connects. Acting as an intermediary for its element, mutable energy changes to match the fluctuations of the reality. However, too much mutable energy can signify restlessness, and too little can indicate an unwillingness to adapt or change. Thus, working with the mutable modality through the signs of Gemini (air), Virgo (earth), Sagittarius (fire), and Pisces (water) can help in matters that require flexibility and connecting ideas to the real world.

Now that you understand how the various modalities by which the classical elements can express themselves, let's look at how this manifests in astrology and through the signs of the zodiac.

# FIRE △

From the candle flame, to the hearth fire, to the brush fire with the power to level houses and forests, the element of fire is the force of life that warms, inspires, and energizes—as well as consumes.

### *Fire Represents Identity/Sense of Self and Energy*

In astrology, fire is often referred to as the energy of identity or sense of vitality—the energy that inspires your body and soul to move in countless ways, whether through art, passion, leadership, creativity, or exercise. Too much fire can manifest as recklessness and uncontrollable explosions or rage, whereas fire deficiencies can appear as a lack of vital energy or difficulty getting excited. At its core, fire represents the flame that "lights the fire" and motivates you to pursue passions, love, and goals.

### *Associated Astrological Signs: Aries, Leo, Sagittarius*

The modalities of fire can be seen in cardinal Aries, the sign that initiates passions and the drive to pursue goals; fixed Leo, which sustains and attracts what it desires in the realms of creative expression and romance; and mutable Sagittarius, which adapts the element of fire for connection through guiding philosophy and spontaneous adventures and social outings.

### *Associated Celestial Bodies: Sun, Mars, Jupiter (shared), Vesta*

Through the sun, we see fire's ability to warm, create, and sustain, and through Mars, we see fire's potential for passion, vitality, and aggression. Some relate Jupiter—the planet of expansion—to fire as well as to the element of air in some astrological practices.

# EARTH ▽

From the mountains that give shape to the earth, to the rumbling earthquakes, to the very ground we build our homes and walk upon, the principle of the earth is vital—it is the foundation upon which humans navigate and experience life.

## Earth Represents Physical Reality and Stability

In astrology, the earth relates to the physical and material realm—the things that you can touch and engage with your senses. The physical manifestation of life around you, your body, your possessions, and even money all fall under the jurisdiction of this classical element. Like the seedling that needs soil to grow, the element of earth provides people with the foundation, stability, and strength upon which to grow. An overabundance of earth can manifest as unmoving, unchanging, and stubborn energy, while a lack of earth can be seen as ungroundedness, a disconnection to reality, or a struggle with material boundaries. Working with earth can remedy restless, ungrounded energy and help you handle the mundane reality of everyday life.

While grounded in practicality and wisdom, the earth is sometimes slow-moving (like a crystal taking millions of years to grow). The earth is what gives form to creation and, through things like food and abundance, supplies what we need to subsist.

## Associated Astrological Signs: Capricorn, Taurus, Virgo

Cardinal earth is expressed through Capricorn, who initiates material manifestation and establishes structure. Earth's stabilizing abilities take center stage in fixed Taurus. And mutable Virgo, through her practicality and organization, connects through community and the harvest of goals that are actualized in the material realm.

## Associated Celestial Bodies: Saturn, Venus, Ceres, Chiron

Saturn encapsulates earth's properties of restraint, stability, and structure. Venus represents earth's ability to nurture, nourish, and revel in the physical pleasures of life.

# WATER ▽

Covering a majority of the planet via deep oceans, raging rapids, placid lakes, and trickling streams, water is the fluid element that represents your capacity to *feel*.

## *Water Represents Feeling and Intuition*

In astrology, the element of water invites you to tune in to your intuition, feelings, and imagination; helps you plunge deep into your subconscious for healing; and encourages you to learn to "go with the flow" in the currents of life. From cross-cultural mythos depicting water as the starting point from which all life emerged, water relates to human emotions and souls—it is the energy and power that move us. Like the groundwater that slips beneath the grass, seeps through the dirt, and roars in caves below, its impact may not always be perceived, but the power of water is always there, deep under the surface.

An overflow of water energy can manifest as turbulent emotional waves or escapism, while a lack or block of water energy can be seen as a general coldness or disconnection from emotions or empathy. Working with water through its respective signs can help enhance your understanding of your emotions; promote forgiveness, compassion, peace, and sympathy; and inspire a strong connection to intuition.

## *Associated Astrological Signs: Cancer, Scorpio, Pisces*

With her ability to connect to emotion and intuition, Cancer represents water's cardinal energy. Through fixed Scorpio, you can experience water's ability to hold fast to intensity and dive deep into water's depths, while still rising to the surface. And you can witness water's mutable ability through Pisces, the sign that goes with the flow and dissolves barriers in connecting to others. Using the expression of water through these signs, you can help focus and heighten your spellwork around matters of intuition, understanding, healing, and emotion.

## *Associated Celestial Bodies: Moon, Neptune, Juno*

On our planet, you can see water influenced by the movement of the moon—the celestial body that relates to your intuition, emotion, and motherly relationships. Through Neptune, you can work with water's unique capacity to dissolve and blend—which is great for magick related to unity, healing, and accessing the depths of psychic, cosmic information.

# AIR ◇

From the air that permeates your lungs, helping you form words and communicate thoughts, to the hawk that glides above and looks down below, air is all about thought, communication, and perspective.

## *Air Represents Communication and Knowledge*

This element can reveal how you think, communicate, and reason, and can even show you how you might be recognized for your thoughts and unique ideas. By helping you communicate, socialize, and share ideas, air is an element of connection. From moving pollen and seeds to influencing the ocean's currents and fueling wildfires and the direction they go, air has the power and capacity to influence and move many things.

While too much air can create scattered, anxious, ungrounded, and emotionally distant energy, a lack of air is stagnant and can indicate an absence of vision, insight, or new ideas. Working with air through astrological magick can help you gain information and perspective, as well as help you think clearly, improve your speech, and be quick and precise with your words.

## *Associated Astrological Signs: Libra, Aquarius, Gemini*

Cardinal Libra can help you see all sides of an issue and execute an action based on weighing and balancing the evidence at hand. Fixed air sign Aquarius helps you retain new and unique thoughts, expanding your horizons and perspective beyond what you may have thought possible. Mutable Gemini highlights air's ability to connect, share ideas, and think on your feet.

## *Associated Celestial Bodies: Mercury, Jupiter (shared), Pallas*

The planet Jupiter represents air by bringing in new opportunities and encouraging expansion. In addition, air is expressed through Mercury, which represents messages, communication, and reasoning.

*Chapter 3*

# THE SIGNS

**M**ost people know their sun sign. From daily horoscopes to birth charts to zodiac-designed gifts, the constellations that make up the zodiac are ever-present in life. But did you ever stop to think how you can use these signs in your magick? Whether the Sun is traveling through Gemini, or Mercury is making a beneficial transit through Virgo, or it's Monday and you want to cast Cancer-aligned spells, you can summon these star signs at a key time to enhance your celestial magick.

In this section, you will learn about the zodiac signs—their strengths and challenges, how they can help you achieve certain goals, and how best to capture their energy. For some signs, you'll discover the ancient myths of the constellations that help us glean more information about their symbolic, mythic, and magickal power in the cosmos. You will uncover the various correspondences you can use to summon the ancient power of these constellations—whether day or time, color, or energy centers. Once you are familiar with the basic information about each of the twelve zodiac signs, you can find additional correspondences (such as suggested crystals) and information like planetary hours in the appendices of this book to enhance your spells even more.

# ARIES

| Aries Season | March 21–April 19 |
|---|---|
| Celestial Bodies | Mars |
| House | First House |

## Aries Themes

True to his cardinal fire nature, active Aries leads the charge into the journey through the zodiacal year with zest and vigor. A highly ambitious sign, Aries can break through barriers, conquer challenges, and achieve accomplishments and victories. Aries's symbol, the ram—the horned sheep that charges headfirst—clearly exemplifies the boldness, aggression, and primal power of this sign. Thus, Aries is naturally a great sign to call on for spells that relate to physicality, vitality, and passion. Within the zodiacal wheel, Aries is the spark that initiates your self-awareness and self-actualization in the world.

## Related Myths

Aries's courage and fearlessness are best exemplified through the Greek myth of Crius, the celestial winged ram that rushed in to save the children of King Athamas. Dashing in to save the children from murder, Aries represents the proactive trailblazer that asserts himself and also pushes for what he feels is right. This is the very same ram whose magickal fur becomes the famous Golden Fleece, a symbol of power and authority. A further testament to Aries's cardinal life force energy, this sign was associated with one of the self-actualizing primordial gods (Amun) in Egyptian mythology, and the hardworking agricultural worker in ancient Babylon.

## Magick

You can add a touch of Aries vivacity to any spell or working via celestial timing, cosmic colors, and sacred symbols. The best time to use Aries's power is during Aries season from March 21 through April 19, when both the Sun and the new moon are aligned in Aries.

Even when the Sun is not shining through Aries, however, there are other ways to time your spells to unlock its power. Access its potency during its full moon in Libra season, or find out when the Moon is in Aries during the other months, and the meaning of that moon phase, for added power. You can also call on this constellation when it rises in the night sky the other ten months of the year or when a planet makes an advantageous transit through Aries. And of course, you can use Aries's ruling planet Mars when it is visible in the sky, in Mars's traditional planetary hours (Appendix F), or on Mars-associated Tuesday.

Just like stars emit different spectrums of light and color, you can employ colors in your cosmic magick. Wear or use passionate, bright colors like red, yellow, orange, and white to imbue more Aries passion, positivity, and creativity into your life—and your spells. Adorn your altar with these fiery shades, select jewelry or accessories that feature these colors, or burn corresponding colored candles for added Aries alignment. Integrating symbols such as the ram and the sharp and direct imagery of its horns can add extra potency to your Aries spells. And since Aries is a cardinal fire sign, candle spells or spells that use burning or the imagery of the spark resonate more potently.

# TAURUS

| ♉ | Taurus Season | April 20–May 20 |
| | Celestial Bodies | Venus, Ceres |
| | House | Second House |

## Taurus Themes

A testament to Taurus's steadfastness, this constellation has been observed since the time of early humans, with depictions dating back to the Lascaux caves in France ten thousand to eighteen thousand years ago. Symbolized by the bull—an ancient symbol of wealth, fertility, and abundance—Taurus is a sign of financial stability and prosperity. Through her fixed expression of earth, Taurus is more grounded and firm than the other earth signs, with unmatched dependability, stability, and stubbornness. But she is also ruled by Venus, planet of pleasure and charm. Thus, Taurus is a sign that revels in the senses and the physical pleasure of being alive, enjoying a stable love life and home, and attracting abundance.

With their heavy, powerful bodies, bulls move at their own speed with dominion over the land they roam. Similarly, Taurus reminds you to connect with your body as a vessel of celestial earth, to hone self-confidence in your space, and to remain steadfast in your desires. With a flash of red fabric, bulls remain transfixed on pursuing their ends—an example of Taurus's iron determination in achieving her goals.

## Related Myths

The Greek myth of Zeus and Europa captures the nobility, determination, and romance of this sign. Zeus, in order to draw the attention and admiration of Princess Europa, turns into a bull and joins the king's herd. With patience, and by being the most refined, regal, and beautiful bull in the herd, Zeus's seduction is successful. Europa climbs atop the bull's back, and Zeus carries her away to the island of Crete, where he reveals himself as a god. The couple has three children, one of which ends up being Minos, the famous king of Crete. The key themes of this myth highlight the patient, refined, and alluring nature of Taurus, but also how, through these qualities, you can attract what you desire. In ancient Mesopotamia, the Taurus constellation was seen as the "Bull of Heaven," sent by the goddess Ishtar when the hero Gilgamesh rejected her advances, connecting Taurus to the planet Venus (with which Ishtar was associated).

## Magick

By timing your Taurus spells, you can call upon this heavenly bull to aid your magickal endeavors. Of course, the best time to use Taurus is during its season from April 20 to May 20, when the Sun travels through this sign. Also blessed with the Taurus new moon, this period is beaming with energy to bless Taurus-favorable endeavors with abundance, stability, and fertility.

There are plenty of other ways to time Taurus spells during various parts of the year. Use the alluring Taurus full moon during Scorpio season, or the magick of the Moon and its phases when it passes through Taurus once a month. Use its bright star Aldebaran or the Pleiades star cluster (known as "The Seven Sisters") to uncover Taurus in the night sky the other ten months of the year and cast a celestial spell under these ancient rising stars. You can also cast celestial magick when a planet makes a beneficial transit through Taurus, when its ruling planet Venus is visible in the sky during Venus's planetary hour, or its ruling day of Friday.

Beyond timing, there are other celestial tools you can use to heighten your Taurus magick, such as color and relevant symbols. Varying shades of green can usher in the verdant, abundant energy of Taurus. Flowery colors such as pastel pinks, yellows, blues, oranges, and reds can summon forth Venusian pleasure and attraction. Symbols such as pentacles, flowers, gems, and money can also strengthen your Taurus magick.

# GEMINI

| | Gemini Season | May 21–June 20 |
|---|---|---|
| | Celestial Bodies | Mercury |
| | House | Third House |

## Gemini Themes

A social and intellectual sign, Gemini exemplifies the desire to communicate and exchange information. Associated with the mutable expression of air, Gemini is adaptable and all about sharing ideas and insights, heightening that air energy of connection and communication.

## Related Myths

Throughout various ancient cultures, Gemini has been symbolized by the image of twins. In ancient Egyptian mythology, the constellation was identified with twin goats or the older/younger version of the god Horus; in ancient Arabia, twin peacocks represented Gemini! As you might imagine from his symbolism, Gemini is a sign of duality—incorporating different ideas and views while also being fickle and changing opinions often. Ruled by Mercury, the planet of communication and travel, Gemini is a fast-moving, talkative, and youthful sign.

To fully understand the dualistic, intermediary qualities of Gemini, you can look at the Greek myth of twins Castor and Pollux, from which the two brightest stars in this constellation derive their name. Seduced by the Greek god Zeus, a Spartan queen gave birth to twin sons— Pollux and Castor. Pollux was the son of Zeus, but Castor had been fathered by the queen's husband, Tyndareus (King of Sparta). As a result, Pollux was immortal, and Castor was mortal, a symbol of dichotomy of the self. These siblings were strong and adventurous (as Gemini energy often is) and were extremely bonded, so when Castor died, Pollux pleaded with Zeus to share his immortality with Castor. The twins were transformed into the Gemini constellation, where they could live together in the heavens for eternity. Through sharing interconnectedness and aspects of the self, the twins were able to level the playing field and live on forever. This air sign is all about relating information, good or bad, and connecting with others through his favored element—air.

### Magick

With the luminous Sun shining through Gemini from May 21 to June 20, and an aligned new moon, this period is the most advantageous for ushering forth Gemini-related magick. When you wish to call upon this ancient constellation outside of this time frame, you can gauge the phase during which the Moon will traverse this sign, as well as the Gemini full moon during Sagittarius season. You can cast a Gemini-aligned spell by using a star chart or website to research when this constellation will rise in the night sky the other ten months of the year, and use the bright stars Castor and Pollux (fittingly representing the heads of these two figures) to locate the constellation as you cast your Gemini spell. Keep an eye out for any favorable transits a planet makes through Gemini, or call upon Mercury when it is visible in the sky, on its favorable day of Wednesday, or during its traditional planetary hour (Appendix F).

Colors related to the mind, such as blue for peaceful thinking, white for clarity, yellow for exciting ideas, violet for the third eye, and sky-associated turquoise, are great colors to use to summon Gemini energy into your wardrobe, altar, or magickal tools. Feathers can be used to represent Mercury's winged feet. You can also include matching imagery to represent twins or air-related tools such as swords (since they slash through the air) and incense; these are all great symbols to empower your Gemini spells.

# CANCER

| Cancer Season | June 21–July 22 |
|---|---|
| Celestial Bodies | Moon, Ceres |
| House | Fourth House |

### Cancer Themes

Following chatty Gemini, deeply psychic and sensitive Cancer invites us to retreat into our shells, like the crab that symbolizes it in the sky. As the cardinal expression of water—the element of feeling and of the soul—Cancer is deeply connected to and uses emotion and intuition as an initiating force. With a hard shell and fierce pincers, crabs are protective and strong. But inside, they are soft and vulnerable, revealing an inner sensitive nature. This works because the crab's protective home (the shell) creates a safe and nurturing space to be vulnerable.

Her rulership by the Moon reflects Cancer's psychic, mysterious nature as well as a sense of moodiness, displayed in the moon's pull on the tides. Cancer's depth of emotion and feeling is seen through her capacity for empathy and empath awareness—the act of being connected to other people's emotions. Cancer is believed to have a special relationship with the dwarf planet Ceres (covered in Chapter 5) in astrology, for Ceres highlights Cancer's mothering energy and tendency to nurture and provide security and warmth.

## Related Myths

The protective yet vulnerable qualities of the Cancer sign can be seen in ancient mythology. A giant crab was immortalized in the sky by the goddess Hera after it tried to thwart and pinch Hercules in his battle against the Hydra. The crab Crios was immortalized after battling against a giant squid in an attempt to save Poseidon's sea nymphs.

## Magick

Cancer is especially useful when it comes to redecorating your home environment to be a nurturing space, reassessing personal goals, releasing emotions, or deepening your spiritual connection and inner awareness. June 21–July 22 is the ideal time to tap in to Cancer energy, with both the Sun and new moon aligned in this sign. But since the Moon is the ruling astrological body of Cancer, its presence at any time is a potent way to align Cancer spells.

If none of these options come at a convenient time, you can always use the Moon-ruled Monday or the Moon's traditional "planetary" hour. You can also research what time the Cancer constellation will be in the night sky in your area, and use the bright stars of Leo and Gemini to estimate where it will be. Watching the Delta Cancrids meteor showers associated with this constellation during mid-December to February is a great way to connect to this celestial energy in spellwork too.

Celestial, cooling, calming colors such as light blue, silver or gray, white, or starlight yellow are great shades to decorate your Cancer season altar, wardrobe, or candles. You can also consider pink (for the heart) or light sea-colored tones to reinforce that water energy. Adding lunar or water symbols to your Cancer spellcasting, such as cups, shells, or crab imagery, can also enhance this constellation's themes.

# LEO

| ♌ | Leo Season | July 23–August 22 |
|---|---|---|
| | Celestial Bodies | Sun, Pallas |
| | House | Fifth House |

## *Leo Themes*

As the fixed expression of fire, Leo helps stabilize and secure your sense of creative identity. Like the lion that represents it, Leo exemplifies strength, pride, and radiance. Considered the kings of all beasts, these creatures exude regality and power like no other, and as their ferocious roar indicates, self-expression is important when it comes to this sign. During Leo season, you can hone your unique creativity, boost your inner light, and strengthen your willpower. Ruled by the Sun—the very center of our solar system and the celestial body of our egos and purpose—Leo helps you embody being the star of your own personal universe, amplifying warmth and creative energy. This curates a favorable energy for the performer to express himself to the world. In Leo, the radiant, fierce, warm, loyal, and prideful energies of the Sun take their rightful place in center stage, invoking a time of joy and pleasure. Some believe that Leo also relates to the asteroid Pallas, in its more creative aspect. Here, you can turn your creativity into more of a disciplined art and practice under Pallas's rulership.

## *Related Myths*

One key myth that explains the meaning of the Leo constellation is that of the Nemean lion that Hercules set out to defeat. Considered an invincible beast, the Nemean lion was undefeatable and terrorized citizens. Hercules was tasked with conquering this lion as one of his twelve labors, but no weapon could pierce its skin. Finally, Hercules killed the lion by strangling it—a metaphor of how central self-expression is to themes of Leo.

### Magick

Leo is ruled by the Sun, so there is no better time to use Leo in magick than during Leo season from July 23 to August 22. With the Sun in this sign, as well as a new moon in Leo, this period is vibrant with Leo energy. But even when the Sun isn't in this sign, you can use its power throughout daylight to bless any Leo-aligned magickal endeavors, whether it is sunrise to inspire new beginnings or the midday sun for success and strength. You can also uncover when the Leo constellation is visible at night, using its bright star Regulus to find it, and cast your magick under the generous luminosity of this star that marks the celestial lion's heart.

For spells that require the more emotional aspect of Leo, the Leo full moon in Aquarius season can inspire romance, as well as help you stand out and shine. Other great alignments include Sun-ruled Sunday, the Sun's planetary hour, or when a planet makes a favorable transit through Leo.

Fiery hues of orange can highlight creativity for Leo magick, and red can inspire passion. Yellow is great for optimism and positivity, while green can open your heart or provide abundance. Gold hues are useful for embodying success and invoking the regal energy of this sign into your magick. Symbols such as crowns, the sun, and cats can help further attune your Leo magick.

# VIRGO

| ♍ | Virgo Season | August 23–September 22 |
| | Celestial Bodies | Mercury, Vesta, Ceres, Chiron |
| | House | Sixth House |

### Virgo Themes

As the mutable expression of earth, Virgo is a sign of self-sufficiency, community, and health. Often symbolized by "the Virgin," Virgo is about dedication, service, and purity of the self. As such, Virgo often embodies the energy of the helper who is driven to serve, whether it be other people, the earth, or animals. Combining her rulership by Mercury with her earthen energy, Virgo is highly intellectual, organized, analytical, and practical. Virgo is also a sign that focuses on the body—health, nutrition, and healthy daily habits—the little things that add up to well-being in the long run.

## Related Myths

In myth, Virgo has been associated with a few different deities, such as Dike, the Greek goddess of justice, and Astraea, a goddess of innocence and purity and the caretaker of humanity. (Astraea was supposedly the last deity to leave earth because she was so dedicated to believing in a better humanity!)

Virgo can also be associated with Proserpina/Persephone, daughter of Ceres/Demeter, who was a goddess of spring, youth, and innocence (similar to some of Virgo's qualities). Persephone was stolen away by Hades and made queen of the underworld for half the year, during which time the world experienced fall and winter. When she returned as goddess of spring for the other half of the year, the seasons changed to spring and summer. This story is reminiscent of Virgo's presence before the change of seasons, as well as the theme of abundance and harvest that this period brings.

## Magick

Virgo is very useful for magick related to health, dedication, and daily routines. The best time to use Virgo magick is when the Sun is in this sign, from August 23 to September 22, along with a Virgo new moon. Or, you can time your magick so that the Virgo constellation is viewable at reasonable hours of the night. With its bright blue-white star Spica (which represents the constellation's mythical ear of grain) easily visible when it rises in this night sky, you can call upon the themes of this constellation as you cast your Virgo-themed spells.

You can also use the Moon when it passes through this sign—every twenty-nine and a half days—including the Virgo full moon, which illuminates matters of health, habits, and routines among the go-with-the-flow Pisces season. Similarly, you can use Virgo when a planet makes a favorable transit through this sign or call upon the power of its ruling planet, Mercury, through Mercury's planetary hour or on a Wednesday.

Colors associated with structure, such as dark earth tones like brown, dark blues, grays, and blacks, can highlight the more orderly nature of this time. Colorful tones of green, pink, purple, other flowery colors, and white can call upon the verdant and pure themes of this sign's magick. Since the sign is associated with wheat, harvest tones such as gold can also be great for Virgo spells. Grain sheaths and floral and herb bundles can be great symbols to utilize to enhance your Virgo-themed magick.

# LIBRA

| Ω | Libra Season | September 23–October 22 |
|---|---|---|
| | Celestial Bodies | Venus, Juno |
| | House | Seventh House |

## Libra Themes

Throughout time, the image of the scales (Libra's symbol) has represented justice, equilibrium, balance, and fairness. The cardinal expression of air, Libra initiates energy through mental and social action. Social-loving Venus enhances Libra's social elements and increases this sign's capacity for compassion and connection, though it also enhances Libra's tendency for indecision, as it always sees multiple sides to any story. The romantic who craves social interaction, Libra admires aesthetics and art but also likes to balance and weigh all sides of a situation from multiple perspectives. This is a sign that can help inspire peace and harmony, as well as charm through aesthetics and artistic allure. Besides sharing rulership of Venus with Taurus, Libra can also be related to asteroid Juno (asteroid goddess of commitment), highlighting Libra's tendency for partnerships and connection.

## Related Myths

In mythology, Libra is often associated with the same Greek myth of Astraea as Virgo. While Virgo is said to sometimes represent the goddess Astraea, who acted as a steward of humanity and justice, Libra is believed to represent the scales of balance she would've held. They were a symbol of harmony and fairness, created to remain in the sky to inspire humanity, and are testaments to Libra's capacity for remaining in both the heart and mind, staying empathetic while also fair and just.

## Magick

When the Sun shines in Libra, from September 23 to October 22, and during the Libra new moon, all Libra-related matters will be brought into the light. The luminous Libra full moon amid Aries season highlights romances and pleasure and brings peace and balance to heady Aries energy, and using the power of the Moon whenever it is in Libra every twenty-nine days or so can be potent. Of course, you can also call upon Libra energy whenever the constellation is visible in the night sky or when a planet makes a favorable transit through the sign. Lining up Libra spells to Venus-ruled Fridays or during Venus's planetary hour can be particularly potent as well.

When it comes to Libra colors, anything that highlights her Venus rulership is a great choice: lavender, pinks, magentas, and purples all highlight the soothing, harmonizing energy of this sign. Blue hues are great for promoting communication and serenity for Libra magick. As a color that encompasses (or absorbs) all other colors, black can help connect to the more artsy and poetic aspects of Libra. When adorning your altar for Libra season or enhancing Libra-themed magick, symbols such as the scales, as well as a feather for the element of air, can help you attune further to this sign.

# SCORPIO

| ♏ | Scorpio Season | October 23–November 21 |
|---|---|---|
| | Celestial Bodies | Pluto, Juno |
| | House | Eighth House |

## Scorpio Themes

Few creatures exemplify the extremes, danger, and power of this sign better than the scorpion. As a fixed water sign, Scorpio seeks stability within the realms of emotion but is also deeply sensitive and psychic—though not as sympathetic as her water-element sistren.

Ruled by Pluto, the planet of sex, death, and rebirth, Scorpio's power is as intense as the stinger of the scorpion that represents it. Scorpio seeks to uncover the truth, discover intimacy, and usher in transformation—though that transformation sometimes comes with destruction too. With a single carefully placed sting, the otherwise small and unobtrusive scorpion can suddenly bring you to the brink of death. It is through these extremes that you are forced to let go and face your inner darkness. With her truth-seeking yet mysterious nature, Scorpio likes to understand others but is not so quick to share about herself—a method of securing her own emotional safety. It is for this reason that Scorpio does not like to feel a loss of control and will "sting" in such circumstances.

## Related Myths

While this constellation is associated with many myths throughout many cultures—as part of the Azure Dragon in Chinese myth or the demigod Maui's fishhook in Hawaiian cosmology—the myth commonly associated with the Scorpius constellation is that of Orion from ancient Greece. In this myth, a talented hunter named Orion exclaimed his greatness, killing many beasts. A scorpion was thus sent by the goddess of the earth, Gaia, for threatening her creatures, or by the huntress Artemis, or by Artemis's brother Apollo to defend her honor as the greatest hunter, as no man could claim to be on the same level as the gods. Through its fearlessness and power, the scorpion defeated Orion, showing how even the smallest of creatures can defeat and bring down those who claim greatness and inflate their egos. As a conduit for Pluto, Scorpio shows that overinflated egos lead to demise, whether literal or metaphoric.

## Magick

Whether using this sign to hone your sense of power, uncover truths, or transform, you can call on this sacred creature to enhance your spells. Scorpio spells are especially blessed from October 23 to November 21, when both the Sun and the new moon travel through this sign. The Scorpio full moon amid Taurus season can also be useful for highlighting Scorpio energy for truth, passion, and intimacy, as well as highlighting the balance between steady Taurus and always-transforming Scorpio. You can also use the power of the Moon when it travels through this sign every twenty-nine and a half days. When neither the Sun nor Moon travels through this sign, determine which hour of the night you can see this constellation, and look upon its bright red star Antares (Greek for "rival of Aries"), which marks the heart of passion of this sign, for added celestial power as you cast your Scorpio spells. Given that Pluto does not have a precise corresponding day or hour, you can use Mars's alignments (such as Tuesday) and Mars's planetary hour to provide an extra boost.

When it comes to channeling Scorpio's star power through color, bold and intense choices are the way to go! Red and orange tones are great for Scorpio's passion and creative energies. Dark, bold tones like gray and black can invoke the mystery and intensity behind this sign. Symbols such as the scorpion, sharp stingers or objects, and the phoenix can help enhance your Scorpio spellcasting.

# SAGITTARIUS

| Sagittarius Season | November 22–December 21 |
|---|---|
| Celestial Bodies | Jupiter, Chiron |
| House | Ninth House |

## Sagittarius Themes

Forever pointing his arrow to the center of the galaxy, Sagittarius the Philosopher is the epitome of new beliefs, visions, and higher pursuits. The mutable expression of fire, Sagittarius adapts the passionate, active energy of fire to the real world and is always in pursuit of expansive, boundaryless freedom, fun, and play. Symbolized by the centaur archer—half human, half horse—Sagittarius integrates the worlds of civilization and the wild—balancing the strength and stamina of beasts and healing wisdom of nature, with the beliefs and ethics of a human. The centaur's arrow pointed toward the heavens is symbolic of directing your focus toward the pursuit of larger ideas and perspectives. Sagittarius seeks to uncover wisdom and philosophies about life to explore and expand—via perspective as well as travel and higher education. Always searching the horizon for new opportunities, Sagittarius helps you integrate the expansive energies of Jupiter through hope, optimism, and personal beliefs.

## Related Myths

While some astrologers associate the myth of Chiron with Sagittarius, others associate Chiron with the Centaurus constellation, saying Sagittarius is another centaur altogether. Some believe Sagittarius is actually tied to a satyr named Crotus, son of Pan and father of archery, who cared for the nine muse daughters of Zeus upon Mount Helicon. Throughout these varying myths, Sagittarius is represented as part man, part beast, showing his capacity to integrate knowledge and wisdom from different experiences of life, combining the best of nature and human civilization.

## Magick

From November 22 to December 21, the Sun appears to shine through this sign, and there is a Sagittarius new moon as well—all auspicious times to try magickal endeavors of perspective, expansion, and good luck/optimism. When the Sun is not shining through this sign, it can be just as powerful to use when the constellation rises at night the other months of the year, for Sagittarius's arrow points to a radio source thought to be a supermassive black hole at the heart of our galaxy, adding a powerful energy to spells. Thus, in both astrology and astronomy, Sagittarius is our gateway to perceiving the universe and our place within it.

Of course, you can also use the archer when the Moon passes through this sign every twenty-nine and a half days; during the Sagittarius full moon (in Gemini season), which highlights spiritual insight and big life questions; or when a planet makes a beneficial transit through Sagittarius. Other great considerations for magickal timing include Jupiter's planetary hour or Jupiter-ruled Thursday.

As a fire sign, hues of red, orange, and yellow can enhance and communicate Sagittarius's sense of adventure and creativity. Gold, purple, and white are great colors in magick involving Sagittarius themes of spirituality, beliefs, and ethics. The imagery of the animated, dancing flame and the arrow can enhance your Sagittarius alignment and magick.

# CAPRICORN

| ♑ | Capricorn Season | December 22–January 19 |
| --- | --- | --- |
| | Celestial Bodies | Saturn |
| | House | Tenth House |

## *Capricorn Themes*

Coupling the determination of a mountain goat with the flexibility of a fish, the sea goat Capricorn invokes the cardinal expression of earth, thereby initiating motion and action through the material realm. As a cardinal energy in the realm of earth, Capricorn is a very ambitious sign, seeking achievement, status, and reputation. A sign of hard work and diligence, Capricorn is not afraid to dig her hands into the earth or climb the impossibly steep mountains of success. As an earth sign, Capricorn is interested in the physical—what is solid, concrete, and real—and she can find practicality and use in all things to achieve her desires. Ruled by Saturn, the planet of boundaries and structure, Capricorn shows how a good foundation can lead to long-term success and accomplishment. A motivated sign that brings focus to your career and the material things—

physical accomplishments that can generate wealth and last generations—Capricorn helps you accomplish goals and aspirations (only after checking them for practicality, though) through lessons of discipline and perseverance. Capricorn also helps you check the foundations you have already built for efficiency and stability.

## Related Myths

True to Capricorn's determined yet wild nature, this constellation was known as a sea goat as far back as the time of the Sumerians. In Greek myth, the Capricornus constellation is attributed to the deity of the wild, Pan, who saved the gods countless times. On one such occasion, he warned the gods of the monster Typhon, sent by Gaia. Advising the gods to disguise themselves as animals, Pan turned the lower part of his body into a fish. Since Pan saved the gods so many times, Zeus immortalized him in the night sky for all to see.

This myth highlights Capricorn's resourcefulness and quick thinking. It also shows how earth, while stable and firm most of the time, can be flexible in its determined nature—whether it is Pan half-turning into a fish or a flower pushing its way through cracks in the cement.

## Magick

The time from December 22 to January 19 is particularly abundant with Capricorn energy, with both the Sun and the new moon aligned in this sign. When the Sun isn't in this sign, you can look up when the constellation will be viewable at night and use the Sagittarius and Aquarius constellations to find this otherwise dim star pattern. You can also do Capricorn-related spells when the Moon passes through this sign every twenty-nine and a half days during the Capricorn full moon in Cancer season, providing the energetic scenery to set goals in balance with self-compassion. Saturday and Saturn's planetary hour are great choices as well. There are also five meteor showers associated with the Capricornus constellation that can enhance your Capricorn magick and determination.

When it comes to colors related to Capricorn, dark and earthy tones are the way to go. Black and dark gray are great for crafting boundaries, whereas brown and dark green can call upon the earth aspect of this sign. Deep red is a great choice when you want to capture the determination of Capricorn. Horns, goat and fish tail imagery, and even the shape of the pyramid can enhance your Capricorn seasonal altars and spellcasting.

# AQUARIUS

| | | |
|---|---|---|
| ♒ | **Aquarius Season** | January 20–February 18 |
| | **Celestial Bodies** | Uranus, Pallas |
| | **House** | Eleventh House |

## Aquarius Themes

Symbolized by the cupbearer who spills the water of life from his cup out into the sky and down to the world, Aquarius shares knowledge and genius with humanity. As the fixed expression of air, humanitarian Aquarius brings stability and steadiness to the realm of thought, inspiring real social change through intellectual genius and social revolutions. Ruled by Uranus, the planet of freedom and ingenuity, Aquarius is a sign of innovation, able to collect and apply information and see new and exciting ideas outside of what was thought possible.

Aquarius's ability to visualize countless possibilities makes this a sign of inventiveness and great to call on for solving any problem. With limitless possibilities, Aquarius can visualize the future and often relates to themes of science fiction, technology, and space. Pursuing originality and social reform, Aquarius aligns with the asteroid Pallas. Driven by his nature to be free and original, and to break away from old ideas and narrowing perspectives, Aquarius seeks to benefit humanity at large, while maintaining individuality—and thus will break ties with anything that limits his ability to be himself.

## Related Myths

Although the association with water-bearing goes all the way back to the ancient Babylonian god Ea, also pictured with an overflowing vessel, it is the Greek myth of Ganymede, the cupbearer of the gods, that dominates Western astrology. Yet another subject of Zeus's affection thanks to his beauty, Ganymede was granted eternal youth and served as cupbearer to the deities upon Mount Olympus. His youth can be seen in relation to Aquarius's ability to see limitless possibilities, providing sustenance to the gods. Ganymede eventually rebelled and poured the contents of the vessel out, sharing it with the world. Through Ganymede, Aquarius shows us that once we understand systems of power, we can change them to empower others—thereby highlighting themes of revolution and rebellion.

## *Magick*

The best time to use Aquarius for magick (for example, for individuality and innovation) is from January 20 to February 18, when the Sun appears to travel through this sign. You can gauge when the Moon passes through Aquarius, such as the Aquarius new moon during that period, for blessings and new beginnings around Aquarius themes, or during the Aquarius full moon in Leo season, for inspiring innovation and connection with your unique identity.

Since Uranus wasn't discovered until much later than the other planets (except for Neptune and Pluto), it was not given a planetary hour or day. However, Uranus, Neptune, and Pluto are often referred to as a "higher octave" of planets that *were* given an hour or day. So, while Uranus does not have its own hour, it is considered a higher octave of Mercury, and, as a sign of air, you can use Mercury's planetary hour or Wednesday in your Aquarius magick. Otherwise, you can always call upon this sign's magick during a favorable transit through Aquarius or by gauging when the constellation is viewable in the night sky. Aquarius is thought to have a special connection to the asteroid Pallas, for, just as Aquarius is a visionary and innovative, Pallas appreciates originality and wisdom.

When it comes to the color associations, hues of the mind, such as turquoise, silver, indigos, and purples, can enhance the ethereal, mental magick of this sign. Blues can heighten communication, and light yellow (a connection to Aquarius's brightest star, Sadalsuud, a rare yellow supergiant associated with good fortune and growth) symbolizes inspired ideas and insight. As the cupbearer, the imagery of vessels and cups can help further your Aquarius altars and magick, as well as a feather (for its air-element rulership) and the lightning symbol.

# PISCES

| | Pisces Season | February 19–March 20 |
|---|---|---|
| | Celestial Bodies | Neptune |
| | House | Twelfth House |

## Pisces Themes

Symbolized by two fish, with a keen ability to dive deep into the waters of your subconscious, Pisces is one of the most spiritual, mystical signs— able to disintegrate the boundaries between the material and unseen realms. As the mutable expression of water, Pisces is flexible and adaptable—like sugar stirred into water, Pisces can dissolve barriers and invite understanding and harmony. Pisces connects individuals to a greater whole (think of the movements of a school of fish) and goes with the flow in the currents of life. Depicted as two fish tailing each other in a circle, Pisces's symbol showcases the complexity and ever-moving nature of the spirit. Pisces recognizes the complexity of life and embraces compassion and understanding.

Ruled by Neptune, planet of dreams, Pisces has the capacity for deep spiritual expression, art, and healing. Pisces can sense all things deeply and channels that inspiration through moving arts of all kinds, especially music. As the last sign of the zodiac, watery Pisces helps us embody oneness with the universe, bringing unity by dissolving the self into the greater collective unconscious.

## Related Myths

Despite being ruled by Neptune (Roman god of the ocean), Pisces's most relevant myth is the story of the Roman gods Venus and Cupid and their escape from the monster Typhon. In this myth, the goddess of beauty, Venus, and her son transform into fish to escape the monster's fiery breath, thus saving love and beauty. This myth affirms Venus as the "lower octave" of Pisces-ruler Neptune (since Venus is seen as person-to-person connection and love, versus Neptune as community/universal love), while demonstrating that through flexibility, unity, and unconditional love, a person can escape destruction.

## Magick

Whether you are casting spells for heightening intuitive powers, summoning spiritual dreams, or invoking harmony with healing waters, you can summon Pisces's capacity to dive deep beneath the surface in any magickal working by aligning your celestial spells with divine timing, cosmic colors, and other tools. Use the Sun and the new moon in Pisces between February 19 and March 20 for birthing and blessing new Piscean endeavors. With the moon's cosmic pull upon water, time your watery Pisces spells to certain lunar phases, based on your needs. Call upon the

Moon when it passes through this sign every twenty-nine and a half days or use the Pisces full moon (during busy Virgo season) to invoke spirituality, intuitive dreams, and peace.

Since Pisces's ruler Neptune does not have its own planetary hour, you can use the alignments of Pisces's once-thought-to-be-ruler Jupiter when appropriate, or call upon the Piscean myth, and time your spells to Venus's planetary hour and favored day of Friday. Like the Piscean energy that blends into its surroundings, barely visible beneath the water's surface, Pisces is difficult to see with the naked eye.

When it comes to channeling the power of light through cosmic colors, watery tones of blue, aqua, and sea greens are great for healing, whereas lavender and violet hues can enhance harmony. White can tap in to Pisces's spirituality. All tones can aid in psychic development. Imagery of the ocean, such as water, fish, and starfish all make great choices for symbols to enhance your Piscean magick.

# Chapter 4

# THE HOUSES

O ver thousands of years, the ancients noticed the apparent path of the moon and the sun in the sky, and how they seemed to travel through the twelve signs. They also noticed certain stars and constellations rising with the coming and going of various seasons, and eventually divided the ecliptic (the sun's path in the sky through the twelve signs) not just into twelve signs but twelve fixed areas of sky as well, called the houses. Each house represents universal themes of life, such as material possessions, partnership, and death and transformation. So while the stars moved throughout the night across the celestial sphere, the houses were fixed, with the first house always beginning at the eastern horizon. Each house was given a natural planetary ruler and resonating zodiacal sign.

Dividing the celestial sphere for each of the twelve houses allowed charts to be cast and mapped based on a specific point in time. You can cast a star map for any specific moment, whether it be for a person's birth (called a natal chart), an important life event, the founding of a city or country, or even for answering a question. Astrologers could gather very specific information about a particular moment based upon what was happening in the sky at that time. For example, the Sun (which represents identity) in the seventh house (the house of one-on-one relationships) could indicate that a person's relationships are especially impactful to their identity, as long as other placements are taken into consideration. Or, Aries in the fifth house of playfulness might signify someone who likes to express their creative and playful energy through sports and physical movement.

# HOUSES AND MAGICK

Everyone has each of the twelve houses in their birth chart, and with the ever-turning wheel of the night sky, everyone's houses will capture a different part of the night sky or universe, and thus different constellations. If you like, you can study the placement of your houses based on the time of your birth. But because the houses represent universal, key themes of the experiences of life, you can still connect to the meaning and magick of *each* house regardless of whether you know your chart or not. Then you can harness their meanings for magickal purposes, such as divination, to focus and direct a magickal intention, or to use their ruling celestial body or sign to help you in that area of life.

Occupying twelve key areas of life, the houses can be separated into two parts—the first six houses represent the intrapersonal (dealing specifically with establishing the self in the world), and houses seven through twelve represent the more interpersonal parts of life, such as social dynamics and your relationship to the outside world. You can use the houses in your witchcraft to pinpoint what area of your life you would like to improve or what area you want to manifest something in. By using the natural rulers and celestial affinities to guide what spells you use in Part 2, or what crystals, herbs, and stones you work with, you can bolster a house's balance in your life. And if you know your chart, you can use Appendix E to add correspondences for your sign in a given house. For example, if Aquarius is in your first house, and you are working on your appearance and confidence, you might choose the Golden Fleece Confidence Talisman spell from Aries season and add extra correspondences for Aquarius, combining the magick of your personal first house with that of the natural ruler of that house.

Beyond using the houses to guide where to focus your magick or for visualizing how a particular spell might manifest in the world, you can use the house system for divination. By pulling a tarot or oracle card for each house in a circle, you can get insight into what is going on in your life or even cast a yearly reading (with each house card representing a month too). This can be further amplified by casting any crystals you gather for these spells upon the cards and seeing which stones land in what house, using the dual meaning of the cards and crystals to provide a full-picture image into any situation.

You can also use the houses to guide your intention setting and visualization before casting a spell. Think of it as creating a business plan for what you wish to bring into your life. For example, in the first house, you might ask yourself, how am I going to pursue this initial spark? In the second house, what kind of material goods, money, or physical foundations will bring this into reality? And so forth.

# THE FIRST HOUSE

**Key themes:** Sense of Self, Body, Beginnings
**Associated sign:** Aries
**Associated celestial bodies:** Mars
**Associated element:** Cardinal Fire

Beginning our journey through the celestial wheel, the first house establishes the self in the world. In the birth chart, the position of the first house is determined by the sign that is rising on the eastern horizon of your birthplace, at the precise moment you were born (often called your Ascendant or Rising Sign in natal astrology). The first house establishes the self and the body—how we take up space in the world. Physically, this means your appearance, body, movements, and mannerisms. In the nonphysical realm, this is the energy you come across with—how others perceive you at first. Your sense of self, outer expression, and confidence can all be connected to the first house. The first house also relates to beginnings and "firsts" of all kinds—such as your childhood, new projects, ventures, relationships, and various other new starts, making it great for magick in these areas. Regardless of what sign your first house is in, the natural ruler of the House of the Self is Aries, making Mars and cardinal fire other natural affinities as well. Because this is the house of first beginnings, you can use this energy and celestial correspondences to usher in new starts of all kinds. If you're looking at the houses as a cycle or as steps for magickal manifestation, this is where you establish the energy with which you will pursue your magickal desires, the energy with which they will begin, and/or how they will take up energetic space in the world.

# THE SECOND HOUSE

**Key themes:** Wealth, Resources, Value
**Associated sign:** Taurus
**Associated celestial bodies:** Venus, Ceres
**Associated element:** Fixed Earth

Now that we've established the self through the first house, it's time to support and sustain it in the real world! The second house is all about physical resources and the value you place in them. This house shows your relationship to the material realm and the role physical goods and wealth play in your life: Your relationship to money (how you make, save, and spend it), what resources are available, possessions you value and hold dear, and even shelter—whether it be a property or how you support, sustain, and enjoy your physical body. The second house can also indicate how you make your money and become a master in your trades and desired fields. The value you place on certain goods, your qualities and talents, and how these values line up with how you feel about yourself can curate your sense of self-esteem. By how you interact with the physical realm and use your wealth and possessions, you can communicate what you place value on, or even simply enjoy the bounty of life, sustain your body, and feel good about yourself!

This House of Value relates to fixed earth and the Taurus sign, sharing themes of physical comforts, wealth, values, and materialism for survival. Venus rules this house, making it great to work with for manifesting abundance, developing a healthy sense of self-worth, and creating a life you value.

# THE THIRD HOUSE

**Key themes:** Communication, Reasoning, Speech
**Associated sign:** Gemini
**Associated celestial bodies:** Mercury
**Associated element:** Mutable Air

Now that we have established the existence of the self through the first house and how we physically sustain it through the second, it is time to focus on how we engage with the immediate world around us. The House of Communication offers insight into how you communicate with others or even how you interact with your environment. This includes how you think and understand things, and it can reveal how you articulate and speak; how you might put concepts, ideas, and thoughts into words; and the diction and tone you choose to use. And since communication has to do with the sharing of information, the third house also deals with learning, your learning style, and what kinds of things strike your curiosity to learn, understand, and develop more. Communication is also about how you connect with your environment, in addition to how you speak to others. So, on one hand, peer-like relationships, such as siblings, coworkers, groups, and covens, with which you closely engage or share bonds, can come into focus here (great for networking and making connections!). On the other hand, this is also about the immediate environment you engage with every day, such as your neighborhood.

So, if you want to network and make new connections, work on your communication style, or spark new ideas, the third house is the place to draw your attention. And, as you might guess from its relation to communication, it corresponds to the sign of Gemini, mutable air, and Mercury. The third house can also help you understand how your words manifest reality and how you might use your voice, diction, and immediate surroundings to manifest your intentions.

# THE FOURTH HOUSE

**Key themes:** Shelter, Psyche, Nurturing
**Associated sign:** Cancer
**Associated celestial bodies:** Moon, Ceres
**Associated element:** Cardinal Water

The fourth house is all about the home—the space where you grew up, how you were nurtured, and those who nurtured you. This house focuses on the early foundations of your childhood and how they still impact your psyche and how you experience or perceive things today. It can help you understand your heritage, family traditions, how you were nurtured, and how you nurture others. This includes your relationships with mother-like figures. The fourth house can also hint at what type of home environment you seek as an adult and how you might like to decorate your nest (based on what you need to nurture yourself and feel emotionally secure and safe). It is all about how you maintain an environment to retreat to so that you can protect, shelter, and nourish yourself from the world. This includes privacy and your innermost self—the "you" that rests inside all the barriers of protection, where you can find intimacy within yourself or with others.

Who knows better than Cancer about nourishing the soul, deeply felt emotions, and setting up a protective, nurturing environment? The sign associated with this House of Home, Cancer, the Moon, and Ceres all resonate with fourth house themes, making these astrological bodies key in focusing on this area of life. In magick, you can use the associations and spells of these planets to strengthen this part of your life. Or, the seasonal witch can use Cancer season to focus on such efforts. In magickal manifestation, this house asks you how you might nurture and protect what you are summoning into the world.

# THE FIFTH HOUSE

**Key themes:** Creativity, Romance, Pleasure
**Associated sign:** Leo
**Associated celestial bodies:** Sun, Pallas
**Associated element:** Fixed Fire

After nurturing yourself in the fourth house, it's time to play! The fifth house, the House of Pleasure, is the home of creativity and playfulness. Here, your capacity to let go and have fun takes center stage. This relates to creativity, your sense of playfulness, and your imagination. This includes anything that is a creative extension of the self—whether it be the arts, theater, or even children. At times, this means how you might interact and relate to kids, and at other times, this is about your inner child and how you create joy. Romances and the playful, teasing, flirtatious beginnings of relationships also play a role in this house, hence its association with lovers and love affairs. In a birth chart, this house can indicate what you find joy in, the role creativity plays in your life, and what kind of hobbies you might enjoy.

If you struggle with engaging in pleasure and just having pure fun, this is the house to bolster with your magick! Artists who have trouble letting go and engaging with the playfulness part of being creative can re-harness that here. By using Leo, the Sun, and fixed fire correspondences (with which this house is related), or even your own fifth house sign, you can explore the depths of your creativity, expand your imagination, have more fun, and even flirt a little bit with life! For those looking to make a career in creative arts, this can be a great place to focus your magick.

# THE SIXTH HOUSE

**Key themes:** Daily Routines, Health, Work
**Associated sign:** Virgo
**Associated celestial bodies:** Vesta, Mercury
**Associated element:** Mutable Earth

While the fifth house reminds us that there is time to play, there is also a time to work. This comes into focus in the sixth house, the house of self-improvement, service, and health. Specifically, this house highlights your daily routines—the little steps you take every day to maintain and improve your goals and health. The sixth house relates to how you maintain physical health—such as your daily habits, routines, and diet. Other themes include what you might do for daily work, self-discipline, planning, and the things you worry about (and thus take care of) on a consistent basis. In essence, this house brings focus to the things we do each day. Since this house deals with how you spend your time, it can also reveal information about what exactly you're devoted to and the overall balance of your life. It can also help you discover the best ways to be service-oriented and work to benefit others.

You can strengthen this part of your life by working with Virgo, Mercury, Vesta, and mutable earth through magick. Here, you can focus magick on daily habits, worries (putting worries to use through action and prevention), and what kind of tangible actions you take to support your magick. If you're using the houses to represent magickal manifestation or for reflection, this house asks what you need to be consistent with, or what you need to do each day to let your desire grow and exist in the world.

# THE SEVENTH HOUSE

**Key themes:** Partnerships, Marriage, One-on-One Dynamics
**Associated sign:** Libra
**Associated celestial bodies:** Venus, Juno
**Associated element:** Cardinal Air

The seventh house marks the journey into the other half of the cycle of the houses, moving us from the realm of the individual-focused themes in houses one through six into the realm of the interpersonal. And to start that journey, the seventh house brings our attention to one-on-one relationships: partnerships, committed relationships, friendships, and counseling and business dynamics. Hence, this house is often associated with marriage but, oddly enough, also with enemies, which are technically another form of one-on-one connection. Like all relationships, these bonds can reveal hidden parts of yourself that only really arise as you navigate opening up to another in a more personal way. Whether good or bad connections, this House of Partnerships is all about the close bonds you form with people on a one-on-one basis and can reveal how you might approach such relationships, what these connections reveal about you, the types of relationships you prefer, and how these key bonds might be important to you in the larger scheme of life and identity.

The seventh house is often associated with Libra, as well as its corresponding element of cardinal air and the celestial bodies Juno and Venus, making all of these celestial figures great to call upon for helping seventh house matters. If you're using the cycle of the houses to bring something into your life, the seventh house is the part of the journey of manifestation that represents how close relationships impact whatever you are manifesting. In love magick, this house is about taking that bond to the next level and confronting your relationship fears. If doing magick for a business, the seventh house can help you determine what kind of business and financial relationships you might form (such as with financial situations or a business partner) to take your business to the next level.

# THE EIGHTH HOUSE

**Key themes:** Loss, Transformation, Death and Rebirth
**Associated sign:** Scorpio
**Associated celestial bodies:** Pluto, Juno
**Associated element:** Fixed Water

While the seventh house dealt with forming close bonds, you also have to deal with the loss of those relationships or even losing parts of yourself as a result of relationship changes. Often called the House of Sex and Death, the eighth house is where you grieve and cope with loss, whether it be the loss of a loved one, a piece of yourself, or significant and earth-shattering changes in life. This part of the chart relates to transformation of all kinds, such as relationship endings, the birth of something new, or even the final transformation: death. These experiences force you to confront your deepest fears, pushing you uncomfortably to healing and, eventually, to rebirth. Thus the eighth house also relates to the hidden, powerful aspects of life—the spaces in between, the secret parts of life that are still unknown, such as the occult, psychic connections, or inner work. This house also relates to certain types of partnerships—specifically, to transformations that occur through relationships and the ways you merge with others, including sexual partnerships, emotional unions and interactions, and even financial arrangements (like inheritance).

If you are looking to work with the psychic realm or spirits, or deepen your knowledge of the occult, this is the house to focus your magick on. The eighth house is associated with Scorpio, Pluto, Juno, and fixed water, so using spells or correspondences for these associations empowers such magick. And while painful, this is also the place to go to be vulnerable and to access the deepest parts of yourself, to bring in big changes in magick.

# THE NINTH HOUSE

**Key themes:** Beliefs, Foreign Travel, Expansion
**Associated sign:** Sagittarius
**Associated celestial bodies:** Jupiter, Chiron
**Associated element:** Mutable Fire

After immense transformations (like those experienced in the eighth house), you might search for new meaning and spiritual guidance in life. This is where the ninth house comes into play. The House of Philosophy and beliefs, the ninth house focuses on how you grow and expand yourself, through themes of faith, finding meaning, and foreign travel. Here, you'll reflect on the belief systems and ethics that guide you and your sense of faith or religion—the higher beliefs that guide your perspective.

Foreign and long-distance travel often come into play here, as the exposure and experience you glean from such adventures expand your awareness of the world, internally and externally. Another way this concept manifests is through higher education: the place where you actively seek to expand and improve your knowledge, whether through formal education, such as law or ethics, or through spiritual teachings and institutions—even astrology! As this house also deals with ethics, legal matters may also come up here. All in all, the ninth house takes your sights off the mundane and onto something greater: a concept or vision that guides your life.

This house corresponds to Sagittarius, whose arrow aims ever higher in the sky and toward the center of the galaxy. Its associations with Jupiter, Chiron, and mutable fire also come into play here, making related spells, herbs, stones, and power beneficial for work with ninth house themes of spiritual wisdom and higher perspective, travels, moving to new horizons, or opening up a world of opportunity. This is the place to discover where to expand your magickal education (such as reading this book!) and reflect on the interplay of your belief systems, perspectives, and faith.

# THE TENTH HOUSE

**Key themes:** Achievements, Vocation, Reputation
**Associated sign:** Capricorn
**Associated celestial bodies:** Saturn
**Associated element:** Cardinal Earth

With a higher vision in mind to guide you and keep you strong, the wheel of the houses now brings your focus to accomplishment and success. The tenth house, often called the House of Social Status or Career, is where these ideas manifest. Therefore, this is the house that is associated with your vocation and your reputation in life. This is where how you achieve your goals interacts with the world, manifesting in success, accomplishments, and what you become known for. You often encounter authority figures as you climb the ladders of success; thus, this house reveals your relationship with authority, tradition, fatherlike figures, and even what you might be like as an authority figure. At a greater level, this house shows what you work hard toward, your discipline, and what you accomplish—such as what career you achieve success in, and how this contributes to society's perception of you.

Do you have important goals you wish to accomplish in your lifetime, or are you looking to achieve renown for your work? You can use this house's association with determined Capricorn to pursue your life goals, Saturn to help you master your vocation and navigate the ladder of authority, and cardinal earth to initiate tangible results.

# THE ELEVENTH HOUSE

**Key themes:** Community, Humanitarianism, Ideals
**Associated sign:** Aquarius
**Associated celestial bodies:** Uranus, Pallas
**Associated element:** Fixed Air

The eleventh house focuses on your ideals, your vision for the future, and how you interact with social groups to achieve greater change in the world. While the seventh house indicates close partnerships, the eleventh house of community expands to peer groups, including friend groups or organizations and collectives, and what kind of ideals you strive for. On a more personal level, this is about your groups of friends and how you connect with others over shared interests such as hobbies or group experiences. On a more abstract level, this house is about your greater ideals and dreams for the future of society and what kinds of communities and movements you connect with to achieve these ideals in the world. For example, maybe you engage with a witchcraft community! Here, you uncover what types of social causes are important to you and how they influence the groups you associate with. It is through these connections that we can support one another and craft significant change in the world.

If you wish to connect to a greater community and lend your magick to humanitarian causes or an ideal for the future of the world, this is the house to focus on. You can inquire as to what sign this house lies within on your birth chart, or even which planets fall within it, to glean how you might operate in such group dynamics or even what interests and causes are more likely to be beneficial and excite you. This house is associated with Aquarius, and its correspondences of Uranus, fixed air, and Pallas. By looking at correspondences of these signs, resonating spells, and spell ingredients, you can bolster this house.

# THE TWELFTH HOUSE

**Key themes:** Spiritual Healing, Escape, Transcendence
**Associated sign:** Pisces
**Associated celestial bodies:** Neptune
**Associated element:** Mutable Water

The twelfth and last house brings the journey around the wheel to an end. This is where you undo everything and connect to the greater whole. Think of it as coming home after a long day—this is the space where you unwind, take off the mask you wore all day, and digest the day's events. Some might unwind through meditation and reflection, seeking spiritual understanding and healing. Others might momentarily lose themselves in their imagination, unwinding through things like fantasy books or games to temporarily get away from reality. Others may have a more difficult time digesting their day and will cope with substances. This house speaks to how you might escape, whether in good, bad, or extreme ways. Often referred to as the House of Self-Undoing, the twelfth house holds the potential for what can connect you to a great sense of spirituality and the hidden fears and wounds that can send you into escapism and addiction.

Once you've regrouped after your long day and reflected, you might head to bed and enter the realm of dreams. Here, your mind accesses the subconscious, processing messages, meanings, and events of the day. In the deeper realms of sleep, you can dissolve your sense of self and connect to the collective consciousness of the watery dream realm, where there is no solid reality. In other words, the twelfth house is about pulling apart the threads of your reality and connecting to the cosmic flow of life. Through transcending the self, some harness psychic abilities and other matters of mysticism. Just as the destruction of a star gives life to new matter, the twelfth house prepares the way for spiritual healing and rebirth in the first house, continuing the cycle.

If you wish to connect to a greater sense of spirituality, psychic ability, and healing, this house can be a great place to focus your intentions and spells. Associated with Pisces, Neptune, and mutable water, this is where you can work dream magick. You can use these associations to guide what crystals or herbs you use in such spells or even in the spells in Part 2. In the scheme of the greater wheel for setting magickal intentions and focuses, this is where you might find deeper spiritual meaning in what you wish to manifest, or learn how something in your life might unravel, to be woven into something new.

## Chapter 5

# CELESTIAL BODIES

In ancient Babylon, priests and prophets would observe and map the movement of the planets from atop their tiered towers and temples to the gods, determining the wills of deities over the affairs of humans. Whether planets were seen as gods themselves or as symbols of a god's will, every planet in our solar system has myth and meaning that can be channeled into your magick. In modern astrology, the planets (and other key astrological bodies like the Sun) are the directors of the celestial stage, driving what is taking place based on where they reside in the sky.

The houses these planets occupy are the stage (area of life they are influencing), and the signs are the various archetypes and characters that express and act out their energy. In a birth chart, the planets represent aspects of personality, with the planets closest to the earth (called inner planets) indicating key personal information, such as the way someone might talk or think, or the kinds of things they might be drawn to. The farther out in the solar system, the longer a planet's transit might take and the more subtle and generational in nature its impact might be—though it is no less powerful (these are called the outer planets).

Whether you want to call on Mars for vitality and force to better stand up for yourself, or tap in to Neptune to channel spiritual information, you can engage planetary transits as a way to focus your intention and magick. You can also use planets' positions in the sky as fortuitous occasions for manifestation and healing in particular areas of your life. You can even customize and advance your magick according to your own planetary placement using Appendix B.

# THE SUN

| | Elements | Fire |
|---|---|---|
| ◉ | Key themes | Identity, Sense of Purpose, Creativity and Self-Expression, Vitality |
| | Associations | Leo, Fifth House |

The center of the solar system and the star that defines our very existence in the universe, the sun symbolizes your root identity in astrology and provides insight into the way you might express your life's purpose. While it's not a planet, the sun is no less of a celestial influence. It represents your creative life force and personal consciousness and speaks to your unique, creative expression and individuality. It helps you to be the creator of your life, manifesting your desires and bringing them into the world with confidence. Connecting to the sun's energy within your chart (such as through your sun sign) can help you shine, create, and share your warmth and gifts with the world.

Throughout many cultures, the sun has been associated with creative and "Creator" archetype energy. In Egyptian mythology, the sun god Ra was combined with the self-actuated deity Amun to form Amun-Ra, the supreme or chief god. In Greek mythology, Apollo rode his chariot across the sky, carrying the sun to mark the day. As a god of healing, the arts, music, and prophecy, Apollo exemplifies the versatility of the power of the sun in magick.

## Magick

In healing magick, the sun relates to the heart—the organ that sustains life and vitality for the rest of the body. Solar magick might be just the ticket when your sense of self is diminished or when you lack confidence in yourself. Aligning your magick to the sun can bless efforts of success, creativity, leadership, and warmth. As such, it is no wonder that the Sun is the ruler of regal Leo, making Leo season and Leo transits powerful for solar magick. The sun is also associated with Sunday and has its own planetary hour.

## Times of Day

The sun has extra astrological times you can use to call upon its power. As the earth goes around the sun, it rotates, creating the twenty-four-hour cycle of the day, where one side of the earth is illuminated by solar light and power, and the other part is serenaded by stars sprinkled across the darkness of the cosmos. Thus, the movement of the sun throughout the day holds the combined power of the earth's fertility and the sun's capacity for creation. Using the power of this cycle can help you manifest specific desires into the world. Here is more information about what type of magick is best for each time of day:

- **Twilight:** The time between night and day, when the sky is not quite dark enough to allow visibility of all the stars or bright enough to illuminate the world. Only the brightest celestial bodies might be visible at this time. It is a time of limbo and is useful for magick related to transformation, alchemy, and creation.

- **Dawn/Sunrise:** As the sun rises above the horizon and illuminates and defines the world, the dawning of a new day brings in the energy of new beginnings. It is a potent time to conduct magick related to birthing things into the world.

- **Morning:** The morning brings the growth of the sun's strength and is thus a time of increase. Use this time for magickal efforts toward increasing or growing something.

- **Midday/Noon:** This is when the sun reaches its highest peak in the sky. It's a powerful time for magick that is aimed at manifesting energies of all kinds or at efforts to stand out and succeed.

- **Afternoon:** At this point, the sun begins its decline in the sky. In the afternoon, try spells or other magick that require a time of wisdom for revisiting or reanalyzing situations.

- **Dusk/Sunset:** A key time for matters that require banishment as a metaphorical way to "snuff out" the light on something. For example, you might try a cleansing at this point, particularly with matters that require rebirth or change. You can then manifest a new and different beginning for the matter with the upcoming dawn.

### Wheel of the Year

As the earth orbits the sun, we experience the changing of seasons that define the year. Due in part to the earth's axis, and in part to the earth's position around the sun, there are significant times of year that combine earth and solar magick. You will learn about these days in Chapter 6.

# THE MOON

| | | |
|---|---|---|
| ☾ | **Elements** | Water |
| | **Key themes** | Emotions, Intuition, the Soul |
| | **Associations** | Cancer, Fourth House |

The most luminous body in the night sky, the moon has captivated humankind since the dawn of time. In fact, due to its gravitational pull on water and its ability to stabilize the earth's axis, the moon likely contributed to the evolution of life on earth. In astrology, the moon symbolizes your emotional nature, or the intuitive part of you that uses your emotions for guidance. Adding context, texture, and color to life, emotions help you find fulfillment and meaning. In this way, the intuitive and emotional guidance of the moon acts like a compass, helping you fully realize your purpose (which the sun can help you identify). In fact, some people believe a person's moon sign symbolizes the soul, and, given the moon's influence over water (the element of feeling and the soul), that isn't much of a stretch.

Ceaselessly changing form and shape in the sky through its phases, yet showing the earth only one side of its face, the moon can exude a sense of mystery and indicate hidden messages and your subconscious—the side of yourself that you don't usually see but that impacts you nonetheless. The moon is a body of reflection—just as it reflects the sun's light. This receptive energy helps you process and receive messages through dreams, feelings, and intuition.

While once also associated with male gods, the moon since has largely become linked with feminine deities in the Western world. Thus, in Western astrology, the moon is a symbol of traditionally mother-like figures and the home—things that provide nurturing and protective energy. Just like the moon nurtures humanity through balancing the seasons and impacting the tides, it can reveal how you have been nurtured in the past, and how you might like to be nurtured in your life. Thus the moon, even in magick, is often regarded as the guardian of the past, helping you access your subconscious.

## Magick

The Moon's nurturing, psychic, and emotional power can be used through its connection with Cancer. It can also be called upon during Moon-ruled Monday or the Moon's planetary hour. However, the Moon has an added layer of magickal timing that the planets do not—the phases of the moon.

As the moon orbits the earth, alignments among the earth, sun, and moon give way to the various lunar phases. When it comes to using the moon for magick, these alignments can provide opportunities for power-ful magickal enhancement. Here is a brief overview of the lunar phases' magickal meanings, as well as occasional special alignments like eclipses. (For more in-depth information and the moon's meanings through the various zodiacal signs, you can check out my book *Moon, Magic, Mixology.*)

### Waxing Cycle

This is a time when the moon appears to grow in both light and power. It is a time of growth and increase, and it is great for magick related to manifestation.

- **New Moon:** When the moon makes a 0-degree alignment with the sun and is not visible in the sky, it is called a new moon. At this point, the moon will always be in the same sign as the sun. Use this time for setting intentions, rebirth, and relaxation.

- **Waxing Crescent:** This is the time when the moon is visible as a sliver in the sky; it looks like a backward *C*. Magick at this time can focus on venturing into the unknown, hope, faith, and starting off on a new journey.

- **First Quarter:** At this point, the moon is half a circle in the sky, or 50 percent full. Spells related to balance and decision-making or pushing forward are especially powerful now. You might notice tensions and challenges that arise as your desires begin to come to fruition.

- **Waxing Gibbous:** The moon is mostly full. This is a time of confirma-tion, affirmation, and optimism, as the end goal is in sight. Refine your goals and cooperate with others.

- **Full Moon:** A full moon occurs when the moon is 100 percent illuminated. The waxing cycle is complete, so it is time for magick related to integration and manifestation. At this point, the moon is always directly opposite the sun and in the opposite sign. This opposition can heighten emotions and produce tension but also provide balance and rewards.

### Waning Cycle

During this cycle, the moon's light begins to decrease; it is a time of giving gratitude, release, cleansing, and banishment.

- **Waning Gibbous:** The moon is still mostly full but is just beginning to decrease in light. The rewards of the full moon can still be harvested. It is a time for magick related to gratitude, sharing, and reflection.

- **Third/Last Quarter:** At this point, there is 50 percent illumination and diminishing moonlight. Sync your magick by focusing on graceful endings and release.

- **Waning Crescent:** Now the moon is more dark than it is bright—it is a small sliver in the sky. It's a time to wrap up leftover matters, surrender, banish, and end things.

- **Dark Moon:** The moon is not visible, but it is not quite at 0-degree alignment with the sun. Magick that deals with the liminal (the threshold or space in between, such as between endings and new beginnings) is enhanced. This includes themes of rebirth, cleansing, banishment, mystery, transformation/alchemy, and inner work. This is also a great time to rest before the rebirth that comes with the new moon.

### Occasional Moons

As part of our unique celestial placement, with the moon orbiting the earth and the earth orbiting the sun, there are some astronomical alignments that are more rare and more powerful than others, such as eclipses and supermoons. The following section provides more information about these special times and how they can amplify your magick.

- **Eclipses:** These occur multiple times a year and involve particular placements of the earth, moon, and sun in a way that obstructs the moon or sun from view. They usually occur in pairs and represent an intense coupling of energy and deep, profound healing and insights. They also mark an energetic pattern of a cycle that can last for months.

- **Solar Eclipse:** A solar eclipse occurs when the moon aligns between the earth and the sun, blocking the sun from view. It can only occur during a new moon and will only last a few minutes. It is a time of dynamic, powerful energy, great for reflecting on the balance of the astrological meanings and powers of the Sun and Moon in your life. While this time can be energetically chaotic and unpredictable, it is also a new moon. As such, it is an ultrapowerful time to focus on new beginnings, new life paths, moving through obstacles, and tapping in to a new perspective. Look at what sign an eclipse is in to better understand its power.

- **Lunar Eclipse:** A lunar eclipse is a time when the earth aligns perfectly between the moon and the sun, with the earth's shadow casting darkness and/or discoloration upon the moon as it obstructs the sun's rays from the moon. As this can only occur when the moon is full, a lunar eclipse is often referred to as "a supercharged full moon." It is a time of wildness and high emotions and can also reveal hidden emotions and bring a powerful opportunity for change and healing.

# MERCURY

| ☿ | Elements | Air |
|---|----------|-----|
| | Key themes | Communication, the Mind, Information, Reasoning |
| | Associations | Gemini, Virgo, Third and Sixth Houses |

Named after the Roman winged-footed messenger deity, Mercury is true to its namesake, governing the realms of communication, intellect, and information. Associated with the element of air, this planet can provide insight into how you think and speak, ways you communicate, and in what types of environments you communicate best. True to its messenger nature in mythology, Mercury travels closest to the Sun and is also the fastest. Adorned with winged shoes that allowed him to relay information quickly,

Mercury is one of the few gods that can travel all three realms—that of the gods, humankind, and the underworld. This flexibility translates to its astrology and can aid you in receiving information and in travels, whether they be spiritual or physical.

Mercury is flexible—it can take on the qualities of whatever energy or planet it is forming an alignment with. So, when looking at Mercury, you'll need to see what planets it is forming an astrological alignment with. Be wary, however: As a symbol of communication and the mind, Mercury can also take on the role of trickster (thanks to its air element cunning and wit) and can be changeable and inauthentic at times. So, when working with this planetary energy, be sure to balance the mind with the heart and be clear on your intention to ensure you manifest the outcome you want.

### *Magick*

Mercury can strengthen spells related to information, travel, reasoning, and communication. Mercury's rulership over communication and reason can be seen through its two signs, Gemini and Virgo. Gemini is known for ideas and communication (the socializer), and Virgo is known for her ability to organize and think critically. Thus, these signs' respective seasons and beneficial transits are great opportunities for Mercury-blessed magick. Mercury's planetary hour and ruling day of Wednesday are also great times to call upon this planet's power.

If you're looking to call on this planetary power for communication, Mercury can open the throat for effective, clear communication. True to its air sign nature, the planet is also associated with the respiratory and central nervous system, through which you communicate from both outside of and within the body. Thus, spells that use the power of words and chants or your own preferred communication style are a great way to call upon Mercury in magick.

# VENUS

| | | |
|---|---|---|
| ♀ | **Elements** | Earth, Water |
| | **Key themes** | Beauty, Attraction, Abundance |
| | **Associations** | Taurus, Libra, Second and Seventh Houses |

The hottest planet in the solar system and the closest to the earth, Venus—the planet of attraction—has special importance to humanity. The brightest of the planets, Venus is often referred to as the morning or evening star, as during some parts of the year, she precedes dawn, and during others, she is the first to follow dusk. Named after the Roman goddess of beauty and love, her counterparts include the Scandinavian goddess Freya, the Greek goddess Aphrodite, and the ancient Babylonian goddess Ishtar. With the realm of love, romance, and luxury as her domain, it is no wonder that Venus has such importance. However, her power extends beyond basic concepts of love in astrology. Venus also indicates what you might attract or charm, how you connect with others, and how you express yourself through aesthetics, partnerships, and even wealth.

Venus celebrates the beauty in all things, such as art and other aesthetics. As goddess of pleasure, she also can lead you to discover what kinds of things you appreciate; where you find value, peace, and comfort; and how you enjoy the finer things in life. Style, harmony, artistic sense, and luxuries like salons and restaurants fall under her governance.

Often described as a lower octave of Neptune, Venus can bring healing and harmony. However, whereas Neptune represents universal love and getting lost in fantasy, Venus is romance: the person-to-person connections and expressive art, but not necessarily being consumed by those things.

### Magick

When it comes to magick, aligning your spells to Venus-ruled Friday or Venus's planetary hour can enhance efforts around love, beauty, harmony, and attracting abundance and gifts. Glamor magick that involves the way you dress or that uses aromas and colors is powerful when connected to Venus, as are aesthetically pleasing altars or curating magick in a space through interior design. You can also time related spells during transits through its signs of Libra and Taurus, where Venus illustrates its romantic and relationship energy. Through Libra, Venus highlights its associations with social graces, artistic sense of beauty, socialization, and romance. In Taurus, Venus illustrates its aspects of enjoying abundance of any kind, pleasures and indulgences, and enduring relationships. By tapping in to Venus at the heart, you can open yourself up to connection as well as receptivity. It can also aid female sex organs and various body glands in healing magick. As her namesake is thought to have risen from the ocean foam, seashells can be powerful imagery to use in Venus planetary spells.

# MARS

| ♂ | Elements | Fire |
|---|---|---|
| | Key themes | Action, Physical Energy, Passion |
| | Associations | Aries, First House |

Named after the Roman god of war and victory, Mars represents action and how you pursue goals and aspirations in the world. Mars is where you exert yourself—energetically and physically—in the world. A person's Mars sign can indicate how they might pursue their desires; their energy levels; their sexuality and what initiates their passion; and what sparks their physical desire, drive, and temperament.

Like its red, rusty appearance (due to iron-rich minerals on its surface), Mars is associated with fire and can indicate your sexual passion, drive, and temperament. Like the spark of the flame, Mars can signify what sparks your attraction, both in physical passion and in your motivation. Empowering efforts of strength, courage, athleticism, energy, and vitality, Mars helps you be more independent by taking initiative and going after what you want. Matters such as battles (even metaphorical ones), competition, challenges, sports, defense, law, military, and physical activities all fall under this planet's domain. However, too much Mars can signify aggression and even craft selfishness in the face of individual pursuit. So, with this fiery planet, it is key to direct its energy in conscious ways, such as through action, motivation, and physical exertion.

## Magick
In magick, Mars can bolster efforts to overcome obstacles, revitalize energy, and achieve goals and victories. Even spells that require physical movement to raise and focus energy do well under Mars's guidance. Aligning spells to Tuesday or Mars's planetary hour can help you summon forth this planet's powerful energy. As the planetary ruler of Aries, you can tap in to Mars's energy through this sign to inspire courage and charge fearlessly into uncharted territories. In ancient Rome, Mars's main festivals occurred during March, which was named for this deity. This same month coincides with the start of Aries season, making March a superior time for overcoming obstacles, igniting action, victory, and pursuing goals and visions.

Attuning your consciousness and energy to Mars can help bolster your energy centers and allow for more powerful results in your magick. When someone is angry, they might say the phrase "makes my blood boil"; in line with this, Mars rules blood within the body, and in healing magick, Mars can be used for circulation and efforts that focus on strength, muscles, adrenal glands, and male sex organs.

# JUPITER

| ♃ | Elements | Air, Fire |
|---|---|---|
| | Key themes | Expansion, Good Fortune, Optimism |
| | Associations | Sagittarius, Ninth House |

More than twice as massive as all the other planets combined, this gas giant is fittingly known as a planet of expansion in astrology; it can expand your perspective and (like its powerful magnetic field) attract luck and good fortune. Jupiter was the main deity in the Roman pantheon, ruling the other gods as well as humankind, bestowing blessings to favored ones while dealing justice (law) to others. Benefactor in both myth and astrology, and akin to its numerous moons as a planet, Jupiter can connect you with patrons who can help you advance your aspirations.

As ruler of Sagittarius, subjects like philosophy, religion, foreign travel, higher education, values, and ethics all fall under Jupiter's rulership as ways of expanding how you see the world and what you believe is possible. Helping you find meaning, establish personal ethics and beliefs, and pursue self-improvement, Jupiter aids you in finding optimism and faith in even the gravest of times. This mindset, in turn, uncovers opportunities and opens new doors.

While Jupiter can be a helpful benefactor, too much of anything is not good! A glass can only hold so much liquid before it overflows and creates a mess, and a flawed foundation cannot support a secure, abundant home. To truly use the benefits of this planet, it is important to have a healthy relationship with Jupiter and harness its structural power first, to give a firm, grounded support for the abundance you seek to take form. Read on to uncover how to use this planet's energy in your celestial magick.

## *Magick*

Working with Jupiter in your magick can help open new doors, invoke opportunities, and bless almost any endeavor. When it comes to timing, gain Jupiter's favor in your magick by using Thursday and Jupiter's planetary hour. You can also tune in to its magick through its ruling sign of Sagittarius or even its old (before the discovery of Neptune) sign of Pisces on occasions when you feel that may be helpful. Powerful Jupiter transits can also be beneficial for new opportunities, expansive ventures, luck, and even successful risk-taking. Use these transits to ponder the big questions, grow, and expand.

Much like it inspires expansion, Jupiter can be used in healing magick to inspire spiritual and physical growth (the process in the body it governs), as well as to balance and heal the body's largest gland (the liver), where the body manages overindulgence.

# SATURN

| ♄ | Elements | Earth |
|---|---|---|
| | Key themes | Responsibility, Structure, Boundaries |
| | Associations | Capricorn, Tenth House |

Famous for its rings, which were likely formed by pieces of comets, asteroids, and moons that were torn apart by the planet's powerful gravity (that imagery really highlights the planet of restriction, doesn't it?), Saturn showcases the harshness but also the rewards of life and reality. The planet of boundaries and limitations, Saturn teaches structure and responsibility, helping you achieve growth through experience. Breaking the pattern of naming planets after the major Roman gods, Saturn is named for the titan that preceded them—the father of Jupiter (Kronos in Greek myth), who ate all his children for fear of being overtaken by them, until Jupiter/Zeus freed them all. Through this myth, you can glean the themes of authority, tradition, power structures, and harsh restrictions this planet is known for, which is probably why it has a negative connotation. However, it is these very limits and challenges that, once learned, help you harness discipline and control and, with time, manifest lasting results.

Prior to absorbing Greek myth, Saturn was an agricultural deity in Rome. Fittingly, agriculture is an occupation that deals with time and cycles, requiring patience, discipline, and hard work in order to gain wealth and abundance. Through these aspects, you can learn responsibility and cultivate rewards that come with recognizing structures and rules as you bring your desires into the physical realm. Like the harvest scythe, Saturn shows that we "reap what we sow," good or bad. Such cause and effect can often highlight inadequacies, but through work, Saturn shows us how to transform weakness into strengths and obtain mastery, and that your greatest weaknesses can indeed become your greatest strengths.

### Magick

Harnessing the power of Saturn in your magick can be beneficial for long-term success, stability, and learning to master anything—even things you once considered your weaknesses. As the planet of limitations, Saturn is great for protection magick and setting up firm physical and energetic boundaries. For healing magick, Saturn can help strengthen the skeletal system that provides structure for the body. When seeking Saturn's favor, try spells on Saturday (for which this planet was named) and/or during Saturn's planetary hour. You can also harness the power of this planet through Capricorn, where Saturn is determined and focuses on achievements and what is real, material, and tangible. Saturn was once thought to rule Aquarius (before the discovery of Uranus), so you can use this sign's power when looking to break rigid rules set by Saturn once you have gleaned the wisdom and mastery in a particular area. Saturn transits can feel tricky, but try to use these times to reflect on how to use structure for your benefit in your magick, whether it be protection, integrating lessons, or building lasting structures.

# URANUS

| | Elements | Air |
|---|---|---|
| | Key themes | Freedom, Genius, the Future |
| | Associations | Aquarius, Eleventh House |

Like the Greek god of the open sky, Ouranos, for whom this planet was named, Uranus expanded the realm of possibility and human knowledge to the fact that other planets and celestial bodies existed past Saturn, beyond the limits of the human eye. The discovery of Uranus in 1781 ushered in an era of revolutions and futuristic, scientific discoveries, establishing this planet in astrology as one of rebellion, future, and science. Often referred to as the higher octave of Mercury, Uranus represents ingenuity, sudden insights, and quick thinking, and relates to lightning and electricity.

Ruler of Aquarius, Uranus seeks freedom and liberation, awakening you to new thoughts and ideas that expand the realm of possibility. Breaking the planetary norm of spinning on its axis, Uranus spins on its side, so that its poles take turns facing the sun. This abnormal, eccentric behavior is mirrored in Uranus's astrology, highlighting themes of individuality and uniqueness within us all.

While Uranus breaks the rules set by Saturn, when these two planets work together, meaningful change happens that can truly improve society. While Uranus seeks freedom, it also speaks to the need to establish discipline before fully being able to use its benefits. In other words, you need to learn the rules before you break them.

## *Magick*

In magick, Uranus can offer an unpredictable energy and manifest in unexpected ways. However, this can be just the energy to call upon in matters of genius, innovation, and liberation. Working with Uranus can usher in change and movement when you're stagnant—just be sure to prepare for the unexpected. Magick that deals with revolution and humanitarianism does well here, as does magick that revolves around technology or uses technology as a tool. Use Uranus's cosmic power to innovate your life or even improve how you do your magick!

Considered the higher octave of Mercury, Wednesdays and Mercury's hour can be beneficial times to connect to this celestial power. You can also use the power of this planet through its sign Aquarius, especially for abandoning old labels and notions and embracing innovation and new identities.

Since this planet rules the electrical impulses within the body, through working with Uranus, you can harness regular "sparks" of genius and innovation in your craft.

# NEPTUNE

| | Elements | Water |
|---|---|---|
| ♆ | Key themes | Collective Unconscious, Psychic Connection, Transcendence |
| | Associations | Pisces, Twelfth House |

Like the god of the sea for whom it was named, watery Neptune washes away and dissolves boundaries, wounds, and perceptions of reality with its energetic waves, and unifies all in its vast, healing oceans. Helping you transcend earthly bonds, Neptune invites you to lose yourself and merge into the greater whole, ushering in new dimensions of reality and consciousness. Here, Neptune inspires the artist who can merge their consciousness to the greater universe and channel ethereal works of art, as well as the psychic who can become a clear cosmic channel of information from other planes of existence. Ruling the arts, poetry, and music, this planet calls forth spiritual experiences that can produce inspired, otherworldly, and vibration-raising works such as symphonies and orchestral pieces. And as can be seen through go-with-the-flow Pisces, Neptune inspires unity through these spiritual, artistic expressions and experiences. Here is where you fantasize and engage in the symbolism of dreams to access the subconscious and the psychic.

Through working with Neptune, you can become a clear psychic channel. But this type of work can lead to extreme sensitivity, which can cloud your sense of clarity and muddy your ability to discern. So, working with Saturn or grounding with earth energy is important before exploring the cosmic and consuming power of water-element Neptune, to help establish reality and ground your energy to boundaries of the physical plane. While working with boundaries may not seem so glamorous, it can heighten your experience with Neptune in a much more productive way.

## Magick

You can bless your spells with profound psychic insight and artistic inspiration—as well as become a clearer channel to the cosmos in all of your celestial magick—by connecting to Neptune. Use its cosmic power of water to soothe and heal and to foster greater understanding and compassion. Magick that relates to dreams and symbolism excels under Neptune's watch, which is great for incorporating the magick of symbols into your spells (such as the astrological glyphs!), or even in using art as a form of magick or to channel psychic information. Such work with Neptune will empower your third eye, which corresponds to a part of the body that Neptune rules—the pineal gland.

Given that Neptune was one of the planets discovered later in human civilization and is considered a higher octave of Venus, you can use Friday or Venus's hour for effective Neptune magick. You can also work with Neptune through Pisces, where its influences of artistic inspiration, psychic consciousness, and unity really come through, inviting peace in any situation!

# PLUTO

| | Elements | Water |
|---|---|---|
| | Key themes | Transformation, Endings, Truth |
| | Associations | Scorpio, Eighth House |

Like the Roman god of the underworld it's named after, this powerful and intense planet rules themes of endings, rebirth, truth, and transformation in astrology. Both the transformer and destroyer, Pluto is a celestial body of extremes. It forces you to surrender and be vulnerable in your search for personal power and inner knowing. While Pluto can usher in experiences that cause drastic, sudden, and extreme changes, it also helps clear the way to rejuvenate and renew—just like the phoenix that is reborn in the ashes of the flames that consumed it or the wildfire that clears the land to make way for new growth. Because Pluto is the slowest-moving "planet"— taking around twenty years to move through one sign—the sign it is in often relates to a generation.

Officially considered a dwarf planet, Pluto is one of the outermost planets, existing in the Kuiper Belt (an interstellar belt on the outskirts of the solar system) just beyond the orbit of Neptune, connecting humans with the primal energy of the beginnings of our solar system. Similarly, it connects you with your own primal energy and desires. Through its rulership of Scorpio, you can see these Plutonian themes of mystery, power, the occult, and sex.

Even before Pluto was discovered, astronomers suspected there was a celestial body in its position due to the gravitational pull it has upon Neptune. Similarly, its themes can seem to sneak up on you, crafting drastic passion, endings, and transformations. Stripping you of your sense of security, Pluto eliminates any falsehoods you've been under and reveals your vulnerability and inner truth. While this process may be difficult at times, it is through vulnerability that you can see your true self and achieve a greater spiritual awareness.

### Magick

When it comes to your magick, Pluto can bring a powerful energy to matters of truth, psychic awareness, personal power, and passion. For the zesty transformative power of this celestial body, you can use Tuesday or Mars's planetary hour for casting spells, as Mars is considered the lower octave of Pluto. Tapping in to beneficial Scorpio transits can help you channel the primal power of this planet as well. However, some Pluto themes may benefit from other planetary bodies, so use discretion on what resonates best with your intention. For example, if you are undergoing a life-shattering transformation in your love life, reflecting on Venus, or the second house, or even working with the hidden wounds and subconscious realm of the Moon and Neptune can help focus the work you are doing.

Pluto transforms all it touches, many times irrevocably, so don't work with this planet lightly, unless you are ready to face the truth and permanently change your perceptions of life. At the same time, rejuvenation, endings, and rebirth are facts of every aspect of life—even your own body, as seen in the process of the death and rebirth of cells in the body (the process Pluto governs). Meditating on this can bring you harmony and attune you to the energy of rebirthing a whole new you (spiritually and physically), in preparation for transformation in your life.

# RETROGRADES

Who hasn't heard of the disruptive Mercury retrograde? This period when the planet of communication moves backward in the sky is fraught with communication mishaps, misunderstandings, and technology and transportation issues. However, Mercury is not the only planet to experience a retrograde period. During Venus retrograde, relationships tend to be tested and past lovers resurface. During Mars retrograde, forward momentum and motivation hit a standstill, inspiring anger and frustration.

Retrogrades are periods when a planet appears to be going backward in the sky. Of course, this is not actually the case but is due to the earth's position in the solar system in relation to the planets. The frequency and length of retrograde periods depend on that planet's orbital period. Some retrogrades, like Mars and Venus, occur every couple of years. Others happen at much longer intervals. Some, like Mercury, we experience three or so times in a single year.

As with anything moving backward in life, retrogrades can bring up delays, unroot hidden issues, and raise tensions in the area that planet rules. The sign the planet will be in at this time "revisits" the energy of that planet in that sign, and the house in which it occurs in your natal chart affects what areas of your life might be impacted. At the core, retrogrades emphasize "re"—they are a time to revisit, relax, redo, and reflect on its themes. Old projects can be revisited, old friendships reignited, or closure regained.

When it comes to magick, retrograde periods are not times to usher forth new beginnings, move matters ahead, or manifest desires in the area of life the retrograde planet rules. However, they are a time of healing and offer the opportunity to revisit and retune in that area. There will almost always be one planet in retrograde, so be vigilant with that planet's energy in your life and your use of it in magick. This is a time to recalibrate and let the retrograde reveal what you need to work on with that planet so that when the planet moves forward again, your relationship and power with that aspect will be even stronger and cosmically aligned.

# OTHER CELESTIAL OBJECTS

The debris from when the solar system was first created formed asteroids, comets, and other rocky debris that orbit in the night sky. Because such bodies are invisible to the human eye, the first of these objects wasn't discovered until 1801. While these celestial objects may not have been worshipped by ancient peoples in the same way the planets were, they are no less powerful in their astrological impact today.

Asteroids are the rocky remains from when the solar system was first created, around 4.6 billion years ago. They orbit the sun like the other celestial bodies, and most stay in a belt located between Mars and Jupiter.

These asteroids are all made up of different groupings of families of different ages.

In this section, you will learn about some of the more established asteroids and other celestial objects often used within astrology. More celestial bodies are always being found, and astrology as a practice is still uncovering how these discoveries fit in. Named after different ancient mythological figures, much like the planets were, these celestial bodies are thought to unlock new themes being unraveled in human consciousness and reality as they are discovered. And like their namesakes, they can provide key themes for reflection, healing, and magick. To learn current thoughts about these bodies in detail, check out the books *Astrology for Yourself* and *Asteroid Goddesses* by Douglas Bloch and Demetra George.

## Dwarf Planet Ceres

| | | |
|---|---|---|
| | Key themes | Unconditional Love, Nurturing, Repeated Loss |
| | Associated signs | Taurus, Cancer, Virgo |
| | Associated element | Earth |

The first celestial body to be discovered within the asteroid belt, Ceres is so large and different from the other asteroids that it was reclassified as a dwarf planet. And this abundant body has lots to share with humanity! Named after the Roman goddess of agriculture, Ceres takes on the roles of her mythological character in astrology—she is the great mother who nurtures and loves unconditionally.

Ruling the domains of agriculture (grain, fertility, abundance) in myth, Ceres provides metaphorical sustenance and nourishment in astrology as well and helps life thrive. She teaches you to love yourself and others unconditionally and to develop self-worth and acceptance. As symbolized by the loss of her child for half the year to Hades (a story explored in Chapter 3), Ceres symbolizes mother-child relationships and experiences of recurrent loss in the process of learning to let go.

### Magick

While the astrological power of bodies such as Ceres is still being established, you can tap in to and access the power of this astrological body in your magick for abundance, unconditional and self-love, and releasing grief. Ceres is a key archetype asteroid to work with for nourishment, providing what you need to thrive and grow, and for connecting to nature. Her themes can be most easily accessed through spells related to the signs of nurturing Taurus, caring Cancer, and virtuous Virgo (explored in more detail in Chapters 8, 10, and 12, respectively). Harvest symbols such as the sickle, sheaths of wheat, and a cornucopia (bountiful with fruits for sustenance and nurturance) can empower your spellwork with this asteroid.

## Vesta Asteroid

| | | |
|---|---|---|
| | **Key themes** | Discipline, Dedication, Self-Work |
| | **Associated signs** | Virgo, Scorpio |
| | **Associated element** | Fire |

The second-largest body in the asteroid belt and named after the goddess of the hearth, asteroid Vesta represents discipline, focus, commitment, and self-work. Like the flickering flame it's named after, Vesta exemplifies one of the largest ranges of brightness of a rocky body (it can be both very dim and very bright) within our solar system, possibly due to darker materials deposited from other asteroids, like soot from a flame. Vesta can help you integrate and focus energy, much like a hearth fire consumes the fuel you give it and maintains a steady flame for the house in return. In ancient Rome, the Vestal Virgins tended to Vesta's perpetually burning fire within her temple, an example of how you must continuously tend fires (or, metaphorically, remain committed to a cause). As goddess of the hearth fire that provides warmth for the home, Vesta was also considered a patron deity of bakers. Through her steady hearth fire, sustenance and prosperity can be achieved.

### Magick
Tapping in to the power of this asteroid can bolster your spells related to dedication, commitment, and fueling your inner flame. Vesta is thought to relate most closely with two signs: Virgo and Scorpio. Through Virgo, Vesta's themes of self-work, focus, and commitment can be more easily accessed. Through Scorpio, Vesta's power can be used for inner truth and transformation, as well as to unravel false ideas of and guilt around sexuality, for this deity was later associated with the idea of virginity.

Fire magick can be a great way to use Vesta's power, harnessing the focus and precision of her flame, which you can also use for cleansing, to connect to the purity of the self and to the sacred—specifically, how you feed your inner flame to make it controlled and deliver just the right amount of heat to your endeavors. Tap in to the power of kitchen witchery and baking when working with this astrological power.

## Juno Asteroid

| | | |
|---|---|---|
| ⚵ | **Key themes** | Relationship Balance, Power Dynamics, Social Prestige |
| | **Associated signs** | Libra, Scorpio |
| | **Associated element** | Water |

Taking its name from the Roman goddess of marriage, women, and the money-making mint (as Juno was inscribed on Roman coins), Juno represents meaningful one-to-one relationships, the power dynamics within them, and social position. A once-powerful goddess who suddenly found her power diminished within her marriage, Juno represents power dynamics within relationships of all kinds. Constantly coping with Jupiter's infidelity in mythology, themes around possessiveness, fidelity, and abuse all fall under her domain, as well as a person's needs within a relationship. While this certainly pertains to romantic relationships and commitment, it can also relate to other one-on-one relationships—such as in business, friendships, and careers. As consort to the chief deity Jupiter, Juno is responsible for social prestige and power as well.

### Magick

In magick, you can call on Juno for matters of balance within relationships, as well as social prestige, personal power, and money. With themes resonating most closely with Libra and Scorpio, Juno's power can be tapped through these signs in your celestial magick. Through Libra, you can experience Juno's relation to equality within relationships and marriage, as well as social prestige, reputation, and status. Through Scorpio, you can experience the depth of intimacy and meaning within relationships, as well as business and personal power.

# Pallas Asteroid

| | Key themes | Originality, Creative Wisdom, Social Causes |
|---|---|---|
| | Associated signs | Leo, Libra, Aquarius |
| | Associated element | Air |

Named after Greek goddess and warrior of wisdom Pallas Athena, in astrology, the Pallas asteroid couples warrior skills with wisdom, inspiring justice, balance, and insight. Springing forth from Zeus's/Jupiter's head in mythology, Pallas represents your mind's capacity to create, whether it be through artisanal professions or your own reality via thoughts and perceptions. Known in mythology as a talented weaver with mental acuity, Pallas can highlight originality and wisdom in the creative arts and aid those who pursue vocations in that area. Mythical Athena's unique birth and depiction as a feminine, chaste goddess of bravery and strength show her capacity to break gender roles and ideas of sexuality. Father-daughter relationships can also be exemplified through this asteroid, as seen in Pallas Athena's relationship with her father, Zeus, in mythology.

### Magick

Modern astrologers are still unraveling the power and associations of asteroids. Pallas's energies may best relate to the signs of Leo, Libra, and Aquarius. Through Leo, Pallas's power as patron of the arts, strength, and success shine through, helping people embrace their originality through creativity. Through Libra, Pallas highlights air-like qualities of justice, balance, and diplomacy. And through Aquarius, Pallas resonates with themes of humanitarianism and social justice, as well as sudden flashes of genius and unique eccentricities.

# Chiron

| | Key themes | Healing from Wounds, Holistic Health, Wisdom |
|---|---|---|
| | Associated signs | Virgo, Sagittarius |
| | Associated element | Unknown |

Originally thought to be an asteroid, the comet Chiron represents healing and holistic knowledge gained from your personal wounds. Believed to originally be part of the Kuiper Belt (like Pluto)—an interstellar belt on the outskirts of the solar system filled with some of the most primitive bodies from when the solar system was formed—and traveling all the way out to Saturn and Uranus, Chiron is believed by some to be an energetic intermediary, connecting humanity to galactic information.

To understand more about Chiron in astrology, it's helpful to look at his myth. A unique centaur adopted by Apollo (god of light, poetry, and healing), Chiron learned the healing arts, medicine, music, and divination/prophecy through Apollo, and archery and hunting through Artemis, Apollo's sister. This unique upbringing crafted a compassionate, wise centaur who artfully combined the skills of nature and of humans. Half man, half horse, Chiron helps you connect to and understand nature on a deeper level. He bridges the natural and human worlds, uncovering and combining the wisdom found within each.

Chiron was accidentally shot with a poisoned arrow by Hercules, one of his mentees. In agony and unable to die due to his immortality, Chiron was placed in the sky by Zeus/Jupiter to relieve him of his pain. In some myths, Chiron even traded his immortality for the sake of Prometheus, who was chained to a rock and punished—showing how even in his moment of pain, Chiron still sought to uplift and help others. A story of alchemy, Chiron encourages you to transform your wounds into wisdom, and can help you use empathy to assist others as they process their personal pains.

### Magick

Accessing the celestial power of this comet can heighten the power of healing, wisdom, mastery spells, and even prophecy. Through their witchcraft, witches often engage in healing their own wounds and look to the healing power of the natural world. As such, Chiron can be a powerful energy for astrological witches to connect to and to use in healing magick of all kinds. Sharing themes with Virgo and Sagittarius, Chiron can be more easily accessed through spells related to these signs, whether it be during their Sun seasons, Moons, or other planetary transits. You can use Virgo to access the healing cures found in nature and share that knowledge and medicine with others. Through Sagittarius, you can more easily connect to Chiron's prophesying abilities and wisdom when it comes to spiritual aspects of healing from wounds. In both, you can uncover Chiron's themes of holistic health.

# Chapter 6

# COSMIC WITCHCRAFT ESSENTIALS

Whether it be the celestial witch's cauldron lighting up with fire in the dark of the night, or the reflection of the stars in a cup of tea, there are various tools that will help you contain, channel, and attune your celestial magick. Now that you are familiar with the astrological signs, celestial bodies, and houses that create the myth, meaning, and power of the night sky, it is time to learn the celestial correspondences that will help you draw down their power right into your very hands. You'll learn how to use relevant crystals, potent foods and herbs, and key energy centers in your spellcasting to connect with astrological themes.

## SPELLCASTING TOOLS

Before you get ready to cast a cosmic spell, it is important to be familiar with some of the tools you will be using and their celestial correspondences. Many of these tools will be familiar to you, and in fact, you may already have some on hand. Anything you don't have, you may be able to find at thrift stores or inexpensive shops—there is no reason to break the bank!

- **Bowl:** A vessel to hold the elemental magick of water or other liquids, a bowl is a great tool for a variety of spells based on water signs, such as water scrying, dissolving spells, or even making magickal mists and mixtures. For scrying, it is ideal to have a black bowl.

- **Teacup or glass:** When mixing up an imbibable potion, having a favorite cup to heighten your cosmic experience can really take your magick the extra mile. Cups are symbolic vessels for what you wish to hold and bring into your life, so make sure you have one you like and resonate with!

- **Cauldron or fireproof dish:** Few symbols bring to mind the image of a witch more than a cauldron does. A cast iron cauldron is best for magick that involves fire, but any fireproof dish or container will do. You can use the dish to hold candles.

- **Bell:** Having a bell or two will come in handy with air and sound spells, and you can usually find inexpensive ones. Bells are great tools for summoning and calling things to you on the astral plane, and they can also be used for cleansing energy with sacred sound.

- **Wand:** Often made of wood or metal, wands are useful (and gorgeous) tools for channeling and directing cosmic energy. (In this spell book, you will be crafting a cinnamon money wand.) You can use a quart crystal point as a wand as well.

- **Sacred space:** While not necessarily a cosmic "tool," having a space, no matter how small, to attune to and channel cosmic energy is important. A place where you can quiet your mind and raise your awareness to the stars will help you really tune in to the cosmos. Additionally, you may consider having an outdoor space, allowing you to gaze directly at the power of the night sky as you do your workings.

- **Oil:** Used in witchcraft to anoint candles, crystals, talismans, and the body with another layer of the power of plants, oil blends and conjure oils are made of essential oils, sometimes infused with herbs and diluted with a base oil, such as olive oil or almond oil. For the sake of accessibility and cost-effectiveness, this book uses kitchen oils (such as coconut, almond, and olive oil) in place of full oil blends, since they still carry the power of the herbal ingredient from which they are made (for example, olive oil carries the herbal power of olives). However, feel free to purchase mixed oil blends from your local witchcraft vendors, or use the Neptune Deep Healing Oil in Chapter 18 as an example of how you might make your own. Oils are great for providing a sticky surface on a standing candle, which allows herb blends to stick to the candle. You can add to the power of such oils or even your basic olive oil by charging them during certain astrological events, similar to making moon water, or by infusing it with a certain herb.

# INTERSTELLAR INGREDIENTS

Each plant or spice has an energetic resonance that can help you summon a specific energy—such as strength or wisdom, for example—from the stars. The ingredients listed in this book have been selected for their accessibility at most grocery stores, whether in the spice section or as fresh produce. For more detailed and diverse planetary ingredients, check out *Cunningham's Encyclopedia of Magical Herbs* by Scott Cunningham or *Llewellyn's Complete Book of Correspondences* by Sandra Kynes.

In the following table, you will find magickal and astrological correspondences combined for the ingredients used in Part 2. This list is by no means exhaustive—there are different magickal and astrological schools of thought and approaches regarding such correspondences—but these will serve your purposes for this book.

| Ingredient | Planet and Element Association(s) | Key Themes |
|---|---|---|
| Agave | Mars, Fire | Lust, Love, Beauty, Youth, Life Cycles, Coming to Power |
| Allspice | Mars, Jupiter, Earth, Fire | Money, Abundance, Luck, Success, Healing |
| Almond | Mercury, Air | Money, Healing, Prosperity, Wisdom, Success, Romance |
| Anise | Jupiter, Air | Purification, Protection, Clarity, Psychic Ability, Spirit |
| Apple | Venus, Water | Love, Healing, Longevity, Fertility, Wisdom, Magick |
| Bay Leaf | Sun, Fire, Air | Protection, Strength, Prophecy, Healing, Purification, Wisdom, Success |
| Basil | Mars, Pluto, Venus, Fire | Affection, Protection, Divination, Mental Clarity, Decision-Making, Banishing Negative Energy |
| Blackberry | Moon, Venus, Water | Healing, Grounding, Lust, Money |
| Black Pepper | Mars, Fire | Protection, Purification, Banishment, Grounding |

| Ingredient | Planet and Element Association(s) | Key Themes |
|---|---|---|
| Calendula | Sun, Fire | Happiness, Prophecy, Luck, Strength, Dreams |
| Cayenne | Mars, Fire | Passion, Heat, Jinx-Breaking, Repellent/Protection, Banishment |
| Caraway | Mercury, Air | Love, Lust, Protection, Healing, Mind |
| Cardamom | Venus, Water | Love, Sex, Luck |
| Chamomile | Sun, Water, Air | Money, Peace, Love, Purification, Communication |
| Cinnamon | Sun, Fire | Vibration-Raising, Power, Lust, Love, Success, Spirituality, Psychic Ability |
| Coconut | Moon, Water | Spirituality, Love, Inner Purification, Psychic Awareness |
| Coffee | Mars, Fire | Mind, Physical Energy, Divination |
| Clove | Jupiter, Fire | Comfort, Exorcism, Love/Sex, Money/Riches, Purification, Protection, Vibration-Raising, Spirituality, Stop Gossip |
| Cumin | Mars, Fire | Protection, Peace, Fidelity, Happiness |
| Dill | Mercury, Fire | Luck, Soothe/Peace, Love/Sensuality, Abundance/Money, Protection |
| Egg | All Elements | Protection, Rebirth/New Life, Cleansing, Abundance, Healing, Divination |
| Fennel | Mercury, Fire | Strength, Protection, Cleansing, Healing |
| Garlic | Mars, Fire | Protection, Health |
| Ginger | Mars, Fire | Health, Healing, Love, Money, Abundance, Success, Power |
| Honey | Sun | Spirituality, Purification, Health, Harmony, Love, Sex, Happiness, Wisdom |

| Ingredient | Planet and Element Association(s) | Key Themes |
|---|---|---|
| Jasmine | Moon, Mercury | Love, Money, Abundance, Spirituality, Prophecy, Dreams |
| Lavender | Mercury, Air | Love, Purification, Dreams, Peace, Longevity, Protection, Happiness |
| Lemon | Moon, Water | Creativity, Fidelity, Friendship, Happiness, Joy, Longevity, Love, Purification |
| Lime | Sun, Fire | Healing, Love, Hex-Breaking, Protection |
| Maple | Jupiter, Air, Earth | Love, Grounding, Longevity, Money |
| Marjoram | Mercury, Air | Love, Peace, Protection, Grief, Health |
| Mint | Peppermint: Mercury, Spearmint: Venus | Mind, Clarity, Abundance, Divination, Psychic Ability, Love, Protection, Calm |
| Nutmeg | Jupiter, Fire | Luck, Money, Wishes, Health, Fidelity |
| Olive | Sun, Air | Spirituality, Blessings, Health/Healing, Peace, Sensuality |
| Orange | Sun, Fire | Love, Well-Being, Divination, Money, Beauty, Purification, Creativity/Inspiration, Luck, |
| Poppy | Moon, Water | Dreams, Fertility, Abundance, Love, Sleep/Rest, Money, Luck |
| Rose | Venus, Water | Love, Healing, Spirituality, Beauty, Psychic Powers, Luck |
| Rosemary | Sun, Mercury, Moon | Protection, Memory, Mind, Love, Clarity, Purification, Healing, Peace |
| Saffron | Sun, Fire | Strength, Psychic Ability, Happiness, Love, Healing, Lust |
| Sage | Jupiter, Mercury, Air | Spirituality, Longevity, Wisdom, Protection, Wishes, Focus, Health, Purification |

| Ingredient | Planet and Element Association(s) | Key Themes |
|---|---|---|
| Salt | Earth | Grounding, Protection, Purification |
| Sugarcane | Venus, Water | Love, Lust, Money, Abundance, Attraction |
| Thyme | Venus, Water | Love, Psychic Awareness, Purification, Healing, Health, Courage, Peace |
| Vanilla | Venus, Water | Love, Sexuality, Energy, Mind, Peace, Money |
| Walnut | Sun, Fire | Health/Healing, Mind, Wishes |

# USING CRYSTALS TO CONNECT TO THE COSMOS

Various stones, crystals, and minerals have been used for their energetic powers and beauty throughout time. Each sign has certain stones that are associated with it. The meditations in Chapters 8, 13, and 16 can help you learn to work with crystal energy in astrological magick. You'll tune in to the stone's energetic frequency to amplify your spells.

The stones in this book were chosen to help correspond with the astrological themes and energy of each sign's season as well as being more affordable alternatives to traditional birthstones. If you cannot find some of the stones used in Part 2, feel free to switch them for a sign's correspondences (see Appendix D), or use this section to make sure the energy matches! For example, if you can't find ethically sourced lapis lazuli, you can check Appendix D for other stones that correspond with Libra or that sign, or reference this section for other suitable alternatives. Try your best to source your stones ethically so that you can contribute to a healthier cosmos. You can do this by developing relationships with your local crystal seller, going to gem shows and (politely) asking crystal dealers, or even finding miners on small business websites (like *Etsy*) who source stones directly from the earth. Remember to be polite when inquiring, as small businesses are often doing the best they can.

A brief overview of stones used in Part 2 is given here, but for more in-depth information about each stone, check out *The Book of Stones* by

Robert Simmons and Naisha Ahsian. Or, for even more information or options as to the intertwining of astrology and stones, look for books such as *Judy Hall's Crystal Zodiac*.

| Stone | Purpose |
| --- | --- |
| Amethyst | Amethyst is a great stone for developing intuitive abilities and peace and harmony. It can also help you connect to the divine source and to spiritual wisdom. |
| Aquamarine | This stone is useful for communicating your innermost truths and with spirit. Like calming, rhythmic waves, aquamarine promotes peace as well as intellect and safe travel. |
| Blue Apatite | Aiding psychic abilities and accessing knowledge, blue apatite is a great stone for lucid dreaming, vision, and open communication. |
| Blue Lace Agate | A powerful communication stone, blue lace agate inspires calm thought, relaxation, and clear communication. |
| Bloodstone | Inspiring courage, vitality, and strength, bloodstone aids you in enduring and fulfilling commitments and aspirations, even in the face of obstacles and change. |
| Carnelian | Since it invokes courage and boldness, carnelian inspires leadership as well as physical vitality and energy. |
| Citrine | Inspiring positive energy, citrine will help connect you to your inner inspiration and will promote joy, happiness, and prosperity. |
| Clear Quartz | A wonderful stone for programming, clear quartz will amplify and direct energy, inspire clarity of mind, and enhance memory. |
| Emerald | Usher in prosperity and connect to divine love as you find your inner worth with emerald. |
| Fluorite | A focusing stone, helping to clear the mind of debris, fluorite soothes anxiety and worry. It is an effective stone for clear thinking and productivity. |
| Garnet | Connect to passion, inner motivation, and your survival instincts with this stone. Garnet will help feed the fire you need to pursue your aspirations! |

| Stone | Purpose |
|-------|---------|
| Hematite | A powerful grounder and protector, hematite connects you to the earth's energy, absorbs negative energy, and balances and soothes. |
| Labradorite | An excellent stone for opening psychic abilities, labradorite helps and protects you as you develop your intuitive abilities. Great for times of transition and change. |
| Lapis Lazuli | This stone will help you access other realms and communicate with your guides, making it a good choice for psychic development and clear communication. |
| Moonstone | Helps you to connect to your higher self and intuition while inviting a calm sense of purpose and resolve. Invokes creativity and inner power into your life and is great for safe travel. |
| Mother-of-Pearl | Containing the healing and soothing power of the sea, mother-of-pearl promotes your intuition, self-expression, emotional balance, and sense of clarity. |
| Orange Calcite | Orange calcite is a stone of creativity, sexuality, playfulness, and confidence. As it brings solar energy into your energetic field, this stone invites balance, joy, and hope. |
| Peridot | A powerful ally for abundance, prosperity, and heart healing, peridot connects you to universal love, opening you up to joy and prosperity. |
| Pyrite | Associated with luck and prosperity, pyrite can also promote vitality, ground you to the earth, deflect negative energy, and enhance your will and inspiration. |
| Rose Quartz | Rose quartz connects you with universal love, inviting peace, comfort, and gratefulness as you recognize the beauty within yourself and all around you. |
| Ruby | Stimulating passion, expression, and awareness at the heart level, ruby balances the heart and inspires bliss. It's also effective in spells for success. |
| Rutilated Quartz | This is a powerful amplifier that works well with all energy centers. It can help you connect to the divine source, manifest creativity, and channel psychic communication. |
| Selenite | Wonderful for connecting to your higher self, selenite is known for its cleansing and protective properties. |

| Stone | Purpose |
| --- | --- |
| Smoky Quartz | A grounding, protective stone that helps filter out unwanted energy. It also helps ground higher frequencies for manifestation. |
| Sunstone | A crystal of confidence, strength, courage, and joy, sunstone's solar connection inspires personal expansion and leadership. |

# THE STARS, SEASONS, AND WHEEL OF THE YEAR

As the earth orbits the sun and spins along its axis, revealing different parts of the celestial sky, it also creates our seasonal experience. Steadied by the gravitational pull of the moon at different points of our orbit around the sun, we experience the change and power of the seasons through the equinoxes and solstices.

Cultures across the timeline of humanity have worshipped the spring and fall equinoxes and summer and winter solstices through various celebrations. These days are especially powerful occasions for astrological magick. In this section, you'll learn about what's known as the "Wheel of the Year" in witchcraft and pagan traditions, and the astrological power and potency of these special days. The Wheel of the Year is the cycle of natural holidays and celebrations of seasonal changes throughout the year, and astrological importance can be found within them. Some days, like Yule and Litha, fall during an astrological solstice. Others, like Samhain and Beltane, are often celebrated on more fixed days but do also have astrological alignments that mark the halfway point between transitions of the seasons. This gives you the option of a fixed day to celebrate or a day when the sun reaches this astrological cross-quarter/halfway mark (perfect for the busy witch whom the celebrations always seem to sneak up on!). It is important to note that, while both the Northern and Southern Hemispheres experience the various zodiacal signs at the same time (such as the Sun in Leo), these two parts of the earth experience opposite seasons. The meaning of the signs is the same, but the seasonal energies will be different. With astrological apps and websites, a quick search will uncover the day of such astrological alignments for the year.

## Spring Equinox

Marking the astrological new year, the spring equinox is one of two days of the entire year when the hours of light and darkness are held in equal balance for a brief time. From this day forward, the hours of daylight grow, and the hours of night and darkness wane. This equinox also summons springlike themes of abundance, growth, rebirth, and renewal. In the Northern Hemisphere, the spring equinox swiftly evokes the zodiac seasons of Aries, Taurus, and Gemini, while ushering in the season of Libra, Scorpio, and Sagittarius in the southern part of the hemisphere.

## Beltane

Whether celebrated as Beltane or May Day, this day comes in the middle of spring and is a time of excitement, growth, renewal, and sensuality. While many witches in the Northern Hemisphere celebrate this as a traditional holiday on May 1, the astrologically correct day would occur when the Sun is at 15 degrees Taurus (which would change every year). For those in the Southern Hemisphere, 15 degrees Taurus will mark your Samhain celebrations.

## Summer Solstice

At the tail end of Gemini season in the North and Sagittarius season in the South, the summer solstice is the day when daylight lasts the longest and nighttime is at its shortest—thus, the longest day of the year. The official start of summer, this solstice is a time of culmination, power, and manifestation. From this day forward, the daylight wanes ever so slowly but still remains in its power. This change of season invokes the themes and energy of the Sun in Cancer, Leo, and Virgo in the Northern Hemisphere, and Capricorn, Aquarius, and Pisces in the Southern.

## Lammas/Lughnasadh

The first of the three harvests, Lammas (also known as Lughnasadh in the pagan world) is a cross-quarter day marking the halfway point between the summer solstice and the fall equinox. It is a time to share, express gratitude, and celebrate the bounty and the blessings of the harvest season yet to come. Many witches observe this holiday on August 1 or 2, but if you wish to honor this day as a cross-quarter day, Lammas will be when the Sun is at 15 degrees Leo. For those in the Southern Hemisphere, 15 degrees Leo will mark your Imbolc celebrations.

## Fall/Autumn Equinox

Fall gets its name from the decline, or fall, of the astrological year, so it makes sense that the fall, or autumn, equinox represents the time of decrease. Like the spring equinox, this day is a time of equal daylight and dark hours. However, from this day forward, the hours of darkness will begin to become longer than the hours of light. The fall equinox invokes a time of loss, letting go, and reflection but also of gratitude and the harvest season. This time calls in the zodiacal seasons of Libra, Scorpio, and Sagittarius in the Northern Hemisphere but does not come until Aries season in the South, followed by the Sun in Taurus and Gemini.

## Samhain

Marking the midway point between the fall equinox and the winter solstice, Samhain is the final of the three harvests. A time of bounty that also marks the transition from light to dark, it is a time of loss, the dead, endings, and letting go. Many people celebrate this day around October 31, but if you wish to celebrate it as an astrological cross-quarter day, Samhain would be when the Sun is at 15 degrees Scorpio. In the Southern Hemisphere, 15 degrees Scorpio will mark Beltane.

## Winter Solstice

The winter solstice brings the longest night of the year and is the official start of winter—a time of decrease, internal reflection, and transformation. In the Northern Hemisphere, this day calls in Capricorn season, followed by Aquarius, and then Pisces. In the Southern Hemisphere, the winter solstice falls at the early beginnings of Cancer season, followed by Leo, and then Virgo. From this day forward, the hours of daylight will grow again, so this is often viewed as a day of rebirth, of hope, and of promise.

## Imbolc/Candlemas

Whether you celebrate it on February 1 or 2, or as a cross-quarter day when the Sun is at 15 degrees Aquarius, Imbolc honors the coming spring, for the daylight hours are visibly increasing as the night hours begin to wane. This is a time of cleansing, renewal, and hope. In the Northern Hemisphere, the cross-quarter celebration of Imbolc will be when the Sun is at 15 degrees Aquarius, whereas in the Southern Hemisphere, 15 degrees Aquarius will mark Lammas.

# ENERGY CENTERS (CHAKRAS) AND THE COSMOS

Celestial energy doesn't influence only the world around you—you can put it to use for your very own healing! By using the energy centers (points of focused, thematic energy in the etheric or energy body that correspond to various organs and bodily processes), you can attune to the energy of the cosmos for healing and more potent magick.

The energy centers correspond to various organs in the body and different life themes for healing and balance. Often depicted as balls or wheels of energy, you can imagine them as little vortexes of energy that hover above and tunnel down to your physical body (see the diagram of energy center placement in this chapter), through which you let energy into your life.

While many cultures, past and present, use different concepts of energy centers, the energy system most often used in Western metaphysics is based on the chakra system. Originating in ancient India and first appearing in the ancient text called the Vedas, the seven chakras have become popular in the West through the spread of yoga and the new age movement. You can reference the chakra/energy center placements, colors, and original Sanskrit symbols from which they are based in the diagram. However, since the Western usage of chakras has changed significantly from their original system, we will defer to the term "energy center." It is important, however, to learn about and respect the origins of the chakra system, which you can use to expand your knowledge of energy.

You can use the energy centers to align to the healing energy of the cosmos and celestial events, to clear energy blockages to allow for better manifestation, or to strengthen and focus your energy for more powerful spellcasting. In Part 2, you will uncover how the signs, planets, and elements of each zodiacal season can positively bolster these different energy centers. Through meditations, spells, and other methods, you can tap in to each energy center to empower your magick or bring focus for healing. In this section, you will find a brief overview of each energy center, its placement on the body, and themes for each one. Through these energy centers, you will be able to capture the celestial power of the stars for use in healing, manifestation, or spellwork.

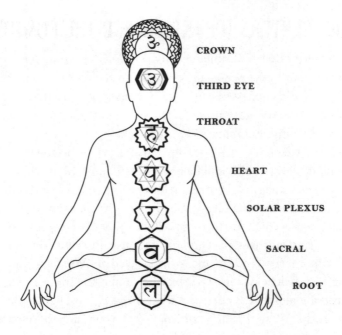

CROWN

THIRD EYE

THROAT

HEART

SOLAR PLEXUS

SACRAL

ROOT

### *Root or Base Energy Center*

Located at the base of the spine, the base center is often depicted as a wheel, ball, or vortex of red light or energy. As you might guess from the name "root," the base energy center deals with our roots—our base needs for survival, ancestry, and familial patterns. This means that themes of survival, safety, security, and even sustenance, income, and scarcity "take root" here.

### *Sacral Energy Center*

Located right below the naval, this orange energy center relates to your creative capacity. The sacral energy center corresponds to themes of sex, creativity, and vitality. Here, you can cultivate your sense of sensuality, enjoy pleasure, and engage your creative urges.

### *Solar Plexus Energy Center*

Often depicted as a ball, wheel, or vortex of yellow light right beneath the breastbone, the third energy center typically deals with a person's sense of self—their confidence, willpower, and purpose. The solar plexus center can also help with matters related to happiness and self-esteem.

### Heart Energy Center

Like its namesake, the heart energy center is located in the center of the breast. Usually shown with green colors, the fourth energy center is where we make heart-to-heart connections—where you experience compassion, warmth, and hope, and where you express your emotions and open up to others. As the center of emotional connection, the heart energy center focuses on the balance of giving and receiving.

### Throat Energy Center

The throat energy center is usually represented with a light blue hue and is located right at the base of the throat. As you might imagine from its location, this energy center is all about communication, language, and how you express your truth into the world.

### Third Eye or Brow Energy Center

The third eye is located just above the middle of the brow. Depicted with indigo or purple colors, this energy center resonates with themes of intuitive/psychic abilities, how you perceive information, and your state of mind. Here, you can inspire mental calm and access your psychic vision.

### Crown Energy Center

The seventh energy center is located at the top of the head, hence the name "crown." A ball, wheel, or vortex of white or purple light, this energy center relates to our connection with spirit and the divine. Here, you can open your awareness to spiritual information and wisdom, as well as your sense of cosmic unity and unconditional love.

### The Energy Centers and Sun Signs

While celestial energy can connect to and influence each energy center in different ways, some zodiacal constellations can empower some energy centers more than others. The following section discusses the relationship between certain constellations and energy centers and explains how you can use this knowledge to fine-tune your celestial spellcasting. Remember, however, that there are no hard-and-fast rules about this. Trust your instincts as to which sign you think might aid a given energy center.

- **Aries:** Aries can help hone the vital and protective energy of the base energy center; the passion, sexuality, and creativity of the sacral; the sense of self and sheer willpower of the solar plexus; and the focus and determination through the brow.

- **Taurus:** Taurus's grounding, fixed energy can empower your base energy center. At the heart, Taurus can help you receive abundance and craft long-lasting romances. Associated with the neck and shoulders, Taurus is sometimes said to aid the throat energy center, allowing you to communicate your truth and boundaries with confidence and steadfastness.

- **Gemini:** It is of little surprise that the throat energy center takes center stage with Gemini, helping fine-tune communication skills. At the third eye energy center, Gemini can help with perceiving information and curating ideas, and if you focus on the sacral or second energy center, these ideas may become more creative.

- **Cancer:** Cancer relates to the heart energy center—the seat of compassion and reciprocity. At the sacral, this sign can help with nurturing energy and mother-child attachments. Connecting with Cancer through the solar plexus center can aid your sense of soul alignment and help you use your emotions to create goals and boundaries that honor you. As an intuitive sign, Cancer can enhance your third eye power for intuitive knowing, even connecting this psychic energy to the heart center, helping those that sense energy through emotion and feeling.

- **Leo:** The two main energy centers often associated with Leo are the heart and solar plexus. At the solar plexus, Leo invokes confidence and willpower, a sense of co-creation with the universe. At the heart, Leo promotes positivity and warmth, aiding your quests to connect with others.

- **Virgo:** The energy center Virgo is most known for is the fifth, or throat, energy center. Ruled by communication planet Mercury, Virgo can help you communicate with practicality, truth, and poise at the throat, or with focus and clear thought at the third eye. Its energy may also help with other energy points, such as the solar plexus for willpower and dedication, or at the sacral, where themes of sacred sexuality may come into play. As an earth sign, Virgo may also help with matters of practicality and realism at the root center.

*Part I: Understanding Astrology and Magick*

- **Libra:** The two most commonly associated energy centers for Libra energy are the heart and the sacral. At the heart, Libra invites open connection, compassion, and empathy—especially when connecting to others. At the sacral, Libra's Venus-ruled zest for pleasure and creative expression through aesthetics comes into play. However, you could also work with Libra (as an air sign) around the throat to promote more loving communication, or at the third eye to help with perceiving information.

- **Scorpio:** By connecting to Scorpio through the sacral center, you can bolster creative energy and inspire intimacy and sexuality. At the base energy center, Scorpio relates to your baser instincts and drives, or what some might consider to be your "shadow" aspect.

- **Sagittarius:** One of the key energy centers often associated with Sagittarius is the solar plexus, where Sagittarius can help you hone your sense of optimism, your confidence, and your spiritual sense of self as it relates to your beliefs. At the third eye center, Sagittarius can heighten your sense of prophecy and awareness, and at the crown, Sagittarius can aid your connection to your higher mind.

- **Capricorn:** At the root energy center, this sign helps provide stability, structure, and sustenance, while at the crown, Capricorn can aid with setting aligned goals and discernment.

- **Aquarius:** Aquarius can especially aid the throat, brow, and crown centers in preparation for heightened magick. At the throat, Aquarius can help you communicate your ideas, thoughts, and truth, and at the brow, Aquarius can improve your perception and ideas. At the crown, Aquarius can invoke divine flashes of insight and genius.

- **Pisces:** Pisces can be especially beneficial for strengthening psychic abilities at the brow, or spiritual enlightenment and cosmic connection at the crown.

## The Energy Centers and Celestial Bodies

Each of the planets has cosmic energy associations that can be used to empower different aspects of the energy centers. The asteroids/comets are not included, as their connections are still being explored.

- **The Sun:** Associated with one's sense of identity and purpose, the Sun resonates most strongly with the solar plexus or third energy center.

Here, it can help usher in warmth, positivity, and confidence in your sense of self and purpose. The Sun also relates to the heart center in how you share your warmth with others.

- **The Moon:** Ruling your emotional sense, the Moon can empower your connection to your higher self at the crown, your psychic insight at the third eye, as well as help balance your empathic abilities and emotions and protect and nurture yourself at the heart. Ruling fluids, the Moon can also have resonance with the sacral energy center.

- **Mars:** As suitable for one who rules passionate urges, Mars relates to the sacral energy center. It also relates to the solar plexus energy center for issues related to willpower and sense of self. For matters of vitality and survival, Mars can strengthen the root or base energy center.

- **Mercury:** Communicative Mercury takes center stage when it comes to opening up the throat energy center for clear and concise communication. Mercury can also especially help at the brow or third eye energy center for ideas and quick thinking.

- **Venus:** Ruling love and sense of attraction, it is of little surprise that Venus can boost your sacral and heart energy centers. At the heart, she also helps you draw in abundance and gifts and connect to others.

- **Jupiter:** Jupiter helps you hone the person you wish to be and radiate optimism and magnetism via the solar plexus energy center. While at the third eye, Jupiter helps you expand your vision and perceive new paths and possibilities. At the crown energy center, Jupiter inspires wisdom and personal growth.

- **Saturn:** At the base energy center, Saturn can help you be more grounded in reality—and thus also manifest in the material plane, making it effective for money magick. Connecting with Saturn through the brow energy center can help you harness determination and problem solve, while at the crown, it can enhance wisdom and even tap in to ancestral wisdom.

- **Uranus:** Uranus can also empower your energy body for more effective and aligned magick, such as inspiring vision and insights about the future at the brow and crown energy centers. The solar plexus is also a good place to connect to Uranus in order to help you embrace your uniqueness.

- **Neptune:** Associated with the pineal gland (located at the third eye), Neptune can help enhance your psychic knowing at the brow energy center. At the same time, connecting to Neptune through the crown, or seventh energy center, can boost your sense of cosmic unity and unconditional love (you can use the heart center as well!), enhancing spells of harmony and connection.

- **Pluto:** Since it also governs sexual reproduction, Pluto can inspire sensual passion in the sacral energy center. You can also use Pluto to connect yourself to your primal self at the base. Stones such as garnet can be beneficial for this work. And finally, ruling intense transformations and connecting you to your inner truths, Pluto can assist in spirit communication and wisdom at the third eye and crown energy centers.

# HOW TO CAST A CELESTIAL SPELL

Now that you have learned about the cosmos and how various celestial objects influence humankind, it is time to harness their myths, meanings, and magick on a more personal level. In this section, you will uncover various ways to create a spellwork space that will help you strengthen your connection to the stars.

### *Ways to Deepen Your Connection to the Cosmos Ahead of Spellwork*

You've already learned a lot in this book about the cosmos. Still, spending even more time learning new things can help you connect to these powerful astrological energies even more deeply. Here are some examples:

- **Stay current on new astrological developments:** Learning more about the scientific side of astronomy can help you truly understand how unique all these alignments are. For example, you can keep up to date on happenings through reputable scientific websites or social media channels, or download apps for your phone to know what kind of transits are happening on any given day.

- **Stargaze:** One simple way to develop a relationship with the stars is to spend some time each night staring up at them! In no time, you will begin to capture the wonder and magick of existence. Apps like Sky Map can help you identify the constellations just by pointing your phone toward the night sky. You can also use a physical sky map or chart for your area—unique to your longitude and latitude—that, once you set it according to the date and time, will show you what stars are viewable at night in your area. Getting away from light pollution can help you see the stars and planets with more clarity too!

- **Witness meteor showers:** Yet another way you can strengthen your connection to the sky is by witnessing meteor showers. Each constellation has a series of meteor showers associated with it. From making wishes on shooting stars to seeing the beauty of a bright light marking its passage in the night sky, taking time to view these meteor showers can certainly help you strengthen and appreciate their magick.

- **Use a telescope:** A telescope, or even high-quality binoculars, can help you see celestial events that may be hard to see with the naked eye.

- **Be sky-aware:** By using an astrology app, you can be aware of celestial movements, the signs they are in, and even various transits and angles they may form. With this information, you can customize your magick (you can also find some of this data in Appendix F). For example, if you want to use Mercury's power of communication for a particular issue, you could find out the planetary hour of Mercury for the day; wait until a Wednesday; until the Moon is in a Mercury-ruled sign, such as Gemini or Virgo; or see what sign Mercury is in.

- **Purchase a meteorite or tektite:** Not only can you view these celestial objects in the sky; you can also hold them in your hand! Millions of years ago, many celestial objects hit the earth, resulting in craters. These impacts also created special stones like tektites due to heat from the impact. Some meteors have survived impact, and you can purchase a small piece of them, known as a "meteorite." These stones have unique origins that give them powerful ways to connect to celestial energy. Be careful with them, though, as their energy can be intense! Once you are grounded, meditating with them before engaging in celestial magick can help you heighten your experience.

## Preparing to Cast a Celestial Spell

Now that you know some easy ways to deepen your connection to the cosmos, it is time to prepare for spellwork! Here are the steps that can help you prepare to cast the celestial spells in Part 2.

### Arrange a Sacred Space

Having a dedicated space where you can practice your witchcraft can help you make a change of consciousness and more easily connect to cosmic energies. You can make or decorate an altar according to the celestial seasons. For example, a fiery altar decorated for Aries season could have colors of red, orange, and yellow. You might consider adding carnelian and garnet stones or a wand to represent the element of fire, or even cinnamon sticks positioned like the logs in a campfire.

You can add cosmic-themed decorations, such as a starry cloth or even a star projector so the stars and cosmos are projected on your walls as you cast your celestial spells.

All of these things can heighten your cosmic consciousness, but at the end of the day, all you really need is yourself! So do what works best for you.

### Preparing Your Energy

Once you have arranged your celestial spell space to help you consciously connect to the cosmos, there are various steps you can take to prepare your energy for efficient spellwork. Each step is further exemplified in the spells in Part 2, so you will have all the tools in your celestial tool kit to cast powerful star spells.

- **Cleansing and centering:** When you sit down to cast celestial spells, it is a good idea to clear your energy and mind, whether through sound, breath work, or burning cleansing herbs. The meditations in Chapters 9 and 17 and the Energy-Cleansing Herb Bundle spell in Chapter 12 provide great ways to cleanse your mind and energy body, and center back into yourself from your day.

- **Grounding:** After your energy is cleansed and centered, it is recommended to ground your energy. Grounding connects your energy to the earth, which is the center point from which we experience the stars and night sky as they are. It also ensures that your energy remains fully anchored, which is especially important when working with the flow of the cosmos! The Gaia Grounding Meditation in Chapter 8 will help teach you how to ground.

- **Raising your consciousness to the sky:** The final step to help clear the way for celestial spellcasting is to direct your focus and consciousness. You can do this by using the journey of the houses (mentioned in Chapter 5) to visualize the nuances of how your spell's intention could manifest in the world. You can also imagine celestial light shining down upon you from the constellation or celestial body you wish to call upon or meditate with meteorite or tektite for a few moments before spellcasting—but these are powerful stones! So make sure you are grounded and confident in your ability to safely and effectively tap in to their energy and power.

### Learn about Your Birth Chart

A birth chart captures what constellations, planets, and celestial bodies were in what position in the night sky at the exact moment you were born. By gathering information from your birth chart, you can learn where your personal strengths and weaknesses lie, allowing you to use your personal placements to cast more efficient spells. For example, if Mercury is in Virgo, you might know that your mind operates very systemically and appreciates lists, organization, and fine details. Thus, you can use that strength in any spells that require organization. Conversely, if you have a placement that you wish to balance, you can do spells that help temper that energy. For example, if you have a lot of Aries energy and like to rush in, you can use its opposite in the chart—Libra—to cast spells to weigh all sides of a situation before rushing in.

# THE COSMOS AND COLOR

Like the red-orange star Aldebaran of the Taurus constellation, the bluish-white Spica of Virgo, and the yellow supergiant Sadalsuud of Aquarius, the stars emit varying colors in the night sky from which we can glean information, like the heat or distance of that star. A cosmic form of communication through the visible spectrum of light, color projects information that can enhance the resonance and potency of your magick. By aligning the color of your spell candles, the clothes you wear, how you adorn your altar, or the shades you use to decorate your home, you can use the cosmic power of color to amplify your celestial magick. You can even correspond colors to the stars of certain constellations if you wish!

Here, you will uncover the various color meanings of ROYGBIV (the acronym for the sequence of colors in a rainbow and the visible spectrum of light: red, orange, yellow, green, blue, indigo, violet), white, and black to empower your star spells. For any color not listed, such as pink (red + white) or gray (white + black), you can combine meanings of the colors that compose it. You can also enhance your relationship to and under-standing of each color through the energy center section, for each energy center has a corresponding color(s).

Appendix D lists various color options associated with each sign of the zodiac, so you can choose colors for each sign or planet to enhance your magick. But remember that there are many issues, such as physics, vision, cultural and societal interpretations, and personal experience, that impact the way color influences us. Learn to trust your intuition and use the color that you feel best matches your intentions. If you wish to expand your knowledge of using color in celestial magick, you can research the color wheel, color in physics, and chromotherapy.

| | |
|---|---|
| **White** | Reflecting all colors of light of the visible spectrum, white contains all the rays of color within it and thus is often substituted for other colors in candle magick. It is associated with cleansing and purification and may help relaxation and relieving tension. In magick, it is often used for clarity and connecting to spirituality. |
| **Red** | As the color of blood, red has long been associated with life force and vitality. Red is associated with passion, desire, anger, and energy. It can also be used for matters of action, power, or confidence. Red may promote circulation and stimulate your body, mind, energy levels, and appetite, making it great for strength and vitality. |
| **Orange** | Combining the colors of red and yellow (passion and joy), orange is a color of creativity, motivation, sensuality, and play. It is therefore little surprise that orange can improve your mood and increase energy. |
| **Yellow** | A color of brightness, yellow can stimulate the nerves (which is good for energy and excitement, but not good for those prone to anxiety). It can help concentration and, in magick, the flow of new ideas, inspiration, happiness, purification, success, and communication. |
| **Green** | In magick, green is often associated with growth, prosperity, and fertility. A combination of blue (peace) and yellow (joy), green can have a calming effect and inspire contentment and harmony. Like the green hues of plant life, this color is often used for growth and healing magick. |

| | |
|---|---|
| **Blue** | A color of peace and calm, blue may aid in soothing and treating pain, such as migraine pain. In magick, it is often used for communication, tranquility, and dreams. Darker tones of blue, such as navy blue, can carry connotations of organization and structure. |
| **Indigo** | Indigo is often used to calm and relax the mind and may aid mental health. The color between blue and violet, indigo is a very spiritual color, associated with intuition, spiritual wisdom, and information. |
| **Violet** | Often associated with the third eye and/or crown energy center, violet aids in meditation and calming the mind. In magick, it is often used to enhance psychic ability and harmony. Because purple was once an expensive dye, it is associated with royalty, luxury, and wealth. It is the combination of red (passion) and blue (intuition/spirituality). |
| **Black** | Given that black absorbs light, this color is the complete absence of light. In magick, it is often used for matters of protection, mystery, power, and banishment. |

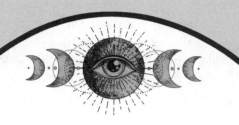

# PART II

## SPELLS FOR EVERY ASTROLOGICAL SEASON

In this part, you will find spells organized by zodiacal season. Each spell includes options for suggested astrological timing, so whether the Sun is shining in Scorpio or there is a favorable Pluto transit you wish to optimize, you will be able to align your desires to any celestial moment. As the Sun moves through each sign along its path of the ecliptic, that sign's energy and themes are especially highlighted in your waking life. To help you maximize this power, each chapter opens with an elemental meditation to harness the cosmic focus of a particular season and a crystal healing spell to attune your energy body to these cosmic energies.

While it's certainly optimal to use spells during their corresponding zodiacal season, each sign's magick can be used at any time if needed. For example, if you want to do the Herbal Pouch to Keep Your Mind Sharp spell from Gemini season, but Mercury is in another sign, or you want to maximize the power of your native Mercury placement, once you have a firm grasp on using the spells in this part, you can use the appendices in this book to mix and match correspondences to individualize your spells. For example, if your Venus is in Virgo, you can add corresponding Virgo herbs to your Venus spells. Also, you'll see specific ingredient amounts listed, but feel free to increase or decrease your amounts to customize the spells to your preferences or what you have on hand.

A note about fire safety: As part of connecting to the element of fire, as well as the element of air through smoke, this book uses spells that involve fire and burning rituals. It is important to make sure that you perform these spells with the utmost vigilance for fire safety and smoke inhalation. Place all candles in a sturdy candleholder to keep them upright, then place them atop a dish for extra safety. Always burn papers and herbs over a large fireproof dish, a cauldron, or outside firepit to ensure embers do not spread. When burning, keep windows open or burn outside over fireproof surfaces, to ensure good ventilation at all times. The spells assume you're using a small or standing candle, like a pillar or "chime" candle, unless otherwise noted. If you need to snuff out your candle before it has burned all the way down, simply be sure to snuff the candle and relight with intention as soon as you are able, until the candle is done.

Whether you are harnessing the power of the cardinal fire spark through the Celestial Spark Meditation in Chapter 7 (to add extra potency anytime you light a candle all year long) or learning how to direct energy via stones for manifestation in the Capricorn Energy Alignment spell (Chapter 16), the spells in these chapters will equip you with power to channel all signs in a variety of ways all year long.

*Chapter 7*

# ARIES SEASON

**Aries Season:** March 21–April 19
**Best Day:** Tuesday
**Best Time of Day:** Mars's Hour, Sunrise

L ike the ram that rushes horns-first and climbs the steepest of mountains, fiery Aries season blesses you with active energy to accomplish anything. With his "can-do" and "get it done" attitude, Aries helps you use the Sun and stars to bless your goals.

Push through barriers, usher motivation, finish old projects and pursue new, exciting ones. In this section, you will find spells that take advantage of astrological Aries energy, along with fiery Mars spells to ignite passion, initiate projects, and bless your endeavors for victory. Now is a key time to connect with the power of cardinal fire and uncover what sparks the light of your soul's inner flame. Aries season also provides the perfect opportunity to look at your first house—in other words, how you project yourself into the world and initially pursue your desires. The perfect alignment between the Sun and new moon in Aries during this period is an effective time to initiate goals and plant seeds for the zodiacal year in alignment with your soul and emotions. The full moon in Libra will temper any aggression and remind you to balance your goals and weigh all sides of the situation. From a Mars-aligned gingerroot spell to inspire passion, to sparking your inner blaze with cardinal fire, to honing the confidence and courage of the ram itself, you will learn to harness the power and potency of this sign and its associated energies.

# Celestial Spark Meditation

———— ✌ ————

**Astrological Timing:** Sunrise, Tuesday, Sunday, Aries New/Full Moon, Sun's/Mars's/Jupiter's Hour

**Celestial Correspondences:** Aries, Mars, Sun, Jupiter

**Energies:** Initializing, Inspiration, Motivation, Passion

Spark the celestial star fire within you! As Aries restarts the zodiacal year, reignite your spark for life with this cardinal fire meditation. Connect to the symbolism of the spark and feed an intention-lit candle with fiery spices like cinnamon and ginger to start your goals and inspired ideas with a bang! Try this meditation when setting intentions for Aries season, sparking new ideas within your creative imagination, or inviting the motivation for new projects.

## You Will Need:

Orange, gold, or red candle

Fireproof dish

½ teaspoon ground cinnamon

½ teaspoon ground ginger

## Directions:

1. In a low-light room or outside before sunrise, sit with your candle. Breathe deeply, clearing your focus. Holding the candle, imagine the celestial energies you want to call on—whether the turn of the seasons, the rebirth of the zodiacal year, or an Aries alignment. Secure the candle on a fireproof dish.

2. Say aloud, "With this flame, [your intention] I do claim." Visualize a spark igniting in your second (or sacral) energy center, and light the candle, considering your intentions. Notice the pop and jump of the spark.

3. Watch the flame move. Just like the spark lit the candle, it will reignite the flame within you. Breathe in that power from the flame.

4. Reflect on what you want to initiate. What sparks the flame within you that is ready to be pursued? What areas of your life need more vitality and motivation? How can you take the first step to support your body to reenergize your vitality and pursue this goal?

*Part II: Spells for Every Astrological Season*

5. Use your finger to mix the spices clockwise in a small dish, drawing the Aries sigil (see Chapter 3 for image). Thinking of your intention, sprinkle the spices a safe distance above the candle flame, symbolically feeding your flame and second energy center, visualizing the heavenly ram blessing your endeavors as the spices create sparks (like little stars) above the flame.

6. Let the candle burn out. Or, snuff it out and repeat the meditation throughout Aries season, burning the candle bit by bit. You can do this meditation whenever you are actively pursuing something.

### Feed the Spark

*You can follow up this spell with the Aries Energy Alignment (in this chapter), using this candle in place of the one required for that spell to help align your energy to this intention. You can also divine what symbols you see in the candle wax at the end or gather the spices left over on your dish to empower other aligned spells as a candle dressing.*

## Aries Energy Alignment

**Astrological Timing:** Sunrise, Tuesday, Sunday, Mars's/Sun's Hour, Aries Quarter/Waxing/Full Moon

**Celestial Correspondences:** Mars, Aries, Sun

**Energies:** Vitality, Passion, Energy

This spell will attune your energy to the vitality and passion of Aries. Revitalizing your body to fuel you with energy to pursue your goals, this energy alignment spell will reinvigorate your lower energy centers. Perform it at sunrise to infuse your body with the power of the morning sun's rays, representative of new beginnings and purpose, or under a favorable Aries or Mars alignment.

### You Will Need:

¼ teaspoon olive oil
Orange or yellow candle
Pinch powdered ginger
Fireproof dish

Citrine
Carnelian
Bloodstone
Smoky quartz, optional

## Directions:

1. Anoint the candle's surface with oil. Place powdered ginger on a small plate and roll the candle through the ginger toward you, visualizing renewed vitality as you do so. Set the candle in the fireproof dish.

2. Hold the stones in your hands, envisioning warming light within them, thinking of your intention. Place the stones by the base of the candle while saying:

   *"By the spark of cardinal fire,*
   *My energy does not tire."*

3. Light the candle, connecting to cardinal fire like you did in the Celestial Spark Meditation (in this chapter). Gazing at the flame, imagine breathing in its energy and exhaling any blockages. Allow the flame to cleanse, consume, and transform these blockages. Take a few breaths and visualize this.

4. Lie down and place the stones in their corresponding energy centers: citrine at the third (solar plexus) energy center, carnelian at the second (sacral) energy center, and bloodstone at the first (root) energy center. Use the image in Chapter 6 for reference on energy center placement. You can also place a smoky quartz between your feet to help keep this energy (and you) grounded.

5. Tune in to the stones on your body, visualizing the candle flame and these energy centers warming with energy. Try to feel the energetic vibration of the stones. If desired, you can visualize the cleansing candle flame in each of your energy centers and chant the words from earlier.

6. After about 20–30 minutes, slowly bring your awareness back to your body, breathing deeply and rotating your wrists and ankles. Arise, and if the candle is still burning, place the stones by its base again. When the candle goes out, you can keep one or all of the stones on your person to keep the energy with you. Repeat as desired when working with Aries energy.

# Limeade Vitali-Tea

——— ✍ ———

**Astrological Timing:** Mars's Hour, Sunrise, Tuesday, Sunday

**Celestial Correspondences:** Mars, Aries, Sun, Scorpio

**Energies:** Vitality, Drive, Determination, Focus

Sometimes your energy and determination need a little boost! Start your day with this Mars-aligned Limeade Vitali-Tea! With energizing Aries-aligned ginger, cayenne, and blackberry; Sun-ruled lime; and the option of rosemary and basil to aid mental determination, this refreshing drink will have you ready to stay focused and take action! Drink this potion when starting your day with the rising sun, as you start on your most important project.

## You Will Need:

2 basil leaves

Pinch powdered ginger

2 blackberries

1 fresh rosemary sprig, optional

Pinch cayenne pepper

1 tablespoon agave syrup

3 tablespoons fresh lime juice

2 tablespoons green tea

## Directions:

1. Place all ingredients except lime juice and green tea in a glass.
2. Muddle these ingredients with a wooden spoon or muddler, visualizing yourself breaking down energy blockages and barriers to your goals. Reflect on the uplifting, natural energy of the ingredients beneath your hands.
3. Pour in lime juice and green tea as you visualize your own metaphorical cup of energy being filled. Add ice, stir, and enjoy as you start your day with a delicious drink and rigor!

# Planting Power

───── ✑ ─────

**Astrological Timing:** Midnight–Sunrise, Aries New Moon, Mars's Hour, Tuesday, Friday (if for passion)

**Celestial Correspondences:** Aries, Mars, Scorpio, Capricorn, Jupiter

**Energies:** Passion, Money, Power

Call upon the power and passion of planet Mars with this gingerroot spell. Bolstered by the added energy of cinnamon and clove to spice things up, this spell will help you enhance energy within yourself, restore motivation for a particular goal, or reignite the passion between you and your lover. In a pinch, you can also use this spell for abundance or power.

## You Will Need:

1–2 fresh gingerroots
Knife or tool for carving
Red candle
½ teaspoon olive oil

Ground cinnamon
Ground clove
Twine

## Directions:

1. Carve your name and the symbols for Mars and Aries on one piece of gingerroot. On the other side, carve up to three key words, such as "power" or "vitality." If you are performing this spell for passion around a specific goal or with a partner, carve their name and/or relevant symbols on an additional root.
2. Light the candle for Mars, and tune in to its power for passion.
3. Anoint root(s) with oil. Sprinkle a mixture of cinnamon and clove on the root(s), covering fully on all sides. You can use any leftover spices from the Celestial Spark Meditation (in this chapter) if you are performing this spell around a similar intention.
4. Encircle the root(s) with twine (if doing two, wrap them both together). Wrap three times, saying:

   *"Flame of Mars, burning bright,*
   *[Passion/Power/Vitality or desired word] be restored this night."*

*Part II: Spells for Every Astrological Season*

5. After saying the chant for the third time, tie the twine and drip wax from your Mars candle over the knot. Set the candle upright, then lay the root(s) to rest and charge by the base of the candle.

6. Once the candle is done burning, bury the root(s) outside in the earth so that the flame of passion will metaphorically take root in your first and second energy centers. As the sun rises in the sky, visualize that its light will strengthen the spell.

# "Light a Fire Under It" Spell

**Astrological Timing:** Midnight–Dawn; Sunrise; Tuesday; Mars's Hour; when Mars is visible in the sky; Aries New/Waxing Moon

**Celestial Correspondences:** Mars, Aries, Capricorn

**Energies:** Action, Initiation, Blockages

We all encounter delays at one time or another. Sometimes, delays can provide an opportunity for introspection and double-checking, but at other times, things just need a little push! As a cardinal fire sign, Aries is the best sign for the job to help initiate some action. Light a fire under your goal to help get things moving!

## You Will Need:

Red candle or tea light
Knife or tool for carving
1 tablespoon olive oil, sunflower oil, or agave syrup
¼ teaspoon ground cayenne pepper
Fireproof dish
2 cinnamon sticks
Piece of paper and writing utensil

## Directions:

1. Use the knife to engrave the Aries, fire, and Mars symbols into the wax of the candle. Anoint with oil. Place cayenne pepper on a small plate and roll the candle through it. Place the candle in the middle of the fireproof dish.

2. Break the cinnamon sticks in half, visualizing yourself breaking down any resistance or blocks to your endeavor. Place the halves

equally around the candle to form a metaphoric crossroads that you are breaking through.

3. Write your intention on the paper and use the oil to draw the Aries or Mars symbol. Anoint with any leftover cayenne to get things moving.

4. Light the candle, visualizing the fires of Aries and Mars, burning bright and strong.

5. Being careful not to burn yourself, hover the paper above the flame so that it gets warm but does not catch fire. Say aloud:

*"Cardinal Fire, light the flame*
*Divine Ram, pursue my aim*
*On this matter [insert intended subject: I/we/name] feel the heat*
*On fast feet this goal we meet."*

6. Carefully fold the warmed paper toward you, then place it under the dish or candle and let the candle burn out. Afterward, you may keep any of the cinnamon pieces on you if desired, rubbing them anytime you need to speed up your work, or burning them as a quickening incense.

## Cosmic Victory Crown

**Astrological Timing:** Midday/Noon, Mars's/Sun's Hour, Tuesday, Sunday, Aries Full Moon

**Celestial Correspondences:** Mars, Aries, Leo, Jupiter, Sun

**Energies:** Victory, Success, Wishes, Leadership

Since Roman times, laurel crowns have been used to signify success. Combine them with the wishing power of bay leaves, and you can craft your very own wishing crown to guarantee success and victory in your endeavors. Using the victory-oriented energy of Mars, Aries, and the Sun, this crown will help you be blessed and achieve victory. Craft it during Aries season, then use it as a talisman or offering for triumph, or wear it anytime you need a magickal booster for success!

## You Will Need:

White or gold candle

Bunch of fresh thyme sprigs

Twine

1 large and 3 small bay leaves, plus extra if desired

Sharpie

Additional decorations, such as ribbons or flowers, optional

Yellow or gold ribbon

Pyrite

## Directions:

1. Sit before your crafting tools. Light the candle to help you attune to Aries's energy.

2. Enjoying the atmosphere of the flame, shape the thyme sprigs into a small circlet, twisting them together and twining them around each other in a circle, reflecting on Aries's power to bend all things with his sheer willpower. Alternatively, if you wish to make a larger circlet to wear, you can use pliable twigs or a premade small circlet from a craft store.

3. Secure the mini circlet by wrapping twine around the thyme, saying aloud:

   *"As I weave this circle of leaves*
   *My success and victory grows by three."*

4. On the largest bay leaf, use the Sharpie to write your specific goal and set aside. On the 3 smaller ones, write one key word each that will help your task, such as "confidence," "power," or "success."

5. Tuck the 3 small bay leaves into the twine, creating your bay leaf success crown. Add more bay leaves in between, if desired. Drip wax from your success candle to further affix the bay leaves to the crown. Add any other decorations you would like.

6. Entwine the yellow or gold ribbon around the crown as you think about your intention to connote success.

7. Burn the large bay leaf like an incense, envisioning your desired outcome coming to pass. Use the smoke to clean your aura, then pass the entire crown through the smoke. Lay the crown on your altar, imagining you are crowning yourself with victory. Place the pyrite in the center. Alternatively, if you feel your crown is at a firesafe distance, you may use it to "crown" your success candle, and let the candle burn in the center of the crown.

8. Once the candle is burnt out, you can crown yourself with this adornment anytime you need some victory. You can also keep it on your altar to crown any further endeavors, use it as a success talisman, or burn it in a fire as an offering for success.

# Golden Fleece Confidence Talisman

**Astrological Timing:** Mars's Hour, Tuesday, Sunday, Aries Full Moon, Midday, Sunrise

**Celestial Correspondences:** Aries, Mars, Jupiter, Sun, Leo

**Energies:** Authority, Confidence, Courage, Leadership

Claim the authority and power of the Golden Fleece and ritually infuse your favorite clothing item as a celestial courage talisman. After being thrown into the heavens, Aries's power lived on in the mortal realm through the famous Golden Fleece, a blessed symbol of authority. Whether taking on leadership roles at work, ushering forth your aspirations, gathering courage in social situations, or simply mustering confidence on a daily basis, you can claim the energetic authority of Aries through this "glamor magick" spell. By attuning a piece of clothing or jewelry to the powers of the Golden Fleece, you can carry that sense of authority, courage, and confidence with you anywhere.

## You Will Need:
Paper and writing utensil
Fireproof dish or cauldron
2 fresh thyme sprigs
2 basil leaves

½ teaspoon powdered ginger, divided
Gold, yellow, or red clothing or jewelry

## Directions:
1. On a small piece of paper, draw the sigil for Aries. Alternatively, you can print out an image with the likeness of the mythical ram. Gaze upon it and settle its power in your mind. Say aloud:

    *"Heavenly Ram, courageous and dominant*
    *Grant me your power to be confident."*

2. Place the paper on the bottom of your fireproof dish.

3. Twist the bottom half of the thyme sprigs together, with the tops curling out, and place them atop the paper in your dish (to replicate the Aries symbol).

4. Place basil leaves within the thyme curls to represent the ram's eyes of determination. Sprinkle ⅓ of the ginger over the creation to evoke power and action.

5. Place your hands above the dish and, visualizing a bright heavenly light, set the paper alight. The fresh ingredients may not burn perfectly, but they should smoke.

6. Sprinkle another ⅓ of the ginger above the fire as you repeat the chant, creating little sparks. Visualize the ram blessing your magick.

7. Take the item you wish to charge and safely pass it through the smoke three times. Gently waft some of the smoke toward your body to bless yourself. Lay the item down, sprinkle it with remaining ginger, and let it rest and charge up overnight (if performing spell at night) or midday if performing in the morning.

## Fire-Starter Spell for Success

———— ❧ ————

**Astrological Timing:** Tuesday, Sunday, Aries New/Waxing Moon, Favorable Mars Transits, Beltane, Summer Solstice

**Celestial Correspondences:** Aries, Mars, Jupiter, Vesta

**Energies:** New Endeavors, Success, Blessings

To get a fire going, all you need is some good kindling and a spark! Use the power of cardinal fire to start any project, and feed the fire of success with this fire-starter spell. With Aries and fire herbs for success and manifestation, you will create an aromatic fire-starting bundle to feed a literal (and spiritual) fire to help jump-start a new project, along with a cleansing, blessing smoke to help you bless this endeavor. Feed to a (safe) fire or craft a smaller version to burn in your cauldron. The amount of spices will vary depending on how much you choose to use.

## You Will Need:

Paper from a newspaper or paper bag

Sharpie

1 teaspoon or more ground clove

1 teaspoon or more ground ginger

1 teaspoon or more ground cinnamon

1 teaspoon or more ground nutmeg

Twine

3 bay leaves

1 cinnamon stick

## Directions:

1. Use the Sharpie to write on the paper what you want to accomplish in the form of a positive affirmation (a simple statement written in the present tense, such as "I am abundant" or "This project starts with ease"). Be sure to be as specific as possible!

2. Thinking of your intention, sprinkle the ground spices on the paper one by one in a clockwise direction. You can do this in whatever circular pattern you like, creating a little spice mandala. As you place each spice, think of its specific energies (listed in Chapter 6) and how it will fuel the fire of this endeavor.

3. Fold or roll the paper toward you, wrapping the spices up with the paper like a present, and secure with twine.

4. Use the Sharpie to write three key words on each bay leaf that would aid your endeavor, such as "success," "courage," or "motivation." Secure the bay leaves to the outside of the spice bundle with twine, adding in the cinnamon stick for manifestation. You may wish to use a smaller piece rather than a whole cinnamon stick if you are burning in a small cauldron.

5. Use the bundle to help start a fire, letting its aromatic magickal smoke cleanse and bless you and your endeavor. As it burns, recite aloud three times:

*"Motivated and inspired, by the power of this fire*
*Excitedly, quickly, I start and finish this project [or your intention]*
*successfully."*

### Start with Success

*You can follow up this spell by making the Cosmic Victory Crown (in this chapter) to help bless the endeavor with further success and to accompany this bundle as a spell or offering to burn together.*

# Chapter 8

# TAURUS SEASON

**Taurus Season:** April 20–May 20
**Best Day:** Friday
**Best Time of Day:** Venus's Hour, Midday–Afternoon, Midnight

Following the fiery, energetic Aries season, Taurus pumps the brakes and brings your focus back to the ground, to the foundation upon which you walk and the soil you use to plant and nourish your intentions. Symbolized by the bull, an ancient totem of abundance, fertility, divinity, and wealth, Taurus season brings a focus to the material realm. A fixed earth sign ruled by Venus and associated with the second house, this time shines a celestial light on finances, reveling in physical pleasures, and engaging the senses.

In the Northern Hemisphere, this time accompanies spring, providing the fertile land in which to manifest abundance and enjoy the sights, sounds, smells, and textures of the lush, verdant life all around. In the Southern Hemisphere, Taurus season comes amid fall, the perfect time to focus on abundance as you work your way through the harvest season. Regardless of location, this time heralds the Taurus new moon (the perfect time to plant enduring intentions for abundant blessings) and the Scorpio full moon. Harness Taurus's fixed nature and stand your ground with the Stand Your Ground Spell, or tap in to this sign's green thumb and bless a plant ally with a Planetary Plant Blessing. Whether you are accessing this fixed earth energy to build firm foundations for stability or working with Venus for beauty and earthly pleasures or the asteroid Ceres for sustenance and abundance, Taurus season is the time to build a bountiful foundation for wealth and to enjoy the pleasures of life.

# Gaia Grounding Meditation

———— ❧ ————

**Astrological Timing:** Venus's/Saturn's Hour, Friday, Saturday

**Celestial Correspondences:** Taurus, Venus, Saturn, Capricorn, Mercury, Virgo

**Energies:** Grounding, Slowing Down, Reflection, Boundaries

Through grounding and connecting to the element of earth, like Taurus, you will learn to slow down and develop boundaries that respect your sacred divinity, and thus clear the way to manifest your desires in the real world. In this meditation, you will learn how to ground and connect with the earth as a celestial body. Whether grounding your energy before spell-work, setting intentions for Taurus season, or centering yourself to clear the way for stable, secure manifestation, this hematite grounding meditation is sure to help!

## You Will Need:

Hematite

## Directions:

1. Go outside, find a place with grass and greenery (if possible), and gaze at the scenery around you. Breathe in the scent of the air, the sounds, the feel of the breeze on your skin.
2. Bring your awareness to your feet and the ground beneath them. You can be barefoot if you wish. This is the earth that supports and nurtures you and all life—your very own planet.
3. Sit down and place your hands on the earth. Notice the firmness of the ground. Breathe into your first energy center, bringing your awareness and focus to your feet, legs, and bottom.
4. At this time, you may wish to hold your hematite. Feel the weight of it in your hand—a measure of gravity's pull upon it. Reflect on how this stone is made of iron and, similarly, how the earth's core is made of iron (and nickel) as well—a matching vibration. Tune your awareness in to the stone's vibration.
5. Gaze at the stone's surface, which provides a mirror of reflection. Take some time to set intentions for Taurus season.

6. A fixed earth sign, Taurus is the most stubborn of the signs. She remains centered in herself and maintains her boundaries. Ask yourself some Taurus questions, such as: How can *you* bring more stability into your life and establish boundaries for yourself? Like the providing earth, what nurtures you? How can you slow down and connect more with the pleasures of life? And finally, how can you provide a stable foundation and tend to your own earth, to attract abundance and help it flourish?

7. With these reflections in mind, close your eyes and breathe in, feeling the weight of the stone in your hand. You can use these revelations to guide your Taurus season magick. You can also choose to keep the hematite with you to help you stay centered in yourself at all times and as a reminder to slow down and savor the moment.

## *Taurus Energy Alignment*

**Astrological Timing:** Venus's Hour, Friday

**Celestial Correspondences:** Taurus, Venus, Libra

**Energies:** Self-Worth, Attraction, Abundance

Call down Taurus and Venus, attune to the star power of manifestation, and craft an energetic aura to draw whatever you desire. Using salt to ground and cleanse any blockages and Taurus-aligned stones such as lapis lazuli, emerald, and rutilated quartz, this divine crystal layout will have you feeling like the stardust that you are. You can use this spell to hone your sense of self-worth, feel luscious and divine, or call down the stars to draw your desires to you. This crystal spell will cleanse and bring comfort and abundance your way.

### You Will Need:

Lapis lazuli

Emerald, if possible, or rose quartz

Rutilated quartz, if possible, or pyrite

¼ cup (or desired amount) salt (can use salt blend from Healing Salt Mixture in this chapter)

# Directions:

1. Place your stones in a bowl filled with salt. Place your hands above the bowl and think of the grounding, cleansing properties of the earth. Sprinkle some of the salt over the stones, visualizing the steady energy of the heavenly bull blessing them. If you wish, you can take a moment to perform the Gaia Grounding Meditation (in this chapter).

2. Remove the stones from the bowl and place bowl by your feet. Lie down and place the stones one by one on their corresponding energy centers—lapis for truth and divine communication at your throat, emerald for abundance at the heart (or rose quartz for self-love and value), and rutilated quartz (or pyrite) at your root for manifestation on the physical plane. (Review the image in Chapter 6 if you need a reminder of energy center locations.)

3. Tune in to the weight of the stones on your body, breathing in that sensation. Visualize the stones slowly melting into your body with their weight, resonating within your body.

4. Beneath you, feel the support of the earth providing a foundation for you to lie and move upon, its slow and steady pulse of gravity pulling you in. Breathe slowly, tuning your awareness slowly to the stones on your body and the earth beneath your body.

5. Spend 20–30 minutes here, then consciously breathe deeply and bring your awareness to your body. Rotate your shoulders, neck, wrists, and ankles, and slowly arise.

6. Breathe any leftover energy to be cleansed into the salt, then add water, stir counterclockwise, and pour mixture down the drain.

# Stand Your Ground Spell

—— ❧ ——

**Astrological Timing:** Dawn–Midday, Tuesday, Saturday, Taurus Waning–New Moon, Saturn's Hour

**Celestial Correspondences:** Taurus, Capricorn, Aries, Saturn

**Energies:** Standing Your Ground, Resistance, Exercising Self-Worth and Affirming Values

Learn to stand your ground like a Taurus! If you need to establish your boundaries, respect yourself, and affirm your values, try this spell. A fixed earth sign, Taurus is known as one of the most steadfast, stubborn signs—combining the properties of fixed energy with the firm, solid properties of earth. Use this powerful energy to express self-respect and self-love. The kinesthetic action of standing a stick in the dirt combined with astrological alignment will help you affirm Taurus energy. If you like, you can turn this stick into an outdoor altar and a metaphorical maypole—a symbol of fertility and abundance.

## You Will Need:

4–5 strong sticks
Small piece of paper and writing
    utensil

Twine
Rocks
Flowers or greenery, optional

## Directions:

1. Gather the sticks, one for each of the four elements, or one for each of the five points of the pentacle. As you walk through nature, focus on grounding and centering your energy. Return to a safe spot where you can conduct the spell and/or arrange your private altar.
2. On the paper, write the matter on which you need to stay grounded, or you can write a declaration of intention.
3. Roll the paper up tightly around one of the sticks and secure with twine. Then bind all of the sticks together with twine.
4. Hold the bundle of sticks in your hand and force them into the ground, saying aloud:

   *"Fixed Earth, steadfast Taurus*
   *With these sticks bound,*
   *Help me stand my ground."*

5. Reinforce the bundle with rocks at the base to symbolize keeping you grounded.

6. Feel free to decorate this space as an outdoor altar to the self or even as a mini-maypole, dressing it with plants, seasonal offerings, and flowers. (It will disintegrate with time, but it isn't meant to last forever.)

# *Planetary Plant Blessing*

———— ✍ ————

**Astrological Timing:** Venus's Hour, Friday, New–Waxing Gibbous Moons, Taurus Moon

**Celestial Correspondences:** Ceres, Venus, Taurus, Capricorn, Virgo

**Energies:** New Beginnings, Protection, Nurturing, Growth

Inspire abundance and growth in your life while nourishing plant life with this Planetary Plant Blessing. Channeling the fertile energies of Taurus, Ceres, and Venus, you will bless a plant and a corresponding endeavor while providing protection as both grow. Whether you're tending to your seasonal garden, looking to connect with a plant as a magickal ally, or simply blessing the earth and plant in gratitude, this protective, fertilizing, and energizing mixture will nurture and inspire protected growth under Taurus and Venus influences. You'll want equal parts of each of the first four ingredients, so plan accordingly based on what you're planting in.

## You Will Need:

Eggshells, washed and crushed
Epsom salt
Baking soda
Ground cinnamon

Piece of paper and writing utensil
Stick or quartz crystal, optional
Seeds or seed paper

## Directions:

1. Decide what endeavor to birth or nurture in your life, and what plant might aid it. Reference Chapter 6 of this book, other plant magick books, and/or look up what seasonal plants thrive in your area. When in doubt, easy herbs such as mint and basil are great options!

2. In a bowl, mix equal parts eggshells for protection and birthing something new; Epsom salt for magnesium, sulfur, and protection; baking soda to protect your plant from fungus; and cinnamon for protection from pests and for spirituality and manifestation.
3. Write your intention on the paper. If planting outside, dig an appropriately sized hole, visualizing any blockages being uprooted. If planting in a pot, fill up with soil, leaving 4 inches to the top. Place your intention paper in the soil and cover with more soil, leaving ½ inch or more for a final layer.
4. Thinking of your intention, use your finger, stick, or quartz crystal to draw a five-pointed star in the dirt and then encircle it (to create a pentagram). Dig a little hole in the center of the star, then bury the seeds and cover them.
5. Fill the pentagram outline with your eggshell mixture, thinking of its properties. Place your hand above it all, visualizing your intention and the plant growing. Lightly water.
6. Research proper plant care and reengage with the plant as needed, using the time to connect to this ally and refocus on your aspiration. As Taurus knows, going slow and steady, day by day with your goals, will help you go further in the long run.

## Cosmic Crystal Rose Water

—————— ✌ ——————

**Astrological Timing:** Dawn–Midday, Venus's Hour, Friday, Spring Equinox, when Venus is visible as the morning star, Libra/Taurus Moons

**Celestial Correspondences:** Venus, Taurus, Libra, Sun, Leo

**Energies:** Beauty, Well-Being, Renewal

The power of water has been used throughout time to capture energy—rose water is one of many examples. A common creation for beauty, rose water gets a cosmic upgrade in this spell. Combining solarized rose petals for beauty, rose quartz for universal love, and peridot for wellness and radiance, this rose water makes a great mist to revitalize, reenergize, and glamorize your aura with spring energy! For optimum astrological alignment, craft the mist at dawn on the day of the spring equinox to combine the spring equinox's energies of growth and beauty with the renewing energy of dawn. Alternatively, it can be done during a sunny dawn on Venus-ruled Friday or when Venus is viewable as the morning star right before sunrise.

## You Will Need:

1 tablespoon dried rose petals or 1 handful fresh rose petals

Peridot

Rose quartz

½ cup purified or spring water (enough to fill your spray bottle)

1 (2-ounce) mister or spray bottle

5 drops lavender essential oil, optional

5 drops orange essential oil, optional

4 tablespoons alcohol or aloe, optional

## Directions:

1. At dawn, place your rose petals, peridot, and rose quartz in a glass bowl. Place your hands over the items, visualizing your intention and their energies growing, like the sun's morning light.

2. Pour in the water, visualizing your metaphorical cup filling with radiance. Place your hands over the water and say aloud:

   *"Dew of dawn and of Venus,*
   *Whose radiance shines so bright and breaks the night,*
   *Bring to me your blessings of beauty,*
   *With the growing sunlight."*

3. Let the water heat up under the sunlight, creating a light, natural tea. When the sun reaches its peak around noon or 1 p.m., pour the water into the spray bottle. Use it every morning on your face or body, or even spray it on your clothes to bless your day with radiance and bring blessings your way. You may wish to add essential oil as well. Add alcohol to preserve the mixture; otherwise, refrigerate and use within 7 days.

# Venus Retrograde Spell

———— ❧ ————

**Astrological Timing:** Dusk, Venus's/Mercury's Hour, Friday, Venus as evening star, Venus Retrograde, Libra/Taurus Moons

**Celestial Correspondences:** Venus, Libra, Taurus, Virgo, Scorpio, Pluto

**Energies:** Hope, Clarity, Reconciliation

Like any retrograde, Venus retrograde provides a time to reflect and review. However, Venus retrograde in particular can cause disturbances in relationships, bringing past and unresolved issues to the surface. At times, this can mean relationships ending. Whether a relationship is already on the rocks or old wounds resurface out of nowhere, this Venus-aligned evening star spell can help you gain vision and clarity through the dark of the night. Cast this spell to provide guidance during turbulent times of love, to sustain love during dark times, or to help keep your heart steady and hopeful during heartbreak and loss.

## You Will Need:

½ teaspoon dried rose petals
¼ teaspoon ground thyme
¼ teaspoon ground rosemary

Small pink or white candle
¼–½ teaspoon honey
Fireproof dish or candleholder

## Directions:

1. When Venus is visible as the evening star or during Venus retrograde, go out at sunset with your items. Alternatively, perform from a windowsill.
2. Mix rose petals, thyme, and rosemary in a bowl, breathing in their calming, soothing aroma. Use your finger to draw Venus's symbol (see Chapter 5) in the mixture.
3. Anoint the candle with honey, starting at the top and moving it down the candle toward you, bringing in soothing and healing energy. When the candle has been anointed, sprinkle the herb mixture atop the candle, letting the honey capture and secure the herbs in place.
4. Place candle in the candleholder or adhere to fireproof dish, and place your hands around the candle. Envision your intention.

5. Light the candle and, as the sun sets, ponder how everything in life comes to an end, to be reborn again—just like the sun rises again in the morning. Watch or visualize Venus appearing in the sky as it darkens, the brightest celestial body to greet the night. Say the prayer:

*"O Venus, evening star*
*Who after dusk, lights the sky from afar*
*Bless this candlelight*
*That like you, it might beam bright*
*To hold my heart open*
*That hope of love, might not be broken."*

6. Visualize Venus growing bright with guidance, and let the candle burn down within sight.

# Cosmic Coin Spell

———— ❧ ————

**Astrological Timing:** Venus's Hour, Friday, Midday, Taurus New/Full Moon, Waxing Moons

**Celestial Correspondences:** Ceres, Taurus, Venus, Jupiter

**Energies:** Money, Finances, Abundance

Taurus season offers a potent time to focus on the second house of finance. With the blessings of this fruitful sign, fertile Venus, and bountiful Ceres, the ground is a perfect place to plant the seeds of financial prosperity and abundance. Manifest your money goals and call upon the archetypes of these celestial connections as you summon the stars to bless you with abundance!

## You Will Need:

Piece of paper and writing utensil
¼ teaspoon vanilla extract
5 pennies
1 teaspoon poppy seeds
1 teaspoon sugar

Emerald (good for nurturing abundant energy) or pyrite (good for money-related matters)

## Directions:

1. On the paper, write your intentions. Do you need money to pay a bill? Seed money for a future endeavor? Get as specific as possible as to what you need.
2. Anoint the corners and center of the paper with the vanilla, fold it toward you, and place it in the center of a dish.
3. Form a five-pointed star (a symbol sacred to earth) with the pennies along the edges of the paper. Sprinkle poppy seeds in a clockwise circle on the dish around the paper. Repeat with the sugar to entice energy in.
4. Hold the emerald in your hands, feel its weight and vibration, and envision abundance coming to you. Place it atop the center of the paper. Hover your hands above the dish, and say aloud:

   *"Venus, planet of attraction,*
   *Bless me with your benefaction.*
   *Asteroid goddess of the grain,*
   *Bless me with your abundant gain."*

5. Imagine the energy of Ceres and Venus providing you with blessings and the dish growing with the requested money. Repeat three times, or more if desired.
6. Leave the dish as is, and continue to add more blessings every once in a while. You can also keep cash or bills in the dish. When your goals manifest, or whenever you feel inspired, plant the pennies outside in dirt, along with any offering you feel is right.

## *Venus Abundance Sugar Bowl*

**Astrological Timing:** Midday, Venus's Hour, Friday, Venus Transits, Taurus/Libra Moons

**Celestial Correspondences:** Venus, Taurus, Libra, Leo

**Energies:** Attraction, Harmony, Love, Manifestation

Draw your desires and create a harmonious environment for manifestation with this alluring sugar bowl spell. With Taurus's fixed energy and the attracting powers of Venus, now is the time to call your desires to you.

In ancient times, bulls were symbols of prosperity, wealth, and divinity. Using Venus-ruled sugar and herbs and rutilated quartz to draw in your desired goal, anything is within your reach. With this spell, you can summon specific desires or general abundance, or just craft a little spell bowl to keep on your desk for positive, loving energy. The amounts will vary depending on your bowl and how you wish to decorate it!

## You Will Need:

Bowl of sugar, filled most of the way

1 teaspoon–1 tablespoon dried rose petals

1 teaspoon ground cardamom

1 teaspoon ground cinnamon

Piece of paper and writing utensil

Rutilated quartz or rose quartz (for drawing love and harmony) or pyrite (for abundance and money)

Decorative dried flowers, such as roses, rosebuds, lavender

Additional crystals, optional

Vanilla, cinnamon, or preferred aroma or incense

## Directions:

1. Use your finger to draw the symbol for Venus in the sugar as you think of beaconing her energy in your favor (see Chapter 5 for sigil). In the indentation, sprinkle rose petals, cardamom, and cinnamon. Stir the mixture clockwise, thinking of the sugar drawing your desire to you.

2. On the paper, write what you are drawing toward yourself. Hold the paper and rutilated quartz, visualizing that outcome as though it has already happened.

3. Roll the paper toward you, drawing in the object of your intent. Place the paper deep within the sugar and nestle the quartz in the center above it, not buried but resting on the surface.

4. Use your finger to draw the symbol for Taurus in the sugar (see Chapter 3 for the sigil) and decorate the surface of the sugar with dried flowers. Craft a beautiful display to draw your desires, adding any other gems or symbols you might like. While you work, chant:

   *"Like bees to a flower,*
   *I draw my desires with each passing hour."*

5. Hover your hands above the bowl, visualizing your goal, and say the chant one final time.

6. Nestle the incense safely in the sugar (where nothing else will catch fire) and light it, using the alluring aroma to draw your desires to you. Regularly burn incense to continue "feeding" this spell.

# *Healing Salt Mixture*

────── ✑ ──────

**Astrological Timing:** Friday, Afternoon, Libra/Taurus Moons, New Moon, Venus's Hour

**Celestial Correspondences:** Taurus, Cancer, Ceres, Libra, Pisces

**Energies:** Purification, Healing, Home Harmony

With the Sun in Taurus shining a light on themes of security, now is the perfect time to craft a salt blend to cleanse and bless your home! Use this blend to create a barrier of salt to keep the energy of your spellcrafting space pristine (in true Taurus fashion), sprinkle a bit before vacuuming, or keep a bowl of this blessed salt by the door or under your bed. You can also add some of this to a bath or mix it with an equal part of oil (such as coconut or almond oil) to create a salt scrub.

## You Will Need:

¼ cup salt
¼ cup Himalayan salt
½ tablespoon dried sage

1 tablespoon dried rose petals
½ tablespoon thyme

## Directions:

1. In a bowl, mix salts. Sprinkle in sage and stir in a counterclockwise motion, visualizing cleansing away any negative energy.
2. Use your finger to draw the Venus sigil (see Chapter 5) to bring peace and beauty to the home.
3. Sprinkle in rose petals and thyme for healing, purification, and loving energy. Stir clockwise.
4. Use your finger to draw the symbol of the pentagram into the bowl. Hover your hand above the bowl and visualize its cleansing, healing earth energies. You may wish to charge this blend under Venus-ruled Moons, such as Libra or Taurus, or harmonize under the Taurus afternoon Sun.

# Chapter 9

# GEMINI SEASON

**Gemini Season:** May 21–June 20
**Best Day:** Wednesday
**Best Time of Day:** Dawn, Morning, Mercury's Hour

Following physical, material Taurus, quick-footed and clever Gemini brings focus to the realm of communication, quick flexibility, and the mind. Symbolized by the twins, Gemini season is all about connection and sharing information. Allow your mind to go wild with curiosity. Use this time to gather any information you need, whether it be drawing out the truth or networking with others. Call down the planet Mercury to inspire exciting short trips or to bolster your third house of how you communicate.

With the Sun shining through this mutable air sign, the energy is buzzing with celestial information and ideas, inspiring connection, recognition, and communication. Call down Mercury's cosmic power and summon new friends and beneficial contacts with the Mercury's Messenger Letter Spell, or harness Gemini's quick thinking and enthusiastic mind with the lavender, peppermint, and rosemary Herbal Pouch to Keep Your Mind Sharp. You can even temper the effects of Mercury retrograde with the Mercury Retrograde Sachet with hematite, citrine, and agate to help you traverse this otherwise frantic period with tranquility, ease, and safety.

# Cosmic Communication Meditation

———— ✿ ————

**Astrological Timing:** Sunrise, Afternoon, Mercury's Hour, Wednesday, Gemini Moons

**Celestial Correspondences:** Gemini, Mercury, Libra, Aquarius

**Energies:** Connection, Reflection, the Mind

Connect to the cosmic energy of Gemini and the power of mutable air with this communication-focused meditation. Gemini season gives you an opportunity to look at your mind and words—how do you integrate, access, and share new information? By focusing on your breath, you will consciously connect to the element of air and contemplate how this element connects you to all things. Whether preparing and setting intentions for Gemini season, becoming conscious of your communication style, or learning the power of your words (and how this can be used in your celestial spellwork), this Cosmic Communication Meditation will help you communicate, connect, and learn from your environment.

## You Will Need:

Lavender incense, optional

Piece of paper and writing utensil

Blue lace agate or blue apatite, optional

## Directions:

1. Sit down in a calming, quiet place. You can light incense if you wish or hold a stone such as blue lace agate, blue apatite, or another Gemini-aligned stone (see Appendix D). Take a few deep breaths, breathing in the calming aroma and tuning in to the stone in your hand.

2. Breathe deeply into your belly, letting it expand fully with air. Hold the breath, noticing the tension in your body, then exhale, noticing the release. With each breath, bring more awareness to your body, exhaling any tension or drifting thoughts. Tune in to the flow of air in and out of your body.

3. As you breathe, notice how your breath connects you to your environment. What scents or smells that communicate information are you breathing in? Exhale out your mouth and notice the sound

as you blow. Whether it is through your words, sounds, or simply exchanging breath with trees and plants, mutable air helps you communicate and thereby connect.

4. Ask the following questions aloud, attuning your focus to this celestial power and setting your focus on Gemini season. You can notice how your body responds; note the thoughts in your head; or try automatic writing, letting your hand write whatever it wants after you speak the question.
   - How do I use my voice?
   - Are my words aligned with the truth in my heart?
   - How do I think? Is my mind overactive? What are my thought patterns?
   - What is my communication style?

5. Ask any other Gemini-related questions if you wish, using the information in the Gemini section of Chapter 3 to inspire you. Note any further thoughts or ideas that arise in your mind. When satisfied, breathe deeply three times, bringing your awareness back to your body with each breath. Use any information or thoughts you gleaned to guide your spellwork in the rest of this chapter. You can carry the stone with you throughout Gemini season to help you be more mindful of your communication. Feel free to repeat this exercise throughout Gemini season.

## Gemini Energy Alignment

———— ✌ ————

**Astrological Timing:** Sunrise, Afternoon, Mercury's Hour, Wednesday

**Celestial Correspondences:** Gemini, Mercury, Aquarius

**Energies:** Communication, the Mind, Ideas

With the Sun in Gemini and the power of the planet Mercury, Gemini season ushers in a time of communication, new ideas, and connection. Attune your energy centers to this cosmic energy to receive this celestial communication and energetic shift. Through using the vibrational power of blue apatite for communication, harnessing your mind with blue lace agate, or inspiring excitement and new ideas with orange calcite, you can ready your energy body to receive cosmic blessings and prepare for celestial spellwork.

## You Will Need:

Blue lace agate                                    Orange calcite
Blue apatite

## Directions:

1. Lie down in a comfortable place. If possible, sit somewhere with good airflow or a slight breeze.
2. Place the blue lace agate on your sixth (third eye) energy center, the blue apatite on your fifth (throat) energy center, and the orange calcite on the second (sacral) energy center. (Refer to the image in Chapter 6 for a reminder of energy center placements.)
3. Take deep breaths, bringing your awareness to your body with each breath. Try to tune in to the energy of the stones on your body.
4. Focus on the flow of air in and out of your abdomen, breathing deep into your belly. Use the breathing exercise from the Cosmic Communication Meditation (in this chapter) if you wish.
5. As you breathe, visualize that each inhalation allows a blue light to glow in your throat and third eye, getting brighter and brighter with each breath. On the exhalations, breathe away any blockages.
6. Feel power and resonance gathering at your energy centers. Imagine your sacral energy center's orange light growing brighter with excitement and ideas.
7. Reflect on the power of air. Air has the capacity to fuel fire, impact ocean currents, and carve canyons with its powerful gust. How can you use your voice to craft change in your life?
8. Allow your mind to journey, reflecting on Gemini themes. When you're done, slowly breathe awareness back into your body and then into your feet and fingers. Write down your reflections and revelations.

# Safe Travel Spell

———— ✏ ————

**Astrological Timing:** Mercury's Hour, Wednesday, Moon in Gemini/Sagittarius

**Celestial Correspondences:** Gemini, Aquarius, Pisces, Sagittarius

**Energies:** Safe Travel, Protection, Truth, Clarity, Information

With the ability to travel so close to the Sun, Mercury certainly knows a thing or two about safe and exciting journeys! Whether you're taking a short trip this Gemini season or astral traveling in the stars, this bottle charm will help bless you for safe travel. With the air element and Mercury-aligned herbs (such as caraway and fennel for protection, calming peppermint, and star anise for spirit), you are sure to have safe yet insightful and informative trips of all kinds. Use this charm to bless your vehicle, hold it while doing deep spiritual journeys and meditations, or take it with you on an exciting day trip or hike.

## You Will Need:

Small 1½–2½-inch wide-mouthed bottle with lid or stopper
¼ teaspoon fennel seeds
¼ teaspoon caraway seeds
1 small dried rosemary sprig
1 cotton ball
3–5 drops peppermint oil
Blue and yellow embroidery thread or ribbon
1 star anise

## Directions:

1. Sit down before your ingredients and breathe deeply. As you breathe, intentionally connect to the element of air to bless this spellwork with its movability.
2. Sprinkle some fennel seeds into your bottle, breathing in their aroma. Then add caraway seeds. These seeds will visually represent earth within the bottle so that you always stay safely grounded within earth's orbit.
3. Nestle the stem of the rosemary sprig in the seeds so it is reaching up to the top of the bottle, representing your safe, peaceful, and also psychic ability to travel from the ground to the clouds.

4. Tear the cotton ball, as though tearing away any blockages or dangers, separating it so that it is wispy. Nestle the pieces around the top of the rosemary sprig at the top of the bottle to represent clouds. Place peppermint oil atop the cotton ball, infusing it with its aroma.

5. Take a moment and breathe in the scents of the herbal bottle you have just created. Now seal the bottle. Wrap some of the thread around the star anise points, then tie the thread around the neck of the bottle. Keep the bottle by your bed, opening it and smelling its aroma while you think of safe astral-travel dreams, or keep it in your car for safe, smooth journeys, holding it whenever you need its aid. Now you travel safely through the cosmos like a shooting star.

## Let the Truth Shine Spell

— ☙ —

**Astrological Timing:** Midnight, Dawn, Mercury's Hour, Wednesday, Favorable Mercury Transits

**Celestial Correspondences:** Gemini, Scorpio, Mercury, Pluto

**Energies:** Truth, Clarity, Information

Call upon the messenger Mercury to bring information to you with this spell. Gemini loves information, and with blessings from messenger Mercury, you can summon forth answers now more than at any other time. Whether you're looking for important information and ideas or seeking the truth, this spell will help that communication shine clear and bright, like a star in the night sky.

### You Will Need:

Small white or blue candle and candleholder

¼ teaspoon olive oil

1 tablespoon dried peppermint leaves

1 pinch rosemary, ground or dried leaves

Large fireproof dish

5 whole cloves

1 star anise or dried chrysanthemum

## Directions:

1. Anoint the candle with oil. On a small plate, mix 1 pinch peppermint and rosemary, then roll the candle through the mixture. Place the candle in the center of your fireproof dish. Thinking of the information you seek, create a circle around the candle along the outer edge of the dish with the rest of the dried peppermint bits in a clockwise circle, representing completion in cycles and drawing the truth to you.

2. Place the cloves clockwise around the candle, forming a five-pointed star.

3. Bring the star anise up to your nose and breathe in its sharp aroma and power. Visualize your desired information coming to you, and exhale onto the star anise three times before placing it by the base of the candle.

4. Hover your hands around the candle, focusing on your intention, and say:

   *"Candlelight, burning bright,*
   *Let the truth shine, like a star in the night."*

5. Light your candle and let it burn. Once the candle is finished burning, take a little bit of the peppermint from the outer circle, take it outside, and blow it from your hand.

6. You may wish to pack the rest of the herbs (the leftover peppermint circle and cloves and anise) into a sachet or add them to a warm bath.

## Mercury's Messenger Letter Spell

**Astrological Timing:** Dawn, Mercury's/Jupiter's Hour, Wednesday, Thursday, Sunday

**Celestial Correspondences:** Gemini, Mercury, Jupiter, Sun

**Energies:** Connection, Communication, Networking

On the astral plane, among the stars, we are all connected. Call down the planet Mercury and invite these cosmic connections into the material plane with this astral networking letter. Since both air and the mutable modality are all about connection, Gemini season provides premium energy for developing connections of all kinds. Invite new friendships, expand your network of career and business contacts, or rekindle lost connections with this letter-writing spell. Using the energies of Gemini and Mercury alongside the power of air (through smoke), this spell will help call in new relationships and connections.

## You Will Need:

Pen with blue ink

Paper with an envelope

¼–½ teaspoon olive oil

½ teaspoon dried lavender

½ teaspoon dried peppermint

½ teaspoon dried or fresh marjoram

Fireproof dish

## Directions:

1. Brainstorm what type of connections you wish to draw into your life: clients, benefactors, or social connections who can expand your mind and the way you think! Be specific (and realistic) on the time frame during which you are looking to make these connections.

2. Use the pen with blue ink to write a letter of gratitude on the paper. Describe these connections as though you have already made them and are grateful for what they bring to your life. Sign your name.

3. Anoint the edges of the paper with oil, then use the oil to draw the sigil for Mercury (see image in Chapter 5) in the middle over the ink, entrusting that he will deliver your letter. Sprinkle letter with lavender, peppermint, and marjoram to boost the energies of communication and connection. (You can add any other herbs you wish that are relevant to your goal.)

4. Fold your letter into three sections toward you. Place it in the envelope and address it to the desired recipient.

5. Hold the letter by your heart. Visualize making these connections with excitement and gratitude. Say aloud:

   *"Mercury, Planet of Communication, deliver quickly this information; Take my letter to those I seek, so that we may very soon meet."*

6. Outside, over a fireproof dish, safely burn the letter. Watch the smoke, the element of air, dissipating and traveling. Visualize the air reaching your connections.

7. While you are sending this letter—on the astral plane via fire and not physically mailing it—be ready to take advantage of any chance encounters! As you await this connection, assemble any relevant details, such as business cards, to be ready at a moment's notice.

# Herbal Pouch to Keep Your Mind Sharp

---- ✍ ----

**Astrological Timing:** Noon, Mercury's Hour, Wednesday, when Mercury is visible in the sky, Gemini/Virgo Season, Gemini/Virgo Full Moons

**Celestial Correspondences:** Mercury, Sun, Gemini, Virgo

**Energies:** Mental Abilities, Peace, Health/Longevity

Whether you're a writer, student, innovator, or entrepreneur looking for new ideas, you can use the astrological power of both Mercury and the Sun to light up your mind. Using Sun-associated walnut as a symbol for the mind, peppermint to stay sharp, lavender for calm thinking, and rosemary to improve memory, this peaceful, energy-clearing herbal bag will help keep your mind sharp and receptive to information, ideas, and insights. You can even prepare this ahead of Mercury retrograde to help keep your mind clear!

## You Will Need:

Blue or yellow cloth, about 6 inches square

1 walnut, shelled

¼ teaspoon almond oil

½ teaspoon dried lavender

½ teaspoon dried peppermint

½ teaspoon dried rosemary

Twine

## Directions:

1. Right before the sun is about to reach its peak, sit outside with your tools and ingredients. Bask in the sun's radiance, visualizing its light cleansing your energy and lifting your mood and mind.

2. Spread out the cloth before you, then hold the walnut, noticing how it resembles the brain. Visualize this nut shining with celestial light and ideas. Anoint the walnut with the almond oil in a clockwise motion, visualizing new ideas coming through. Anoint one more time with Mercury's sigil (see Chapter 5).

3. Place the walnut in the center of the cloth, then circle it with lavender, then peppermint, then rosemary, thinking of what each herb brings to the spell. Place your hands over these ingredients, visualizing them strengthening your mind with their power.

4. Say aloud:

*"Mercury, who rules the mind;*
*Ruled by air, clear my mind.*
*Draw near to the sun, shining bright;*
*Bring me new ideas, and insights."*

5. Repeat this incantation three times until you feel the herb blend resonate with energy underneath your palms. Close and tie the pouch with twine.
6. Keep the pouch on your work desk or in your pocket when working or studying so you can rub it and repeat the incantation as needed. To keep the magick alive, anoint the bag every Wednesday at noon with a dab of almond oil.

## *Communication Lemonade*

──────  ✍  ──────

**Astrological Timing:** Mercury's Hour, Wednesday, Midday

**Celestial Correspondences:** Gemini, Virgo, Libra, Mercury

**Energies:** Communication, Optimism, the Mind

What better than mint, lemon, and honey to help open and activate your throat? Plus, thanks to Gemini communication herbs, your throat energy center will be buzzing with energy. Share this drink with a friend to inspire clear communication, enjoy before a public speaking engagement, or try it while writing! You can also add natural blue food coloring for a layer of cosmic color magick. Double the ingredients if you want to use a larger glass.

### You Will Need:

7 fresh mint leaves
⅛ teaspoon ground clove
3 leaves fresh sage
1 tablespoon honey
3 tablespoons lemon juice

Ice cubes
½ tablespoon orange juice
1½ tablespoons soda water
1 star anise, for garnish
1 fresh mint sprig, for garnish

## Directions:

1. In a cup, place mint, clove, sage, and honey. Smell the aroma of these ingredients and visualize the scent opening up your throat.
2. Use a wooden spoon or muddler to muddle the ingredients, envisioning stamping out any blockages to communication.
3. Add lemon juice (if needed, you can warm the lemon juice before adding it, to help dissolve the honey once you add it in) and ice and stir clockwise. Top with orange juice and soda water. Garnish with star anise and mint sprig.

## *Mercury Retrograde Sachet*

**Astrological Timing:** Mercury's Hour, Wednesday

**Celestial Correspondences:** Mercury, Gemini, Virgo

**Energies:** Grounding, Clear Communication, Calm Mind

Mercury retrograde is infamous for causing havoc in communication, technology, and travel. But it is also an opportunity for reflection on where you need to slow down or revisit past (but lingering) issues and lessons. Tap in to the benefits of this time—while nullifying and protecting yourself from the Mercury retrograde chaos—with this lavender crystal sachet. The aroma of lavender can relax your mind and soothe communication, and the added power of Mercury-aligned stones can help ground and center you, making this sachet a must-have to keep close by each Mercury retrograde season.

## You Will Need:

Hematite

Citrine

Blue lace agate

Drawstring pouch

1 tablespoon dried lavender

Amber, petrified wood, or a fossil such as ammonite, optional

## Directions:

1. Sit before your tools and breathe deeply, intentionally slowing down your mind and body with each breath. Think about connecting to the element of air.
2. Hold each stone one at a time, tuning in to their energy. Gently place each one in the pouch: hematite, for grounding and protection from emotional waves of others; citrine, for positivity and to help you deflect negative energy; and blue lace agate, for clear communication and a calm mind.
3. Atop the stones, sprinkle lavender for peaceful, clear thinking. If desired, add amber, petrified wood, or a fossil to this sachet bag for grounding wisdom.
4. Hold the pouch, breathing in its aroma and feeling its weight.
5. Carry the pouch with you through Mercury retrograde; keep it in your car or by your desk to help you stay grounded, clear, and peaceful at any moment.

### Make an Amulet

*You can also use the stones to craft an amulet or piece of jewelry. Purchase wire from a craft store and use it to wrap the stones together (using an online tutorial), or collect beads of these stones to create a bracelet or necklace. Amber makes a great bead addition for such an amulet as well!*

# Chapter 10

# CANCER SEASON

**Cancer Season:** June 21–July 22
**Best Day:** Monday, Friday
**Best Time of Day:** Moon's Hour, Dusk, Nighttime

Following airy, talkative Gemini season, Cancer invites you out of the wind, back into the security of your shell. In the realm of cardinal water, it is time to quiet the talking and turn inward to the intuitive power accessible through the realm of feeling.

In the Cancer season, the Moon's guiding light shines clearer. It is a time to tune in to your innate psychic nature; develop inner awareness; and (with the bolstering of Ceres) nurture yourself, those close to you, and your soul's purpose. Attune to the power of cardinal water in your life, and direct your focus to your fourth house of the home. During Cancer season, you will connect to the power of your emotions, strengthen your psychic feeling, and spruce up your home to be sure it is a space of safety and comfort.

## *Moving Water Meditation*

**Astrological Timing:** Moon's Hour, New/Crescent Moon, Monday

**Celestial Correspondences:** Moon, Cancer, Scorpio

**Energies:** Initiation/Action, Emotions, Empathy

Set your focus and intentions for Cancer season by connecting to the flow of emotions and intuition within you. In astrology, water rules the realm of feeling and your soul's intuition and thus can be a powerful ally in your Cancer magick, whether through potions, baths, teas, or magickal mists. This is a great reflection to use when you want to encourage personal growth, intuition, and healing.

## You Will Need:

Body of running water

## Directions:

1. Perform this meditation by a body of running water—whether the tidal ocean, a rushing stream, or even the bathtub faucet (as you fill the bath with water for the Restorative Moon Bath spell later in this chapter). If you don't have a moving body of water available, you can simply close your eyes and visualize one.

2. Breathe deeply and imagine that the rushing water is actually a powerful stream of fast-moving energy, connecting and flowing with everything around it.

3. Reflect on this cardinal expression of water and how it impacts its environment. What does that expression of water offer its surroundings? For example, does that stream of water nurture trees and greenery or perhaps offer sustenance to animal life?

4. Ponder how cardinal water manifests within you. Is it like a small stream of emotions, slowly and quietly making its way through? Or are your emotions more like a gushing waterfall, crashing forward and acting as a powerful (if somewhat chaotic) force in your life? Or are your emotions restricted, like a dam?

5. The cardinal expression of water can help you connect to your subconscious experience and check in with your soul. Neither too little nor too much is healthy. So reflect on which manifestation of cardinal water appears in your life right now by asking yourself the following questions:

   - How can I cater to my soul's growth?
   - How do I nurture myself?
   - How is my home set up? How can I curate my space to provide better nurturance?
   - What is my relationship with my emotions? How do they guide me?

6. Ponder any more questions that come to mind, or refer to the Cancer section in Chapter 3 to guide your mind further into Cancerian energy and meaning. When ready, take a few deep breaths and bring your awareness back to your body. Use any insight you gleaned to guide your magick throughout Cancer season, and feel free to repeat this meditation as desired.

## *Cancer Energy Alignment*

———— ❦ ————

**Astrological Timing:** Moon's/Venus's Hour, Monday, Friday, Cancer Moon

**Celestial Correspondences:** Cancer, Moon, Libra, Taurus

**Energies:** Emotions, Healing, Heart's Intuition

This spell will help you open the flow of emotional, psychic energy and connect to the Moon using Cancer and Moon-aligned stones, such as selenite (named after the Moon goddess Selene), chrysocolla/rose quartz for emotional connection, and moonstone. Through this energy alignment and meditation, you will reveal hidden emotions, enhance your psychic sense, and connect to your feelings and their power. Whether you are preparing the way for other powerful celestial spellwork or just want to open your heart to honoring your emotions and intuition, this crystal body layout will aid you.

### You Will Need:

Cup of cold water
Selenite
Chrysocolla or rose quartz

Ruby
Moonstone

### Directions:

1. Hold the cup in your hands, reflecting on how this cup is a symbol for what you choose to hold within your life and your body. Sip the water, feeling its coldness pass down your throat and chest.

2. Lie down and place the selenite by the base of your skull where the neck meets the head, chrysocolla/rose quartz at your fourth (heart) energy center, ruby at the third (solar plexus) energy center, and moonstone on your second (sacral) energy center. (See Chapter 6 for energy center placement information.)
3. Visualize the moon above you and a waterfall flowing from it into each of your energy centers. Imagine the stones vibrating or humming with energy in response.
4. Focus on visualizing the water from the moon flowing through you, growing from a tiny stream, stronger and stronger, strengthening your psychic connection. Allow your feelings to flow through you and out your feet, back to the earth.
5. After 20–30 minutes, breathe deeply, and slowly bring your awareness back to your body. Arise when ready.

## *Moon Scrying Spell*

**Astrological Timing:** Moon's Hour, Monday, Full/Dark Moon

**Celestial Correspondences:** Cancer, Scorpio, Moon, Chiron, Neptune

**Energies:** Divination, Insight, Intuition

With the intuitive, Moon-guided nature of Cancer, this is the perfect season to practice water-scrying. Scrying is a way of divining images, meanings, and spiritual information through a surface, such as a crystal ball or, in this case, water. The astrological element of water often relates to intuitive feeling and can offer insight and enhance psychic abilities. You can find answers to your questions by scrying with water and Moon- and Cancer-aligned herbs. Perform this spell by candlelight during the dark and new moons, or use the light of the full moon to guide your vision along the water's surface. You can also prepare and charge sacred scrying water during this season to use throughout the year to call down the power of the Moon.

### You Will Need:

Bowl of water

1 teaspoon sea salt

½ dried teaspoon jasmine

½ dried teaspoon rose petals

½ dried teaspoon rosemary leaves

## Directions:

1. Place the bowl of water before you. Encircle the bowl in sea salt, connecting you to the ocean but also offering a circle of protection as you discern the water's message.
2. Place the jasmine, rose petals, and rosemary into the bowl. Mix them together, connecting to their innate energies and petitioning them to help you perceive messages.
3. Say your intention out loud, feeling it resonate through your body, and pour the water into the bowl. Notice how the herbs move in the bowl and if they form any shapes. You can also use your knowledge of the houses and the movement of the herbs to divine information.
4. Allow your eyes to soften, and use the light of the full moon (if full) upon the water to further discern shapes and images. Watch the movement of the water, the reflection of light upon its surface, and any additional shapes the herbs make.

### Enhance Your Lunar Intuition
*You can also use the Restorative Moon Bath (in this chapter) or the Celestial Dreams Tea (Chapter 18) spells to help enhance your connection to water and heighten your sense of intuition, or you can spray the Pisces Moon Psychic Mist before doing this spell (in Chapter 18).*

## Restorative Moon Bath

———— ✇ ————

**Astrological Timing:** Monday, Moon in Cancer, New/Full Moon

**Celestial Correspondences:** Cancer, Moon, Pisces, Libra

**Energies:** Emotional Release, Nourishment, Spiritual Alignment

Like the crab that wishes to rest and restore itself under the sand and ocean waves, Cancer season provides a time to nurture yourself, focus on emotional healing, and boost your spiritual and intuitive development. This floral Cancer- and Moon-aligned bath will help clear your energy fields, promoting the release of restless emotions, soothing your spirit, and reinvigorating your intuition. You can prepare this mix during powerful Cancer times (such as Monday for the Moon or during the Cancer new/full moons) to craft an ultra-charged yet very relaxing bath.

## You Will Need:

1½ cups Epsom salt

¾ cup Himalayan salt

¼ cup baking soda

½ tablespoon dried rose petals

½ tablespoon dried whole
calendula flower

½ tablespoon dried jasmine

5 drops lemon essential oil

5 drops lavender essential oil

1 tablespoon coconut oil,
fractionated or melted

1 fresh or dried rosemary sprig

Moonstone, optional

Rose quartz, optional

## Directions:

1. In a bowl, pour in both salts and baking soda and mix with your hand, feeling the texture of the salt between your fingers.

2. One by one, add the flowers in a clockwise circle around the bowl as you smell the herbal aromas. In the center, add lemon oil, lavender oil, and coconut oil.

3. Mix in the oils with a wooden spoon until you find the aroma calming. Take a deep breath and draw the sigil of the Moon (see Chapter 5), visualizing its luminescence lighting up the glyph.

4. Place the rosemary sprig and stones, if using, in the center of the bowl, and charge it under the moonlight, if desired.

5. This will make about 3 cups. You can remove the stones and rosemary, if desired, and store the mixture in a jar or use part of it right away.

6. To prepare a bath, add 1 cup of the mixture to the bathwater and add the stones (either to the bathwater or along the side of the bath). Use the rosemary sprig to "stir" the bath clockwise, ushering in peace and relaxation. Let the healing Moon- and Cancer-aligned ingredients diffuse, dissolve, and dissipate any tension in your mind, body, or spirit.

# Cosmic Water Cleansing

**Astrological Timing:** Moon's Hour, Monday, Any Full Moon

**Celestial Correspondences:** Cancer, Moon, Pisces

**Energies:** Cleansing, Healing, Purification

Just like the moon's pull creates the ebb and flow of the ocean, it also pulls upon and empowers your emotions and sense of feeling. This cleansing water spell will help you get in touch with those feelings and learn to trust your intuition and the information it provides you. This spell uses cold water to help draw emotions to the surface and cleanse any negative energy from your body. It will also help you practice tuning in to and honoring your emotions as important messengers of psychic and subconscious information.

## You Will Need:

Wide-mouthed jar and lid
1 fresh or dried rosemary sprig
1 fresh or dried thyme sprig
1 tablespoon dried rose petals

Aquamarine
Purified or spring water
Towel

## Directions:

1. In the jar, place herbs, rose petals, and aquamarine. Breathe in the aroma, then pour the water into the jar. Let the liquid charge in the moonlight or infuse in the refrigerator, or you can charge it with the sunrise on the day of the new moon (for on this day, the moon will rise and set with the sun).

2. Once the water has changed color and cooled, take your towel to a sacred space, perhaps where you can enjoy the light of the moon. Remove the aquamarine from the water and hold it in your hand.

3. Close your eyes, tuning in to your breath. Think of the moon above and feel its intuitive, emotional pull upon you.

4. Think about a situation that is bothering you, and notice where in your body you feel an emotional response. Does your throat feel tense? Are your shoulders tight? Visualize the emotion in your body. Where exactly is the emotion? Why is it there? What does it look like or feel like? Does it have a color, texture, or form? Feel free to reference Chapter 6 for guidance on any relevant energy centers.

5. When you feel like you need to cleanse your energy, inhale and place a small handful of the water where you feel the energy in your body. With your exhale, visualize the water drawing the emotion out. Wipe water away with your towel, and repeat until released. You may wish to rinse off more fully in the shower afterward as you visualize any debris going down the drain. (For more significant or

*Part II: Spells for Every Astrological Season*

persistent issues, you may wish to seek energetic guidance from a professional.) Pour any leftover water outside to nurture plants, or store in the refrigerator and repeat, using within seven days.

# *Home Blessing Spritz*

**Astrological Timing:** Moon's Hour, Monday, Friday, Full–New Moons

**Celestial Correspondences:** Cancer, Moon, Ceres, Libra, Taurus

**Energies:** Cleansing, Protection, Consecration

Cancer season brings a focus to domestic life and reminds you how important your home is. It should provide a safe space to nurture yourself and your interests. Using the power of water and ingredients associated with Cancer and the Moon, this mixture will help you cleanse and bless your home with good energy! Perform this spell as part of a regular lunar cleansing ritual or whenever your home's energy feels like it needs an upgrade.

## You Will Need:

1 tablespoon Himalayan or sea salt

½ cup water

1 fresh rosemary sprig

1 tablespoon dried rose petals or 5–10 drops rose essential oil

5 drops jasmine essential oil, optional

2–3 lemon peels

## Directions:

1. Place salt in a bowl. Stir salt with your hand, smelling its scent and thinking of its cleansing properties.
2. Pour in water, and stir counterclockwise with rosemary sprig, visualizing the cleansing power of the ocean and its tides. Drop in rose petals or a few drops of rose oil and jasmine oil, if using.
3. With the rind facing the water, squeeze your lemon peel, sending the oils into the water, crafting a refreshing aroma. Stir clockwise with the rosemary sprig, visualizing protections and healing.
4. Take your bowl around the house, and use the rosemary sprig to fling out the water in all directions for cleansing. Say aloud as you do so:

*"Spirit of water, Mother Moon,*
*With your blessing, I cleanse this room."*

5. Continue until you have blessed all spaces in the house and feel a shift in energy.

# Celestial Cup of Goals

———— ꙮ ————

**Astrological Timing:** Midnight–Sunrise, Monday, Cancer Moon, Full/ New Moon

**Celestial Correspondences:** Cancer, Moon, Ceres

**Energies:** Spiritual Alignment, Aspiration, Contentment

Bring balance into your life and manifest spiritual goals with this special spell. Like the symbol of the overflowing cup of blessings, a cup is a symbol of a container—a metaphor for what you choose to hold in your life. Whatever you wish to bring into your life will take the shape of the container you assign to it (like a liquid). During Cancer season, it is time to assess whether your current goals and activities are still in alignment with your path. In this spell, you will reflect on the power of cardinal water and create a cup altar filled with symbols of goals that will nurture and fill you with contentment. The amounts you use may vary depending on the size of glass you choose.

## You Will Need:

Special glass
½ cup sea salt (for grounding and connecting to the power of water) or sugar (for sweetening and drawing)
2–3 drops jasmine essential oil

Natural quartz point
Dried rose petals or buds
Dried lavender
Dried jasmine
Dried chamomile

## Directions:

1. Think of what kind of goals you would like to have that are in alignment with your spiritual self and needs. What kinds of activities and people feed your spirit and nurture your soul so that you feel restored?

2. Place a layer of sea salt (or sugar) in your cup. Since it is of the sea and also of the earth, the salt will act as a grounding foundation for the spell and represent the physical principle of life. If choosing sugar, the sweetness of this ingredient will draw your goals to you with peace and ease—or, feel free to add both!

3. Mix in a few drops of jasmine oil for fragrance so that you can enjoy its aroma each time you walk by. This scent can remind you of your personal goals.

4. Use the quartz point to stir the salt clockwise, saying aloud:

*"Under the power of moonlight, I bring spiritual balance into my life."*

5. Visualize what this balance might look like for you, then nestle the quartz, point up, in the center of the cup, representing the initiating aspect of water.

6. Think of what goal each flower can represent, then place them one by one with intention in the cup, as a symbol of allowing that goal into the "container" of your life. Hover your hands above the finished scene, visualizing the cup overflowing with abundance in your chosen realms. Charge in the growing moonlight, ideally for the duration of the lunar month (if doing at new moon) or for two weeks until the next new moon.

## *Healing Egg Meditation*

───── ✍ ─────

**Astrological Timing:** Moon's Hour, Monday, Winter Solstice, Dark Moon

**Celestial Correspondences:** Cancer, Ceres, Moon, Virgo, Scorpio

**Energies:** Rebirth, Cleansing, Grief

Use the cleansing, rebirthing, and protective energy of an egg to release grief from old wounds. Countless cultures past and present have associated eggs with water, as well as with rebirth, cleansing, and protection. Moon-ruled Cancer season, which brings a focus to how you were raised and highlights old wounds, is the perfect time to call on the power of an egg to release ancient grief and loss. After doing this spell, you may feel birthed anew and emotionally cleansed.

## You Will Need:

1 egg

Sea salt

White candle

Chrysocolla

## Directions:

1. Think of a situation that you want to release. You might be experiencing grief, contemplating support you didn't receive, or have another topic weighing on you. Breathe deeply as you imagine breathing the situation into the egg.

2. Crack the egg in half, discard the yolk and egg white, and rinse out the shell. Place cleansing sea salt in a bowl. Nestle one eggshell half in the sea salt so that it stands upright, and place the candle in the shell. (You can melt the bottom of the candle to affix it to the shell.)

3. Hover your hands above the candle and visualize being surrounded with healing light and love. See yourself reborn. Crumble the other eggshell half and sprinkle the pieces clockwise in the salt around the candle as an added layer of protection.

4. Hold the chrysocolla to your heart, visualizing healing as you do so. Light the candle. You may wish to lie down with the chrysocolla on your heart energy center or keep it on your person until you feel recovered.

# Chapter 11

# LEO SEASON

**Leo Season:** July 23–August 22
**Best Day:** Sunday
**Best Time of Day:** Sun's Hour, Sunrise, Morning, Midday

Like a bulb blossoming beneath the soil, fiery, fixed Leo ushers you from one season to the next with his creative, romantic energy and spark for social connection. Radiant Leo invites witches out of their shells and into the sun.

Now is the perfect time to focus on producing creative new ideas (and trying new spells!) that highlight your talents and passions. In this section, you will find spells that take advantage of that Leo energy, from heart and solar healing spells to spells for creative self-expression, leadership, confidence, and romance. Connect to your own inner sun to bolster your sense of self or engage your fifth house of playfulness by getting creative! Tap in to Leo themes of resilience, warmth, happiness, and creativity with a seed spell for a successful career—the spells in this section are filled with celestial magick to use during Leo season for confidence, power, and positivity. You'll find yourself shining like the warming sun itself.

## *Fixed Fire Meditation*

**Astrological Timing:** Noon, Sun's Hour, Sunday

**Celestial Correspondences:** Sun, Pallas, Leo, Sagittarius

**Energies:** Focus, Identity, Energy

This fixed fire sign helps you connect to your inner fire. Whether it be solar themes of purpose and identity, fifth house themes of pleasure and romance, or Pallas themes around sharing your creative self with the world through your career, Leo season reminds you to fuel your inner flame. In this spell, reflect on how you share your warmth with the world through your creativity.

## You Will Need:

Candle, preferably orange, gold, red, or yellow

¼ teaspoon olive oil, optional

½ teaspoon ground cinnamon, optional

Candleholder

Fireproof dish

3 whole nutmegs, optional

Sharpie

## Directions:

1. Anoint your candle with oil and a pinch of cinnamon. Place in the candleholder on fireproof dish. Dim the lights in the room.
2. Light the candle (if using a match, you can connect to the cardinal fire imagery from the Celestial Spark Meditation in Chapter 7) and close your eyes, breathing deeply and bringing your awareness to your body.
3. After a few deep breaths, open your eyes and gaze at the candle flame. Notice its movements and how it is the only light in the room. Like the sun and other distant stars light up the dark of the cosmos, helping to define reality, so, too, does this candle flicker within the darkness of your meditative space.
4. Soften your eyes as you gaze, and allow the flickering movement of the light to calm your mind. Notice how the wax keeps the flame steady so that the flame doesn't consume the wick. This is the power of fixed fire—keeping the flame steady and providing consistent warmth and light.
5. Place the nutmegs in a triangle shape around the candle. When you feel ready, ponder the fixed fire, Leo, Sun, fifth house, and Pallas themes by asking yourself these questions:
    - As you rotate the nutmegs around the candle, ask yourself, Like the sun has its orbiting planets, what activities, people, and passions do I have in my orbit?
    - Watching the candlelight shine upon the nutmegs, ponder, "How do I share my light with the world?"

- What kind of steady flames do I have in my life? Which do I wish to maintain?

6. With these questions in mind, pick three things that are important to you. If celebrating your solar return (your birthday), you can pick from goals, mindset key words, hobbies, or a relationship you wish to maintain. Identify three things that are important to you at this time and that you would like to nurture or hold steady in the next year.

7. Use the Sharpie to draw a relevant symbol for each goal or idea onto each nutmeg. Watch the candlelight nurture the nutmeg with its warmth and place your hand above the three nutmegs.

8. Imagine a light within you, especially around your solar plexus and heart energy centers, glowing in harmony with the candle. This is your own inner light. Like the helium and hydrogen that fuel the sun, consider what things fuel your inner fire. Visualize the nutmeg also humming with this light.

9. Sprinkle the remaining cinnamon above the flame and atop the nutmegs, visualizing this Sun-ruled spice nurturing your intentions. Let the candle burn down all the way, then keep the nutmegs on your altar, hold it during magickal meditations, place it in a sachet bag to keep on you, or use it in future spells (such as the Grow Your Passions Spell in this chapter). Take the insight gleaned from this magickal meditation to guide your Leo season spells.

### Energetic Enhancement
*Hold a sunstone during this spell to aid your meditation and empower your own inner light. You can also combine this spell with the Apollo's Chariot Inner Light Spell (in this chapter).*

## Grow Your Passions Spell

————— ✌ —————

**Astrological Timing:** Sunrise, Sun's Hour, Sunday, Leo New Moon

**Celestial Correspondences:** Leo, Sun, Pallas, Mars

**Energies:** Creative Endeavors, Entrepreneurship, Success, Manifestation

Using the sigil of Leo-associated asteroid Pallas for success and wisdom in creative endeavors, this nutmeg seed spell will help you plant the seeds of a long and prosperous future in your heart's calling. With energizing, mind-awakening coffee to symbolize soil, empowered with cinnamon for manifestation and eggshell for protection and birthing, your dreams will be nestled in a potent and powerful soil so they can sprout into reality. The bay leaf is added to represent intention and success, while a whole nutmeg acts as good luck, fidelity toward your goals, and financial abundance.

## You Will Need:

½ cup ground coffee

1¼ teaspoons ground cinnamon, divided

3 saffron threads, torn or ground

½ eggshell

1 cinnamon stick, optional

4-ounce jar with a lid

Sharpie

1 large bay leaf

1 whole nutmeg

Honey, enough to fill rest of jar

Green or gold candle

¼ teaspoon ground nutmeg

## Directions:

1. Wake with the sunrise on either the Leo new moon or a Sunday. Sit before your magickal space, or bring your tools and ingredients outside to bask in the power of the rising sun.
2. In a bowl, place coffee for grounding, empowering energy; 1 teaspoon of the cinnamon for manifestation; saffron for power and solar success; and eggshell to protect and empower your dreams as they are birthed into reality.
3. Stir this mixture clockwise with a wooden spoon (or a cinnamon stick), visualizing your dreams and aspirations having a powerful, nurturing soil in which to grow. Pour into the jar as a symbolic soil for your magick.
4. Use the Sharpie to write the name of your endeavor onto the bay leaf, which is a symbol of success. On the other side, draw the Pallas asteroid sigil (see Chapter 5). Place bay leaf atop the coffee mixture.
5. Hold your nutmeg and visualize your endeavor birthing into reality, growing with success! Imagine the nutmeg growing and glowing with life like the rising sun, and breathe your essence onto it, giving it life. Nestle the nutmeg atop the bay leaf in the mixture.
6. Pour nurturing solar honey—the product of hardworking, busy bees—atop the mixture to fill and preserve the jar. Close the jar.

7. Every Sunday, anoint a gold or green candle with honey and sprinkle with nutmeg and the rest of the cinnamon. Place candle atop the jar and light it to continue to grow your project.

*Other Options*
*Alternatively, you can use the Cosmic Coffee Mix from Chapter 15 instead of the blend used here; then you can sip the Sagittarius coffee each day to continue to connect to the spell and energize your efforts! You can even sweeten it with Solar-Spiced Creativity Syrup (in this chapter). If you are using this spell for a business purpose, you can increase its energy by casting the Mercury's Messenger Letter Spell from Chapter 9 to make good business connections and attract investors on the following Wednesday. Or, cast the Wealth and Abundance Spell from Chapter 15 to help your business grow.*

# Sun-Charged Stone Energy Alignment

**Astrological Timing:** Sunday, Leo Sun, Noon, Leo Moon

**Celestial Correspondences:** Leo, Sun

**Energies:** Joy, Confidence, Positivity/Radiance

In addition to ruling the heart, Leo is associated with the solar plexus energy center, which is your seat of personal power and confidence. With this solar-charged crystal healing session, you can empower your sense of self. Using Leo- and Sun-associated stones of sunstone for confidence, leadership, and happiness; orange calcite for creative expression; and peridot for positivity, joy, and abundance, your confidence will be radiant (like a lion's) in no time.

## You Will Need:

Peridot or ruby                                    Orange calcite
Sunstone

## Directions:

1. On a sunny Sunday morning, place your stones in a safe place to charge with the morning sun.
2. Around noon, remove the stones from the sunlight. Lie down in a comfortable, quiet space. Place the peridot at the heart energy

center, sunstone at the solar plexus energy center, and orange calcite on the sacral energy center.

3. Place your hands above your solar plexus, where the sunstone rests, and think about how the crystals were lying outside with the rising sun. Visualize them aglow with the Leo Sun's power, and imagine a bright yellow or golden light growing within your stomach. Think of the Leo Sun blessing you with confidence, power, and positivity. Lie there for 20–30 minutes, absorbing the stones' warming energy and breathing it in. Breathe deeply. When done, slowly bring your awareness back to your body.

4. You can place the stones in a bag and carry them with you, repeating this energy alignment spell as needed.

## *Solar-Spiced Creativity Syrup*

———— ❧ ————

**Astrological Timing:** Sunrise, Sunday, Sun's Hour, Leo New Moon

**Celestial Correspondences:** Leo, Sun, Aries

**Energies:** Creativity, Inspiration, Success

Many people greet the start of a new day with coffee to revitalize and energize their body and mind. Why not usher in some inspiration and creativity by adding this Sun- and Leo-based syrup to your morning cup of joe? With chamomile for clear ideas, orange for inspiration, cinnamon and clove for success, and saffron for solar strength and power, this honey syrup makes a great addition to coffee, tea, or other morning beverages by enhancing creative energies throughout the day. Craft this Leo/Sun creativity syrup at sunrise, then continue using it every morning as you greet the sun to add a bit of creativity into your day!

### You Will Need:

Glass jar with lid
1 tablespoon dried chamomile
1 orange peel
½ teaspoon ground clove
2 saffron threads
1 cinnamon stick

½ cup water
Citrine
½ cup honey

## Directions:

1. At sunrise, place all ingredients except for the cinnamon, water, citrine, and honey in the jar. As you add each ingredient, think about its properties and smell its aroma.
2. Place your hands above or on either side of the ingredients and visualize that as the sun rises and brings light to the world, so, too, do new ideas light up within you. Imagine light blossoming in the herbs, and once you feel an energetic response from them, use the cinnamon stick to stir the herbs clockwise, calling in creativity. Pour in the water and visualize your sacral and solar plexus energy centers growing with creative power. Add the citrine to the glass.
3. Watch or imagine the sunrise, with the endless orange and bright colors lighting up the previously dark sky. Close the jar, and let the sun heat the infusion throughout the day, keeping it in a spot where it can absorb the sunlight. Alternatively, if you remove the citrine, you can add heated water or heat the mixture in a pot on the stove, if the sun will not warm it enough.
4. At midday, when the sun reaches its peak, add the honey, again stirring clockwise with the cinnamon stick. Bring inside and strain into a bowl. Pour strained liquid back into jar and store in refrigerator for up to three weeks.

### Try Making Sun Tea

*You can also make sun tea the same way! Just choose your favorite tea, add water, and heat in the sun, then add your Solar-Spiced Creativity Syrup for extra solar energies.*

## Lion's Heart Healing Spell

———— ❧ ————

**Astrological Timing:** Noon, Sunday, Leo Full/New Moon

**Celestial Correspondences:** Leo, Sun, Cancer, Chiron, Ceres

**Energies:** Heart Healing and Strength, Self-Expression, Bliss

Leo rules the heart, and when the Sun is radiating in this warm and charismatic sign, it is the perfect time to focus on healing your heart. With peridot for positivity and joy, and ruby for strength of the heart, and thyme for strength, this crystal star spell is designed to support you as you release old wounds. Once you have opened up your heart again, you can find more bliss and feel more free to express yourself.

## You Will Need:

Fireproof dish

12 small fresh thyme sprigs

1½ tablespoons dried rose petals

Burgundy, green, or pink candle
    and candleholder

¼ teaspoon honey

Peridot

Ruby

## Directions:

1. At sunrise/morning, place the fireproof dish on a flat, safe surface (where you will be able to watch the candle burn).

2. Line the outer rim of the dish with all but one of the thyme sprigs. Sprinkle all but a pinch of the rose petals along this thyme circle, in a clockwise manner, creating a beautiful circle of magenta and green for the heart center for healing and strength. Sprinkle remaining rose petals in center of circle and add a pinch of thyme leaves from remaining sprig.

3. Dress your candle with Sun-ruled honey, and roll it toward you through the thyme and rose petals you dropped in the center of the circle, bringing in healing and strength. Secure dressed candle in the center of the dish.

4. Place the peridot and ruby around the base of the candle.

5. Hover your hands above the stones and around the candle, noticing the stones and herb beneath your palms and all the heart-opening, strengthening energies they represent. Visualize a sun rising and opening both within the scene and within your heart center, clearing away blockages and infusing your energy with radiance and positivity.

6. Say aloud three times:

*"Celestial Lion, your power to me impart*
*Grant me your radiant strength of heart."*

7. Light the candle. You can stop here if you like, or lie down and rest the ruby on your heart and the peridot on your third (solar plexus) energy center. Meditate on the image of the rising sun, clearing away all darkness and warming the earth. Imagine the sun doing the same to your heart. Return stones to candle to charge up until the candle

burns all the way down, then keep them on your person to hold in times of need.

8. When you are done, feel free to carry the stones with you, or you can keep the layout in place and put a quartz point in the middle.

*Use a Crystal Body Layout*
*To add another layer of cosmic vibration, meditate using the crystal body layout from the Cancer Energy Alignment in Chapter 10. A sign of the emotions, this layout will help further your healing as the candle burns.*

# Apollo's Chariot Inner Light Spell

— ✧ —

**Astrological Timing:** Sunrise, Sun's Hour, Midday, Sunday, Leo/Aries New/Waxing/Full Moon

**Celestial Correspondences:** Leo, Aries, Sun

**Energies:** Support, Spirituality, Positivity

Renew your inner light with this Sun-aligned support spell. Whether you need to be reminded of your purpose or are looking to usher in creativity, call in the solar chariot of Apollo to light your inner sun as he lights up the sky. Using the power of the rising sun, you will strengthen and renew your own inner light and sense of positivity, or lend solar support to a matter of your choice. You can even do this spell regularly during your sun sign's season to develop a healthier relationship with your personal sun sign— just use Appendix D to add some ingredients for your sign! For example, if your sun sign is in Cancer, you might wish to sprinkle some jasmine or add a few pieces of moonstone to make a flower and crystal grid to bring in blessings for your solar return (otherwise known as your birthday)!

## You Will Need:

Tea light
Toothpick
¼ teaspoon olive oil
½ teaspoon ground cinnamon
Fireproof dish
3 cinnamon sticks

1 tablespoon dried chamomile and/or 5 or more marigold/calendula flowers, or fresh flowers, (or flowers for your sun sign)
Peridot
Yellow or orange candle

# Directions:

1. Just before sunrise, use the toothpick to engrave the tea light with your name and intention. Dab it with a small amount of oil and sprinkle it with a pinch of the cinnamon to increase your energy and spiritual vibration. Place tea light in the center of your fireproof dish.

2. Visualize breaking away any negative energy, then snap each cinnamon stick in half so that you have six pieces. In a clockwise motion, place five of the pieces around the tea light in a star shape. You can use the remaining piece to burn slightly, like incense.

3. Place your flowers in the space between each stick (a safe distance away from the tea light so that they do not catch on fire), thinking of their bright and confident energy. Nestle the peridot beside the tea light, or nestle any Sun-aligned stones inside the flowers.

4. Engrave the candle with the symbol of the sun (see Chapter 5) and light it. As the sun rises, imagine Apollo's chariot carrying the sun across the sky. Use this candle to light the tea light, while saying something like this (you can change these words as needed to match your intention):

   *"As the sun rises again each day anew, the light within me grows and is renewed."*

5. Repeat the words two more times, then sprinkle the remaining ground cinnamon above the flame and over the flowers in a clockwise motion, blessing them with extra energy.

6. Let the tea light burn out. You can snuff the candle if you wish and reuse it to repeat the ritual daily or as needed, or let it burn out on its own. Keep the peridot on you to promote optimism.

### Add Excitement with a Meteor Shower
*If you're looking to renew a sense of excitement or make a wish, perform this spell while watching a meteor shower and use the motion and flash of lighting a match (to light the candle) like the light of a shooting star, blessing and setting your intentions aflame, rather than the rising sun.*

# Coffee Confidence Scrub

————— ✍ —————

**Astrological Timing:** Sunrise, Midday, Afternoon, Sun's Hour, Sunday, Moon in Leo, Leo Transits

**Celestial Correspondences:** Leo, Sun, Aries, Venus

**Energies:** Confidence, Cleansing, Vigor

Cleanse away stagnant energy and claim your confidence with this Coffee Confidence Scrub. Known for their radiating confidence, Leos own their Sun's rulership, exuding confidence and positive energy. Every time you use this scrub, you will metaphorically burn away the old and replace it with new, confident, and exciting energy. Infuse the mixture during daylight hours, then use it throughout Leo season or whenever you need a confidence boost!

## You Will Need:

½ cup coffee grounds

½ cup brown sugar

½ teaspoon ground cinnamon

½ teaspoon ground clove

3 saffron threads, torn into pieces

¼ cup almond oil

½ teaspoon vanilla extract

10 drops orange essential oil or 6 slices orange peel

## Directions:

1. In a bowl, mix together the energizing coffee, sweetening sugar, and spices. Breathe in the aroma of the ingredients and stir clockwise with a spoon, growing your confidence. Use your finger to draw the sigil for Leo (see Chapter 3).

2. In a separate bowl, mix together almond oil, vanilla, and orange essential oil (or squeeze orange peel with rind facing mixture to get natural, fresh oils—and have a leftover orange you can enjoy as a snack, drizzled with honey). Add to the coffee mixture in a clockwise motion.

3. Use immediately and store leftovers in the refrigerator, being sure to use within one week. Every time you use the scrub, visualize it cleansing away old energy and reenergizing your body with confidence, excitement, and creativity.

*Turn This Spell Into a Ritual*
*Leo isn't the only sign able to usher in attention! With the aesthetics of Venus, the connectivity of air, and the power of Juno, the Attention on Me Bell Spell (Chapter 13) would be a great addition to this cosmic spellcasting to ensure you get noticed. Before an evening out, be sure to shower with the coffee scrub, then cast the bell spell before heading out.*

# Binary Star Connection Spell

**Astrological Timing:** Sun's/Venus's Hour, Friday, Leo Moon

**Celestial Correspondences:** Leo, Venus, Sun

**Energies:** Romance, Connection, Inspiration

Binary star systems have two stars that rotate around each other. While at times, Leo wants to be the brightest star in his solar system (like Leo's ruling celestial body, our Sun is), this sign is also about connecting heart-to-heart and sharing your radiance with others. Like the binary star system, invite others' inner stars to shine brightly along with you! Engage your fifth house of pleasure, and deepen your connection with someone as you shine together in harmony with this rotating star spell.

## You Will Need:

2 candles, yellow for friendship or pink for romance and 2 candleholders
Toothpick
Fireproof dish
2 lodestones

1 teaspoon ground cinnamon
1 tablespoon dried rose petals (for love) or dried lavender (for friendship)—or a mixture of both flowers

## Directions:

1. Use the toothpick to engrave one candle with your name and the other with your intended subject or person, adding the Leo sigil to both (see Chapter 3).
2. Place your two candles on the fireproof dish so they stand across from each other.

3. Place the lodestones by the foot of each candle. Lodestones have a natural small magnetic pull and represent the gravity of two stars attracting one another.
4. Use the cinnamon and dried flowers to draw an infinity symbol encircling each candle to represent equal give-and-take.
5. Think of your intention and light the candles. Darken the lights in the room and turn the dish slowly in a clockwise direction five times, saying aloud:

*"Like two sun stars encircling in the night*
*Let me and [name of person] connect by this light."*

6. Watch the candle flames shining together, then let them burn out.

### Strengthen This Spell
*Strengthen the power of this star spell by combining it with another. If you're looking to usher in passion with another person or subject, follow this spell with the Planting Power spell from Aries season (Chapter 7) on the following Tuesday, or heighten the harmony of this spell with the Cosmic Harmony Diffuser Spell from Chapter 13.*

# Chapter 12

# VIRGO SEASON

**Virgo Season:** August 23–September 22
**Best Day:** Wednesday
**Best Time of Day:** Mercury's Hour, Morning/Afternoon

Following fiery Leo season, where we focused on personal identity and inner flame, it's now time for charitable, giving Virgo to sweep in abundance and sharing with her bushels of grain. Ruled by Mercury, earth sign Virgo provides a fertile time to ground the ideas of air into the earth, review the systems in place, and brainstorm how to improve efficiency to make your dreams happen.

Use the power of Mercury and Virgo through spells for efficiency; feed your sixth house by building daily habits; fuel your focus and discipline via working with Vesta; engage the healing power of nature through Chiron; and, finally, manifest, celebrate, and share abundance with Ceres. During this time, the new moon in Virgo will rise with the Sun, providing a blessed time to set intentions and sow the seeds of efficiency, organization, and daily habits. The full moon in Pisces will highlight the balance between going with the flow and being efficient and organized.

## *Earth Energy Meditation*

**Astrological Timing:** Mercury's Hour, Afternoon, Wednesday

**Celestial Correspondences:** Virgo, Ceres, Mercury, Taurus

**Energies:** Material Connection, Reciprocity, Gratitude

As the mutable expression of earth, Virgo is about connecting to earth allies of all kinds. In this meditation, you will learn how to connect to the power of herbs to add their energy to any celestial spell. You'll also engage in reciprocity with nature and recognize and celebrate your relationship with the earth. While rosemary is listed in this spell, feel free to use another herb or even a plant in your very own backyard!

## You Will Need:

Rosemary plant or other herb or
    plant

## Directions:

1. Sit down, breathing deeply. Bring your focus to how the solid earth supports you with each inhale. Relax further into the earth with each exhale.
2. Take the rosemary or other herb in your hand, feeling its textures. Gaze at its colors and breathe in its scent.
3. Place your herb on the ground or on a small plate. Hover your hand above the plant. Slowly raise your hand farther away from the plant, then lower it. Do this slowly, until you begin to notice a shift in buzzing energy—the herb's vibration—under your hand, below your palm. You can also close your eyes as you do this.
4. Next, hover both hands above the herb, feeling its energy. Visualize your seventh (crown) energy center alight and draw that energy down to your hands and then to the herbs, connecting your cosmic energy to the plant's. Spend as long as you need to do this, until you feel an energetic response and shift beneath your hands as if the herb is buzzing along with you.
5. Now that you are connected in energetic resonance to this plant ally, ask yourself the following questions:
   • How is my connection to the earth?
   • How is my connection to my body?
   • How do I serve and engage in reciprocity with the world around me?
6. Feel free to ponder any further questions or themes inspired by the Virgo section in Chapter 3. When ready, give conscious thanks to your plant ally and breathe your focus back into your body.

*Other Uses of This Spell*
*You can repeat this meditation with a variety of plants to connect to their energy and begin to develop a relationship. You can also use this spell to connect to the medicine and power of any herbs or spices you use throughout this book, thus adding the power of mutable earth to all your celestial spells.*

# Virgo Energy Alignment

**Astrological Timing:** Wednesday, Virgo New Moon, Mercury's Hour

**Celestial Correspondences:** Ceres, Virgo, Mercury

**Energies:** Healing, Purification/Cleansing, Grounding, Centering, Discipline

Since Virgo is a sign of service and health, this crystal ritual will help center your energy, attune you to your purpose, and ground your energy—and your mind. Using stones matched to Virgo's capacity for health, work, service, and discipline, as well as the healing capacity of dill, you will align your energy centers to cast powerful Virgo magick to encourage personal healing. Do this spell throughout Virgo season to promote healing or self-discipline or whenever you need a dose of grounded focus to bring your attention back to your body.

## You Will Need:

1 fresh or dried dill or rosemary sprig

Fluorite

Blue lace agate

Citrine

Hematite

## Directions:

1. If possible, set up a space outside where you can easily connect to the energies of nature. Sitting in your healing spot, take the dill or rosemary and brush it against your body, flicking away stagnant energy and infusing your aura with its cleansing, healing vibration.
2. Once you have patted your body down with the herb, lie down and place the stones on their corresponding energy centers (see Chapter 6 for placement information): fluorite at the third eye (for focus), blue lace agate for the throat (to help open your voice), citrine on the

solar plexus (for willpower and positivity), and hematite at the root (for grounding and connection to earth).

3. As you lie there, really feel the weight of the stones on your body. Just as the stones rest on you, you rest on Mother Earth, who supports you with her gravity. Breathe in tune with the earth and allow your body to receive the energy for 20–30 minutes.

4. Bring your focus slowly back to your feet and fingers, and when ready, arise from the session. You may wish to safely burn the herb (if using fresh, you can let it dry for a few days, or just enjoy the smoke from the embers of the fresh herb, knowing it might not burn as well) afterward to cleanse the energy it brushed away, as well as breathe in its healing aroma.

## *Harvest Blessings Cornucopia*

———— ❧ ————

**Astrological Timing:** Wednesday, Sunday, Sun's/Mercury's Hour

**Celestial Correspondences:** Ceres, Virgo, Saturn, Sun

**Energies:** Abundance, Harvest, Blessings

When harvest season comes around, it is a time to focus on gratitude, connect with the community, and usher in further growth. Celebrate the myth and magick of Ceres in her harvest form and thank her for the nourishment she provides by crafting a cornucopia to share with your community and wildlife! By connecting to the archetypal energy of Ceres and celebrating the harvest, you can invite in more abundance and blessings to receive at the remaining harvests.

### You Will Need:

Cornucopia container (available at craft stores, or you can craft your own from a hollowed-out loaf of bread)

Grain stalks, such as wheat, barley, corn, or rye

Local harvest season ingredients such as apples, grapes, or pumpkins

Nontoxic, seasonal flower blooms

Peridot

Green candle

## Directions:

1. Gather your items on your altar or, preferably, on a central community table in your home.
2. Construct your cornucopia, thinking about orchards, fields, and plants alive with growth, and the goddess Ceres blessing it all with her touch. See her magick in the items you place in the cornucopia.
3. Adorn your work with seasonal flowers to symbolize the fertility of life and abundance, then place your cornucopia in the center of the table or altar.
4. Spend a moment admiring your creation and gazing upon the Ceres archetypal energy, holding your peridot. Visualize abundance and sharing that abundance with others. Place the green candle in a safe place nearby and light it for abundance, then place the peridot beside it.
5. Leave the cornucopia out for guests to enjoy and eat from as a symbol of community, and then (being sure not to litter), leave any extra outside for wildlife to enjoy, as wildlife is also sacred to Ceres.

# *Focus Clari-Tea*

#### ——— ∂ ———

**Astrological Timing:** Mercury's Hour, Wednesday, Virgo Moon, Mercury Transits

**Celestial Correspondences:** Virgo, Gemini, Capricorn, Taurus, Mercury, Aries

**Energies:** Focus, Clarity, the Mind

Almost nothing is more calming than a hot cup of tea, its steam warming your face. Using Mercury- and Virgo-aligned herbs, this simple tea potion is bursting with energies of focus, insight, and clarity. Enjoy this beverage before a tarot reading, studying for school, or diving into a work project to help you stay focused and keep your mind sharp through the element of air.

## You Will Need:

9 tablespoons hot water
1 fresh rosemary sprig
3 fresh sage leaves
1 tablespoon honey
Earl Grey tea bag

1 tablespoon lemon juice, optional
Ice, if desired, for a chilled tea
1 fresh mint or rosemary sprig, optional

# Directions:

1. Boil water. In a cup, place rosemary, sage, and ½ tablespoon honey. Breathe in the aroma of these ingredients and connect to their energy.

2. Muddle the herbs with a wooden spoon or muddler, expressing their magickal oils out and into the honey. As you do so, imagine muddling away distractions and refining your focus. Say aloud:

   *"Herbs of cleansing, and of the mind;*
   *Clarity and focus I do find."*

3. Add the tea bag and boiling water. When steeped, you can drink the tea hot or, if you prefer it cold, add another ½ tablespoon honey, 1 tablespoon cleansing lemon, and ice, and garnish with mint or rosemary spring to refresh the mind each time you sip.

### Other Celestial Additions

*Finesse your focus and master your mind by holding a piece of fluorite as you sip this beverage, carrying it with you as you complete your tasks. The Herbal Pouch to Keep Your Mind Sharp (Chapter 9) and the Master(y) Key Spell (Chapter 16) also make great additions!*

## Celestial Caduceus Cure

**Astrological Timing:** Wednesday, Sunday, Mercury's/Sun's Hour

**Celestial Correspondences:** Mercury, Sun, Ceres, Vesta, Chiron

**Energies:** Healing, Physical Well-Being

With this spell, you will create your very own caduceus (the same staff the god Mercury held, often associated with healing) with restorative Virgo-aligned herbs to bring your body into balance or to invoke a remedy. You can leave this staff out in nature as an offering to healing nature spirits, burn it as an offering to the sacred flame of Vesta in a healing ritual, or go all out and create something long-lasting by engraving symbols in the wood and attaching crystals—the choice is up to you!

## You Will Need:

Piece of paper and writing utensil
Short Stick
Twine
Fresh rosemary sprigs, enough to
    twist around your chosen stick

Sharpie
6 bay leaves
2 fresh or dried sage leaves

## Directions:

1. Set your intention for healing—whether it be for a very specific health issue, supporting general good health, or setting healthy daily habits. Write this intention on the paper, wrap it around the thicker end of the stick, and secure it with twine.
2. Next, weave the rosemary up from the base of the stick, like the helix of DNA or two serpents intermingling and shedding skin. Secure with more twine as needed.
3. Next, write your intention down in Sharpie on each of the bay leaves. Separate so that you have two piles of 3 bay leaves each. You can secure them with twine or glue them to the top of your stick to represent wings.
4. Attach sage leaves to the bay leaves to add layers to your wings.
5. Take the herb bundle outside and leave it in nature as a plea to healing nature spirits, or burn safely in a sacred fire to Vesta.

### Create a Full Healing Ritual

*Looking to invite celestial healing balance within your body? Turn this into a full healing ritual by following up this caduceus spell with the Restorative Moon Bath (Chapter 10) or the Virgo Energy Alignment (this chapter), and then keep the Healing Salt Mixture (Chapter 8) next to or under your bed!*

# Harmony Basket

———— ❧ ————

**Astrological Timing:** Mercury's/Venus's Hour, Saturday, Wednesday, Friday

**Celestial Correspondences:** Ceres, Virgo, Saturn, Libra, Vesta, Venus

**Energies:** Harmony, Abundance, Working Together, Community

Virgo season is a time when you can share what you have with your community. In this spell, you'll enchant a basket (a symbol of bounty and sharing) to keep in your home or office to inspire a sense of sharing and working together in harmony, or to reflect on your service and what you share with the world. You can also keep a small basket on your altar for offerings, for abundance blessings from Ceres, or even to hold your spell ingredients or harvest from your garden!

## You Will Need:

Basket

Green, yellow, or white candle

¼ teaspoon olive oil

¼ teaspoon dried lavender

Fireproof dish

Ribbon

## Directions:

1. Sit in your sacred space with your basket and spell items before you.
2. Anoint your candle with oil like a celestial olive branch of peace and harmony. Place the lavender on a small plate and roll the candle through it. Set candle securely on your fireproof dish.
3. Hovering your hands around the candle, envision community, harmony, and any specific intentions—such as a shared chore load around the house or workplace collaboration. Light the candle.
4. As the candle burns, envision that it is a cleansing, warming hearth fire that invites everyone around it. Begin weaving your ribbon through the basket in any way you like, saying something like:

   *"With this ribbon I weave, harmony and unity is achieved."*

5. When done weaving, place the basket a safe distance from the candle so the candle can bless it with its golden light. Let the candle burn all the way down.

*Add Aromatherapy*
*You can add to the cosmic power of this spell by enjoying the scent of the*
*Cosmic Harmony Diffuser Spell from Chapter 13 as you decorate your basket.*
*With its peaceful aroma, the diffuser can craft a harmonious environment. Or,*
*invite further unity with the Flower Power Potion from Chapter 18.*

# Energy-Cleansing Herb Bundle

**Astrological Timing:** Virgo Full/New Moon, Waning Moon, Wednesday, Friday, Sunday

**Celestial Correspondences:** Ceres, Virgo, Mercury, Venus, Sun

**Energies:** Healing, Nature, Cleansing, Purification

Call down cosmic cleansing and promote healing and health with this Virgo herb bundle. Health and routines come into focus during Virgo season, but as a cosmic witch, your magickal and energetic routines are just as important! One such routine is regularly cleansing your energy body. With healing herbs, this cleansing bundle will help clear your space and energy, as well as invoke some health and well-being-oriented energy. Make it once during the Virgo new or full moons and enjoy year-round before or after magick and energy sessions to keep your aura and body as fresh as the night's celestial breeze!

## You Will Need:

3 fresh marjoram or lavender
    sprigs, optional
3 fresh rosemary sprigs

3 fresh thyme sprigs
Twine
Small citrine point, optional

## Directions:

1. Under the light of the Virgo Moon or Virgo Sun, set out your herbs before you. Breathe in their aromas and notice their textures. Take a moment to connect to the herbal energies and give gratitude.
2. Gather the herbs together and use the twine to wrap them from the base of the stems to the tips and back down. Knot twine at the base.

3. You may wish to tie a small citrine point at the base (just be sure you don't burn it) for extra positive, cleansing, affirming energy each time you use the bundle.

4. Hang the bundle upside down and let dry for one to two weeks. When ready to use, unravel a small amount of the twine from the tip of the bundle, set herbs aflame, and then blow out the flame to use the smoke from the embers (just like burning incense). Charged under the Virgo Sun or Moon, you now have a powerful healing bundle to use as needed throughout the celestial year.

# Daily Discipline Vesta Flame Spell

**Astrological Timing:** Wednesday, Saturday, Saturn's/Mercury's Hour

**Celestial Correspondences:** Virgo, Mercury, Vesta, Saturn

**Energies:** Habits, Routines, Focus, Discipline

Virgo and Vesta inspire discipline, daily routines, and habits to help you stay in balance and healthy. With herbs like cumin and rosemary—aligned to Virgo—and the sacred steadiness of Vesta's flame, this spell harnesses the power of celestial myths to help you establish new routines or specific habits. Work this celestial spell during Virgo season or whenever you need a dose of Virgo and Vesta magick in your life for discipline, balance, and health!

## You Will Need:

Piece of paper and writing utensil
White, green, or yellow pillar
   candle
Toothpick
¼–½ teaspoon olive oil

¼ teaspoon dried rosemary
¼ teaspoon dried dill
Fireproof dish
7 cumin seeds

## Directions:

1. Think of the habit you want to begin or improve upon and write it down on the paper. Use the toothpick to engrave a key word of that intention (a shortened version is okay) into the candle.

2. Dab the top of the candle with oil and use your left (receiving) hand to pull the oil down from the top of the candle toward you and your third (solar plexus) energy center. Visualize integrating this new energy into your center as you do so.
3. On a small plate, mix rosemary and dill, then roll the candle through the mixture. Place candle on the fireproof dish.
4. Place the paper under the dish, and hover your hands around candle, thinking of your intention. Visualize your center's inner willpower/ fire resonating with the candle's energy and with this vision.
5. Press the cumin seeds into the candle, creating seven different sections of candle to mark seven days of working on this spell.
6. Whenever you are ready to start your new habit, think of your commitment and light the candle. Say aloud:

> *"Vesta, goddess of the burning flame. Willpower and dedication, I do claim."*

7. Light the candle, visualizing it resonating with your third energy center and both burning bright together.
8. Complete your task while the candle is burning. Let the candle burn until it reaches the first cumin seed marker. Snuff the candle for the day, saying aloud:

> *"The flame holds steady,*
> *Until the next day I am ready."*

9. Each day you do your task, light the candle until it burns down to the next cumin seed marker.

### Change the Pattern
*Sometimes bad habits get in the way of positive changes. Cut away any old patterns at their root with the Cosmic Cord Cutting spell (Chapter 17) or with the Transform Like a Phoenix Spell (Chapter 14) before or while working this spell.*

*Chapter 13*

# LIBRA SEASON

**Libra Season:** September 23–October 22
**Best Day:** Friday
**Best Time of Day:** Venus's Hour, Afternoon

L ike a cool, soothing breeze carrying the alluring scent of roses, Libra season brings your focus up from the earth of hardworking Virgo season to the horizon and bright blue skies. A time of charm, balance, and social connection, this season of cardinal air ruled by Venus reminds you to take a look around to appreciate the beauty of life and the connections you have with those around you.

Represented by the scales, Libra brings a time of balance—which nature demonstrates, for, in both the Northern and Southern Hemispheres, the start of the season is marked by equal hours of light and dark. Now is the time to invoke harmony at parties and social gatherings, cultivate your personal aesthetic and sense of charm, and usher in balance and reciprocity in relationships as seventh house themes of partnerships come into focus. Libra season brings in the new moon in Libra—a time when both Sun and Moon are aligned in this sign, paving the way for new beginnings and efforts favorable to Libra-ruled energies. It also brings the full moon into headstrong Aries, which highlights balance through conflict (between Libra's tendency to balance all sides of a situation and Aries's tendency to rush in without considering all factors). Channel Libra's peaceful energy by sipping on and sharing the rose, lavender, and honey Libra Peace Tea, or invoke an equal balance of give-and-take in relationships through the Relationship Reciprocity Spell.

# Breath of Life Meditation

———— ✐ ————

**Astrological Timing:** Wednesday, Friday, Mercury's/Venus's Hour

**Celestial Correspondences:** Libra, Mercury, Venus, Gemini

**Energies:** Calm, Peace, Focus, Clarity

From the light breeze that dances across your skin to the first gust of a stormy wind, cardinal air promotes communication and thought. In this meditation, you will set your intentions for Libra season and attune to these astrological energies, while also learning to harness the power of your breath. A simple breathing exercise, but magickal nonetheless, you can do this every day to help you connect to and use the power of your voice or breath to communicate with others or to initiate action and change in the real world. And in true Libra fashion, such an exercise can help elicit calm and focus in any situation. You can use this meditation to empower any spell with the element of air, breathing your intention into candles; harnessing the power of your breath through the words and tone you use; or using your breath to connect to your magickal allies, such as herbs or stones.

## You Will Need:

Lapis lazuli

## Directions:

1. Sit comfortably in your meditative space, holding the lapis in your left hand, and take a few deep breaths to get comfortable.
2. Breathe deeply into your belly for four counts, feeling it expand with air. Hold for four counts, noticing the tension, and then exhale, noticing the relief as you release.
3. Continue breathing and counting like this, focusing on your inhalation and exhalation and the cycle of breath entering and exiting your body, feeding each cell with oxygen.
4. Tune in to the energy of the stone. Visualize breathing in light and exhaling any negative or stagnant energy, relaxing your muscles with each passage of air.

5. Finally, visualize your throat energy center opening up as air passes through it, breathing in this light to your solar plexus energy center as the air expands your belly and empowers it.

6. After a few breaths, bring your focus to something you want right now and what it might feel or look like if this came to be. Again attuning to the vibration of the lapis in your hand, breathe this vision three times into your body, feeding this thought with the very breath of life. Then, exhale it into the world with power from your throat and solar plexus centers.

## Libra Energy Alignment

—————— ✌ ——————

**Astrological Timing:** Libra Season, Moon in Libra, Friday, Wednesday, Mercury's/Venus's Hour

**Celestial Correspondences:** Libra, Venus

**Energies:** Peace, Insight, Connection, Calm

Illuminate your mind, throat, and heart with star power using this Libra-aligned body crystal grid. Using stones such as amethyst, you tune your energy in to the cosmos to prepare for Libra season healing and also pave the way for more effective Libra-aligned spellwork. This spell will also promote clear, calm thinking and heartfelt communication and emotion. Feel free to add a smoky quartz between your feet to remain grounded.

### You Will Need:

Rose or vanilla incense

Amethyst

Lapis lazuli

Rose quartz

### Directions:

1. Prepare a place where you will rest for this energy alignment. Light the incense. You may wish to put on relaxing music. Spend a few moments enjoying the aroma, then take your stones and pass them through the smoke, one by one.

2. Lie down. Breathe in, exhale, and place the amethyst on your third eye as you breathe out (see Chapter 6 for placement). Breathe in, exhale, then place the lapis on your throat energy center. Place the rose quartz at your heart energy center.

3. Bring your awareness to the stones on your body and visualize the constellation of the scales in the sky. Imagine a meteor shower originating from this constellation raining down energetic shooting stars that light up your energy centers. Imagine yourself breathing this star power into each of the stones.

4. Focus on the cycle of breath in your body, really tuning your awareness in to this air element. Enjoy for 20–30 minutes, then slowly bring your awareness back to your body, rotating your wrists and ankles and arising from your meditation.

## Cosmic Harmony Diffuser Spell

**Astrological Timing:** Friday, Venus's Hour, Full Moon, Libra Sun

**Celestial Correspondences:** Venus, Mercury, Libra, Pisces, Neptune

**Energies:** Unity, Harmony, Compassion

Spread Libra's sense of peace and harmony and encourage heartfelt communication with this aromatic spell. This diffuser blend will infuse your environment with the calming mental, communicative, and connective energy of this sign. Use it to establish a calm environment before meditating, to bring peace to situations or discussions, or to enchant your home with harmonious energies.

### You Will Need:

1 tablespoon vodka

Jar with lid

1 orange rind piece

10 drops rose essential oil (or several dried rose petals)

10 drops lavender essential oil

½ teaspoon vanilla extract

¼ cup almond oil

Amethyst

Glass bottle with narrow opening

Reed diffuser sticks

### Directions:

1. Add vodka to the jar and infuse with orange rind. Cover with lid and let sit for about 6 hours.

2. After 6 hours, place 2 tablespoons of the infusion in a bowl. Drop in the essential oils and vanilla. Stir in a clockwise motion and breathe in the scent.

3. Add almond oil, then use the amethyst to draw Libra's sigil (see Chapter 3) on the surface of the mixture. Drop the amethyst into the bowl. Hover your hands above the bowl, envisioning this enchanting aroma calming tempers and inspiring reason and harmony.
4. Charge under the full moon in Libra season or under the bright planet Venus in the sky.
5. Transfer to the bottle (remove amethyst if necessary) and add diffuser sticks to allow the scent to permeate the area.

### How to Promote Extra Peace and Unity
*Accompany this spell with the Communication Lemonade from Chapter 9 to inspire calm communication or the Flower Power Potion from Chapter 18 to inspire more peace.*

# Call for Justice Spell

———— ❧ ————

**Astrological Timing:** Thursday, Jupiter's Hour

**Celestial Correspondences:** Libra, Jupiter, Saturn, Mercury, Pallas, Juno

**Energies:** Balance, Justice, Fairness

Invoke interstellar balance with this spell that welcomes justice. You will invoke astrological energy by calling upon the power and myth of Juno and Pallas and the balancing power of Libra to champion what is right. In this spell, you will be burning two different candles (one for each side of the story), letting the one that represents your cause burn all the way down. Cast this cosmic balance spell when you want to bring justice to your side or rebalance the scales in relationships and power dynamics.

## You Will Need:
Appropriate stands for candles
2 white candles
Toothpick
¼ teaspoon olive oil
¼–½ teaspoon dried or fresh thyme

1 bay leaf
Sharpie
Any other symbols as needed, optional (see Step 4)

# Directions:

1. Place the candles depending on your situation. If you want the truth to shine, then perhaps the lighter side of the scale (the candle that's higher in the air) should represent success. Or perhaps with all the facts or any financial winnings, the heavier side of the scale (lower candle) will be the favored position. Or do you prefer a symbolism of balance with two candles at equal height? Gather firesafe equipment, such as stands or tall candleholders, to achieve the appropriate setup and height difference for your spell.
2. Use the toothpick to engrave your name on one candle and the name of the person/situation in question on the other.
3. Anoint the candles with oil. Place thyme on a small plate and roll candle through it. Set the candle representing you on the favored platform and the other candle in the lesser spot.
4. On the bay leaf, write your name with Sharpie and then draw a crown to represent success. Place it underneath or by the "preferred" candle. Add any other symbolism you wish, such as coins for financial winnings, a feather for innocence and purity of heart, or a star anise for truth.
5. Place your hands around your candle and visualize yourself winning or balance restored. Say aloud three times:

   *"Asteroid Juno, Asteroid Pallas,*
   *From this moment forward, heed no more malice.*
   *By what is right, weigh in favor of me this night."*

6. Light both candles. Repeat the chant three more times, then blow out the opposing candle if using for justice, leaving only yours alight. If doing this spell for bringing balance, leave both alight.
7. Once the desired candle(s) is burnt out, keep the bay leaf on your person and throw away the opposing candle.

### Cast Cosmic Success
*Combine this spell with the Cosmic Victory Crown spell from Chapter 7 and help to usher in energy in your favor. You can do this by crafting the crown as your candle burns, placing it by your candle, crowning yourself with it as a symbol of success upon casting this spell, or burning it as an offering.*

# Venus Attraction Fragrance

———— ✥ ————

**Astrological Timing:** Friday, Venus's Hour, under the light of Venus

**Celestial Correspondences:** Libra, Venus, Juno, Scorpio, Taurus

**Energies:** Attraction, Connection, Sensuality, Love

With alluring vanilla, sweetening rose, and the spice of cardamom, this fragrance is sure to enchant all those that interact with you, inviting connection and favor. A Venusian sign also ruled by air, Libra is the perfect season to use the power of scent in your magick. Whether you're looking to gain social favor, connect with others, or attract the things you desire to you, this perfume is sure to do the job!

## You Will Need:

1 vanilla bean
1 tablespoon almond oil
Small glass jar
1 pinch cardamom

12 drops rose essential oil
Small glass bottle with roller top
Tiny rose quartz

## Directions:

1. Under the light of the Libra new moon, cut open the vanilla bean. Slice it into small pieces, breathing in its enticing aroma, and place it with the almond oil in the glass jar. Sprinkle in cardamom, visualizing the shining starlight of Venus and this star sign.
2. Let this oil infuse for 4 weeks, growing in power through the lunar cycle and the Sun in Libra. You may wish to place the oil on your windowsill to charge under the light of the Aries full moon during Libra season. On the next new moon (which would be in Scorpio), add rose oil and the Libra-aligned rose quartz.
3. Place liquid in roller bottle, and anoint your skin each morning before going out, breathing in its enchanting aroma and visualizing your desires being drawn toward you—whether gifts, admiration, romance, or abundance!

# Libra Peace Tea

———— ❧ ————

**Astrological Timing:** Friday, Venus's Hour, Libra or Gemini Transits

**Celestial Correspondences:** Venus, Libra, Mercury, Gemini

**Energies:** Peace, Communication, Connection, Intuition

Libra season brings a time of connection—a period when you may want to use your voice to communicate and engage with others. What better way to open your throat energy center, calm your mind, and invite connection than with a little tea gathering? Engage Venus through sharing drinks and conversation with others while opening and soothing the throat energy center for clear, heartfelt communication. You can also enjoy this Libra Peace Tea alone to calm your mind or to connect to your intuition for Libra-inspired perception.

## You Will Need:

9 tablespoons hot water

1 tablespoon dried rose petals

¼ teaspoon dried lavender

¼ teaspoon dried mint leaves

Special glass or mug

1 tablespoons honey

1 fresh rosemary sprig

¼ ounce fresh lemon juice

## Directions:

1. Boil water. Place loving rose, peaceful lavender, and throat-soothing mint in the glass or mug. Visualize these flowers and herbs opening up, just like your throat, heart, and third eye energy centers, for calm, clear, and loving communication. Breathe in the floral aroma. Pour boiling water over these ingredients and let steep for 2 minutes.

2. Add honey, using the rosemary sprig to stir clockwise, visualizing a peaceful, eloquent gathering or your own peace and intuition. Then add in lemon.

3. Strain (if not doing tea leaf reading; see sidebar) and drink, or make more to share with guests.

### Tea Leaf Reading

*You can use the leftover herbs for tea leaf reading. Instead of straining out the herbs, sip the tea with your question in mind. When the cup is empty, look at the herbs on the bottom of the cup and see where they land. Mentally separating the spaces of the cup by the houses, notice what symbols you see.*

# Attention on Me Bell Spell

———— ✌ ————

**Astrological Timing:** Friday, Venus's/Mercury's Hour

**Celestial Correspondences:** Venus, Juno, Mercury, Gemini

**Energies:** Attention, Connection, Enchantment

During Libra season, asteroid Juno's energy seems more easily accessible and can be called on when you want to adjust your social position. Whether your aim is to network, win favor, or enchant others, this spell will call forth cardinal air energy to help you make cosmic connections. Using the power of sound with a bell, and the enchantment and glamor of a peacock feather (sacred to Juno), you will summon social prestige, be the center of the party, and build or strengthen relationships.

## You Will Need:

Clothing and symbols to match your intentions (see Step 1)

Fireproof dish

¼ teaspoon dried rose petals

¼ teaspoon ground cinnamon

Artificial peacock feather from a craft store or any feather you find to be beautiful

Bell

## Directions:

1. Decide what you want your energy to be, then choose matching clothes, symbols, and accessories that communicate that to the cosmos and help you embody that energy. For example, if you wish to invite playfulness, creativity, and sensuality, you might choose items that are orange.

2. In the fireproof dish, set rose petals and cinnamon aflame, using the feather to fan the smoke and simultaneously anointing the feather with the smoke's power.

3. Ringing the bell, visualize all eyes turning toward you, and wave the feather through your aura, emphasizing your glamor.

4. If you have a small bell, you can keep the bell and feather with you as charms to quietly and subtly ring anytime you desire attention (so long as it isn't noticeable or obnoxious!).

# *Relationship Reciprocity Spell*

**Astrological Timing:** Libra/Virgo New Moon, Friday, Wednesday, Venus's Hour

**Celestial Correspondences:** Libra, Venus, Juno, Sun, Mercury

**Energies:** Communication, Attraction, Harmony, Balance

With the Sun shining in Libra, now is the time to use the power of cardinal air to promote positive relationships through open, loving, and equal communication. Using the symbolism of the infinity sign for balance and give-and-take, Venus-ruled attracting sugar, and the communicative powers of lavender and chamomile, you will draw balance, like-mindedness, and clear communication into any relationship. This spell is effective for both forging new friendships or bringing balance, communication, and reciprocity to a current one.

## You Will Need:

Two pink candles
Toothpick
¼–½ teaspoon honey
1 teaspoon dried lavender
Fireproof dish

1 tablespoon sugar
½ teaspoon chamomile
Yellow ribbon
Rose quartz

## Directions:

1. Use the toothpick to engrave the two candles with the air elemental symbol (see Chapter 2) to represent communication and a balance of the minds.
2. Anoint the candles with honey for attraction, then sprinkle them with a pinch of the lavender to promote healthy communication. Place the candles side by side on the fireproof dish.
3. Pour the sugar into a bowl and draw the symbol for Libra (see Chapter 3) with your finger. Fill the indentation with chamomile

and remaining lavender and stir clockwise with your finger. Set aside.

4. Thinking of your intention, light the two candles and notice the beauty of their equal flames.

5. Sprinkle the sugar mixture in the shape of an infinity symbol around the lit candles, visualizing the equal flow of energy as you do so. Then draw a figure 8 (an upright infinity symbol) from top to bottom, intersecting the first infinity symbol so that you have a four-petaled flower drawn with sugar.

6. Place the yellow ribbon between the two candles to craft a line of connection, being careful to keep it away from the flames.

7. Breathe your intention into the rose quartz and place in the center of your scene at the intersection of the symbols and the ribbon.

8. Let the candles burn down, with fire safety in mind. When the candles are done burning, you can place the rose quartz and sugar into a cloth and use the ribbon to tie it into a little pouch to carry with you until you manifest your intention.

### Helpful Spell Pairings

*This spell matches well with several other options that highlight connection. Thinking of your intention, use the Venus Attraction Fragrance (in this chapter) to continue to charm and attract your social interactions until your intention manifests. Or cast this spell alongside the Binary Star Connection Spell (Chapter 11) to help you connect on a heart-to-heart level.*

# Chapter 14

# SCORPIO SEASON

**Scorpio Season:** October 23–November 21
**Best Day:** Tuesday
**Best Time of Day:** Afternoon, Dusk, Mars's Hour

Small and subtle—but with a piercing stinger that reaches deep—Scorpio season takes us from social, pleasurable Libra season to the truth, power, and potential of Pluto. An invitation to plunge into the depths of emotion, fixed water Scorpio season is a time of surrender, truth, and transformation.

Truth-seeking Scorpio's stinger pierces to the heart of any matter. Bringing you back to the core of your baser instincts, this is a time to face your instinctual, primal, survival-based self and confront unpleasant truths. While sometimes uncomfortable, this work eventually curates understanding of your innermost needs and desires, helping you to be vulnerable, transform yourself, and develop deep wisdom. It also allows for passion, power, and profound intimacy with yourself and others. Use the depth and power of Scorpio's stinger at this time to probe and heal unresolved wounds with the Heart-Softening Tea, or set an energetic boundary to protect your space with the Boundary-Setting Salt Mix. Now is the time to dive deep into matters of the occult for insight and wisdom, to uncover truths, and to explore any inner darkness…as well as look at the fine details in all things, from finances to contracts.

# Water's Reflection Meditation

──────── ✺ ────────

**Astrological Timing:** Monday, Friday, Moon's Hour

**Celestial Correspondences:** Scorpio, Moon, Neptune, Pisces, Cancer

**Energies:** Reflection, Inner Truth, Stillness

Investigate the depths of your soul and reflect on your personal truth with this fixed water meditation. Whether doing some soul searching during Scorpio season or using the power of the Scorpio Moon to meditate and reflect, this water-scrying meditation will help you find your inner truth. This spell will help you set your intentions and uncover what areas of your life can be healed with Scorpio magick during this month.

## You Will Need:

Bowl of water                              Notebook and pen

## Directions:

1. Place the bowl of water before you. Alternatively, you can do this meditation at a closed body of water, such as a lake or a pond. If you wish, you can put on some meditative music or nature sounds, such as the sound of a running stream.
2. Close your eyes and take a few deep breaths. Breathe into your body at the belly and exhale any tensions. After a few deep breaths, when your body feels more relaxed, open your eyes and gaze at the water.
3. Notice the features of your body of water. It has defined boundaries that secure it, in much the same way as Scorpio likes to be secure and steady within her emotions. Now look into the bowl of water— notice that you can see your reflection in it. It is in the stillness of water that you can see your reflection and your truth. Ask yourself the following questions:
   - What is an emotion that has been tugging on you?
   - What is your outlet for your emotions? Do you have the means to channel your feelings?
   - How do you regularly process your emotions?
   - What is it that feeds positive feeling within you?

- What is your connection with sensuality and feeling through your body?
- What is your inner truth?

4. Write down your answers in your notebook, and revisit these questions throughout Scorpio season. The Sun in Scorpio is a good time to reflect on your inner truth and passion and to manifest power and transformation.

# *Scorpio Energy Alignment*

*—— ❧ ——*

**Astrological Timing:** Scorpio Season, Friday, Tuesday, Mars's Hour

**Celestial Correspondences:** Pluto, Mars, Scorpio

**Energies:** Psychic Knowing, Passion, Perception, Truth

Attune your energy to Scorpio season and harness this sign's power of perception, psychic abilities, truth, and passion, or use these qualities to reveal your utmost self. In this crystal layout, labradorite will help heighten your psychic discernment; garnet will work to connect you to your passion and intimacy, as well as what motivates you on a deeper level; and bloodstone will help purify your energy and instill courage and resilience in the face of any obstacles. Together, these stones will help align your energy to both the intuitive powers of this water sign and the primal roots of your passion, desires, and inner truth. Perform this alignment session throughout Scorpio season to harness her energy for healing, or perform it in preparation for any Scorpio-related spellwork to help clear the way for powerful manifestation.

## You Will Need:

Labradorite

Garnet

Bloodstone

Bowl of water

## Directions:

1. Lie down in a comfortable spot. Dip your stones into the bowl of water (the stones are water-safe), thinking about accessing the healing power of fixed water. Wash your hands in this bowl, letting

the water cleanse your hands of any negative energy. Remove your crystals and place the bowl of water by your feet.

2. Lie down with the bowl still near your feet and place the stones on their corresponding energy centers (see Chapter 6 for placement): labradorite for the third eye, garnet for the sacral, and bloodstone for the root.

3. Visualize water flowing through you—a steady stream flowing through your crown, through your body and legs, and into the bowl. See this water cleansing away any stagnant energy with each flow, removing layers of energetic debris and revealing your pure, inner energy.

4. Continue visualizing this stream for 20–30 minutes, feeling the weight and flow of stones on your body and absorbing their energy. When ready, remove the stones, rotate your wrists and ankles to come back to the present moment, and bring your awareness back to your body. Blow out any leftover stagnant energy into the bowl and pour the water outside or down the drain.

# *Heart-Softening Tea*

———— ✍ ————

**Astrological Timing:** Friday, Venus's Hour

**Celestial Correspondences:** Pluto, Scorpio, Venus, Neptune

**Energies:** Surrender, Vulnerability, Healing, Emotions, Truth

With her sharp stinger, Scorpio stings deep into your heart, revealing deep-seated emotions that may be festering within the fixed water of your body. Reveal the iceberg of frozen emotions beneath the surface and dissolve the ice around your heart with this soothing tea. This potion will help you work through any pent-up emotions and release your emotional truth.

## You Will Need:

1 tablespoon dried rose petals
Ice cube tray
4½ ounces hot water
2–3 fresh basil leaves

⅛ teaspoon allspice
1 tablespoon honey

## Directions:

1. Holding the rose petals in your hand, share with the universe the wish that your heart opens up. Place the petals in one ice cube tray slot and pour water over them. Place in freezer.
2. Once the ice cube has frozen, boil the water. Hold the basil leaves between your hands in prayer pose by your heart. Breathe in their aroma and visualize your heart opening up. Place the basil leaves in a mug.
3. Sprinkle in allspice to warm the heart and pour in boiling water. Let steep for 1–2 minutes.
4. Add your rose petal ice cube, watching it melt. Stir in honey clockwise with a spoon to soothe your soul. Next, use the spoon to trace the symbol for Scorpio (Chapter 3).
5. Sip the concoction to soothe your heart, feeling your heart center warm and soften like the ice cube. Alternatively, pour the liquid outside as an offering.

# *Blessed Financial Partnership Spell*

**Astrological Timing:** Friday, Thursday, Jupiter's/Venus's Hour

**Celestial Correspondences:** Scorpio, Juno, Jupiter, Taurus

**Energies:** Finances, Money, Balance, Financial Partnerships

Balance your finances and inspire fruitful, bountiful monetary partnerships with this spell. With both Juno and Scorpio shedding celestial light on money partnerships, now is a great time to either pay off or collect old debts, bring balance to financial arrangements, or bless yourself with abundant, cosmic cash flow!

## You Will Need:

Piece of paper and writing utensil
½ teaspoon almond oil
½ teaspoon ground allspice
½ teaspoon ground clove
½ teaspoon ground ginger
Toothpick

1 large green pillar candle
2 smaller green pillar candles
3 candleholders
1 large fireproof dish
Pyrite

# Directions:

1. Write your intention on the paper. Anoint the paper with a dab of almond oil, fold it toward you, and place it in the bottom of a bowl.
2. Mix the spices together clockwise over the paper in your bowl, visualizing money moving and growing. Use your finger to draw the Scorpio sigil (see Chapter 3) into the mixture.
3. Use the toothpick to engrave the larger candle with two arrows engaged in a circle (like the recycling symbol or two scorpion claws) to represent reciprocity, the cycle of money, and energy exchange. Engrave one of the smaller candles with your name, and the other with your financial partner/institution.
4. Anoint all three candles with almond oil, then sprinkle the spice mixture over them, using just a few pinches, imagining the shared riches rolling in. Set up the candles in holders on a fireproof dish, with the larger candle in the center and the smaller ones on either side. Place your paper underneath the fireproof dish, then place the pyrite next to it.
5. Light the small candles, saying your affirmation. With your intention in mind, move to light the central candle, saying aloud:

*"As I light this candle*
*Money flows.*
*From one to another,*
*Money grows."*

6. Light the central candle. Repeating the chant three times, use the remaining spice mixture to draw one arrow leading from one candle to another on the surface they rest on, and another arrow along the top, again, on the surface. (If this is hard to visualize, look at the Cancer sign symbol in Chapter 3. Imagine the circles on either curved line is a candle, plus one larger candle in the middle.) Visualize the exchange and mutual growth of income as you do or any debts being paid off and your financial freedom growing. Let the candles burn out. Feel free to scoop the spices from the dishes into a sachet bag or cloth and add the pyrite to it to keep with you or on an abundance altar to continue to attract financial gains.

# Sensual Star-Powered Magick Mist

———— ✑ ————

**Astrological Timing:** Friday, Scorpio Moon, Moon in Scorpio, Tuesday

**Celestial Correspondences:** Scorpio, Pluto, Mars, Venus, Juno, Aries, Vesta

**Energies:** Sensuality, Power, Confidence, Protection

Infuse your aura with the mystery, sensuality, confidence, and power of Scorpio with this special body spray. Scorpio is the sign of sex and death, symbolized by a protectively shelled scorpion (with a stinger to ward off unwanted energy, no less), and few other signs know how to hone the sensuality, mystery, power, and protection that this sign does. By crafting this body mist with powerful Scorpio ingredients, you will harness the power of this sign. Whether for a little subtle protection, mystery, or power, this sacred spray will add some Scorpio magick to your everyday life and help you feel confident in your skin.

## You Will Need:

1 tablespoon vodka

Mason jar with lid

1 pinch allspice

1-inch piece vanilla bean

5 drops ginger essential oil

7 drops black pepper essential oil

7 drops blood orange essential oil

2 tablespoons purified water

1 (1-ounce) mister or spray bottle

Small smoky quartz, optional

## Directions:

1. Under the Scorpio full moon/new moon, pour vodka into the Mason jar. Sprinkle in allspice, visualizing Scorpio's star power blessing your efforts, then stir clockwise with vanilla bean while visualizing yourself strutting your stuff with power, mystery, and protection. Add vanilla to jar, close the lid, and let charge under the moon.

2. Two weeks later at the following new/full moon (or one day later, if in a rush), thoroughly strain the vodka. Add essential oils and water and add mixture to spray bottle. Drop in smoky quartz (if using), and let the mister charge once more under the moon phase.

3. Spray when you need a little extra boost of power or protection, or to hone your sense of mystery and sensuality with confidence.

# Safety Pin Protection Charm

––––––– ໑ –––––––

**Astrological Timing:** Tuesday, Saturday, Mars's Hour, Scorpio Moons

**Celestial Correspondences:** Scorpio, Juno, Aries, Mars, Capricorn

**Energies:** Protection, Power, Security

Remind yourself of your inner power in any situation with this fun and easy safety pin charm. Just like the Scorpio is small yet has a powerful sting, you will craft a powerful yet subtle protection charm with a safety pin. By enchanting this symbol (which you can securely tuck into your clothes), you will be imbued with extra protection and a reminder of the strength you carry at all times.

## You Will Need:

Ginger or other spiced incense
Small purple candle
¼ teaspoon coconut oil
¼ teaspoon ground clove
¼ teaspoon ground ginger

¼ teaspoon ground allspice
Fireproof dish
Safety pin
Red/purple/black string, ribbon,
     or embroidery floss

## Directions:

1. Light incense, preparing your mind and space for this spell.
2. Pass your candle through the smoke of the incense and anoint the candle with coconut oil. On a small plate, mix together clove, ginger, and allspice (setting aside a hefty pinch of the mixture for later use) and roll candle through the mixture. Set the candle on your fireproof dish and light it.
3. As the candle burns, pass the safety pin through the smoke of the incense. Open the pin and weave the ribbon or thread securely around and through it, before knotting it when it meets back where it started. Feel free to braid any hanging leftover string. Then sprinkle it with the rest of the spice mixture. Rest the pin by the candle, letting it charge as the candle burns. Then attach the pin to your clothes or another important item as a talisman of protection.

# *Boundary-Setting Salt Mix*

——— ✌ ———

**Astrological Timing:** Tuesday, Mars's Hour, Afternoon, Sunset, Midnight, Scorpio New Moon, Scorpio Moons

**Celestial Correspondences:** Scorpio, Pluto, Mars, Saturn, Capricorn, Aries

**Energies:** Protection, Boundaries, Repellant

If anyone knows a thing or two about boundaries, it's Scorpio. Attuned to Scorpio, as well as her ancient ruler Mars (before the discovery of Pluto), this fiery, sharp spice mixture is sure to drive away unwanted energy.

## You Will Need:

½ cup black salt (such as black lava salt) or sea salt

1 tablespoon cumin seed

1 tablespoon garlic powder

1 tablespoon black pepper

1 tablespoon cayenne pepper

## Directions:

1. If possible, perform this during the Scorpio new moon in Scorpio season. Otherwise, other Scorpio or Mars alignments will do.
2. Add black salt to a bowl. Add equal parts cumin, garlic, and black pepper. Stir in a counterclockwise motion with a spoon.
3. Use your finger to draw the Scorpio sigil (see Chapter 3) into the mixture. In the indentation, sprinkle in cayenne pepper, noting how this hot, red spice fills the "stinger," or point, like a poker that strikes away unwanted energy.
4. Mix together with intention. Use around the outskirts of the home to craft a warding barrier, and keep any extra to dress black candles for protection!

# *Sensual Blackberry Drink*

——— ✌ ———

**Astrological Timing:** Friday, Full Moon, Mars's/Venus's Hour

**Celestial Correspondences:** Pluto, Venus, Mars

**Energies:** Passion, Sensuality, Creativity

Scorpio is a water sign known for her sensuality and ruled by intense, shamanic Pluto, and her season is a potent time to focus on healing your sacral energy center and expressing your life force through sexuality. This potion will help reinvigorate your passion and allow you to embrace your sensuality. Enjoy by yourself or share with a special person.

## You Will Need:

3 blackberries

1 tablespoon agave syrup

Pinch ground ginger

Pinch allspice

¼ teaspoon vanilla extract

2–2½ tablespoons fresh lemon juice

Soda water, to taste

Ice cubes

## Directions:

1. In a glass, use a muddler or spoon to muddle 2 blackberries in agave. Notice how these sensual ingredients mix together.
2. Sprinkle in ginger and allspice, breathing in their enchanting, fiery aroma.
3. Add vanilla, lemon juice, soda water, and ice. Garnish with remaining blackberry.
4. Drink with a partner during the Taurus full moon amid Scorpio season to reignite your passionate flame, or enjoy by yourself to inspire some sacred sensuality or as an energy boost while casting your Scorpio magick.

## Transform Like a Phoenix Spell

**Astrological Timing:** Friday, Full Moon, Waning Moon, Mars's/ Saturn's Hour, Samhain, Afternoon–Midnight

**Celestial Correspondences:** Scorpio, Pluto, Mars, Saturn, Aquarius

**Energies:** Transformation, Banishment, Cleansing

Another symbol associated with Scorpio is the phoenix, an immortal bird that is transformed and born anew after rising from the ashes of a fire. With Scorpio season thinning the veil between the worlds and bringing the witch's new year, now is the perfect time to use this transformative paper-burning spell to usher change and cleanse unwanted things from your life, such as old habits or false beliefs about yourself. Perform this spell under the full moon in Scorpio season or during any Scorpio waning moon to aid in releasing this energy.

## You Will Need:

Piece of paper and writing utensil
Fireproof dish or cauldron
¼ teaspoon cayenne pepper

¼ teaspoon black pepper
Smoky quartz point

## Directions:

1. Bring your tools outside to a well-ventilated and firesafe area.
2. Consider what you wish to eliminate in your life, such as old identities or labels, unhelpful patterns, or unhealthy habits. Write them down on the paper with space between them.
3. Sit by your fireproof dish or cauldron and rip each word away from the paper one by one, imagining Scorpio stinging and eliminating that energy from your life.
4. In a separate dish, blend together cayenne and black pepper. Use the smoky quartz to draw the sigil for Scorpio (see Chapter 3).
5. Set the paper aflame on top of the fireproof dish or cauldron. Sprinkle a small amount of the herb mixture a safe distance above the flame, saying aloud:

   *"Stinger of Scorpio, Fire of the Phoenix*
   *Set these things aflame,*
   *That my true and pure energy,*
   *I now reclaim."*

6. Watch the flame react to the spices and visualize these banishing ingredients burning away falsehoods. Pass the smoky quartz through the smoke, then hold it, visualizing its point diverting energy and filtering out unwanted patterns.
7. When the paper is done burning, bring the ashes to a crossroads to disperse. Keep the smoky quartz with you as you continue to cycle out unwanted energy.

# *Chapter 15*

# SAGITTARIUS SEASON

**Sagittarius Season:** November 22–December 21
**Best Day:** Thursday
**Best Time of Day:** Jupiter's Hour, Midday, Afternoon

Sagittarius season gives you space to rest from the intensity of Scorpio season. With its arrow tailing Scorpio in the sky, Sagittarius redirects Scorpio's themes of truth away from the inner world of introspection and into the outer world of faith and beliefs. With Jupiter's blessing, you will use this time to invoke abundance, optimism, and new opportunities. The comet Chiron's energy also comes into focus now, inviting you to transform the wounds of your past into wisdom and a message to share with others.

Through exploring your ninth house, you will develop a better understanding of your philosophy about the meaning of life at large and how this sense of faith and possibility can strengthen your powers of prophecy, abundance, and healing in your magick. Use the power of mutable fire to set your goals aflame with the Inner Flame Goal-Setting Meditation, or create and charge a special coffee with which to excite your every morning under the Sagittarius new moon and Sun. You can even call upon Jupiter to expand your income and/or invoke new opportunities for expansion.

# Inner Flame Goal-Setting Meditation

———— ✍ ————

**Astrological Timing:** Thursday, Jupiter's Hour, Sagittarius Full Moon

**Celestial Correspondences:** Sagittarius, Jupiter, Mars

**Energies:** Reflection, Alignment, Excitement, Insight

Just as the brightest stars shine blue, you will reflect on the flame of a blue candle and divine the wisdom of this prophetic sign to learn what excites and fuels your inner fire and purpose. When you feed that fire with new goals that are aligned to this season, you will set new expansive, aligned goals with the truth of an archer's mark in Sagittarius-like fashion.

## You Will Need:

Blue candle

¼ teaspoon maple syrup

¼ teaspoon ground anise

¼ teaspoon ground clove

Fireproof dish

2 pieces of paper and writing utensil

## Directions:

1. Anoint the candle with maple syrup, pulling the syrup down from the top of the candle toward you as you visualize calling down the wisdom of your inner light. Sprinkle the candle with anise and clove for inner spiritual truth and personal passion. Set aside remaining mixture.

2. Visualizing the power of this celestial sign, say aloud:

*"Light of the archer, aim ever higher.*
*Flaming arrow, find what feeds my inner fire."*

3. Set the candle in the fireproof dish and light it.

4. Blow lightly with intention toward the flame, watching how your breath influences it. How you feed and guide your inner fire—whether through your beliefs, pursuing opportunities, expanding your mind, or doing things that excite you—determines how brightly it shines and what direction it goes. With that reflection in mind, ask yourself the following questions and write down your

answers. You may even wish to read the questions aloud and see how the flame responds.

- What beliefs are limiting me? What is it time to get let go of?
- In what areas is it time to expand myself?
- What activities or ideas excite me?

5. Write down a new goal on another piece of paper, seal it with maple syrup for love in your efforts and any remaining spices, then burn the paper above the flame, using tongs or dropping it onto the fireproof dish before the flame touches your fingers. Notice how the flame rises and envelopes the paper, feeding your inner fire with this realigned vision.

## *Sagittarius Energy Alignment*

————— ❧ —————

**Astrological Timing:** Nighttime, Thursday, Jupiter's Hour, Sagittarius Full–New Moon

**Celestial Correspondences:** Jupiter, Sun, Sagittarius, Leo, Scorpio

**Energies:** Insight, Prophetic Wisdom, Celestial Manifestation

This healing session will help you call upon cosmic energy and align your energy centers for maximum manifestation potential this Sagittarius season. Inspire the prophetic wisdom, insight, and excitement of this star sign as you reflect on your beliefs and expand your vision. You will use the vibrational alignment of lapis, labradorite, and citrine to help you reflect on your beliefs, expand your vision, and make your aura a vibrational match for Sagittarius season energy. You will then be equipped to find your spiritual center, manifest abundance, or summon opportunities that excite you. You may wish to place a smoky quartz between your feet to help your energy remain grounded.

### You Will Need:

Lapis lazuli
Labradorite
Citrine (for the solar plexus
    energy center)
Fireproof dish

¼ teaspoon dried sage
¼ teaspoon dried rose petals

# Directions:

1. Place the three stones in the fireproof dish. Slowly sprinkle sage and rose petals atop them, envisioning celestial light shining from the heavens to your spellcasting space. Breathe in the scent. You may wish to let this sit for a little bit or charge it under the full moon—but if not, you can move to the next step.

2. Lie down, and place the dish at your feet, removing the stones as you do so. Place the stones on your energy centers as follows (see Chapter 6 for locations): lapis at the crown of your head, labradorite at the brow, and citrine at the solar plexus.

3. Let your energy centers align with the vibrations of the stones. You may wish to visualize the center of the galaxy and your corresponding galaxy center within yourself, or simply visualize starlight illuminating the stones. If not, allow yourself to simply relax.

4. After 20–30 minutes, bring your awareness back to your feet and fingers and slowly arise when ready. Take the dish of sage and rose petals outside and burn it as you ponder any wisdom gained—visualizing the smoke further cleansing and replacing any energy blockages. You may need to waft the embers of the herbs to invite more cleansing smoke.

5. Repeat once a week during Sagittarius season on Thursdays or whenever the Moon graces the sign once a month as needed.

### Other Stone Options
*Combine the stones from this session with those of the other fire season energy alignments (choose your preferred stone for a given energy center if you're using more than one) for a full fire-aligned energy session. You may wish to place smoky quartz between your feet for this to help you ground such energy.*

# Fire Divination Spell

———— ✌ ————

**Astrological Timing:** Thursday, Jupiter's Hour, Chiron Transits, Sagittarius New Moon, Scorpio Full Moon

**Celestial Correspondences:** Jupiter, Sun, Sagittarius, Scorpio, Chiron, Vesta

**Energies:** Prophecy, Insight, Spiritual Alignment

Call down Sagittarius's power for prophecy—and channel your inner visionary—with this fire-scrying spell. Using a blend of Sagittarius-aligned herbs, this scrying ritual will help you divine insight, and its aroma will bless your aura and efforts. For example, if you're asking about how your day will go tomorrow, if the flame burns bright and steadily, you might know your day will go well. If it burns brightly but then dims and goes out, you might divine that your energy will lessen partway through the day. If the flame breaks into two flames that burn together, you may receive aid in accomplishing your tasks. If the flames burn in opposite ends before going out, focus or energy of the day may end up being split in another direction. All this depends on your personal insight and opinion!

## You Will Need:

Fireproof dish or cauldron

Small, square piece of paper and writing utensil

¼ teaspoon olive oil

¼ teaspoon ground anise

## Directions:

1. In a well-ventilated and firesafe space, sit before your fireproof dish with ingredients at hand.
2. Write your question on the paper. Thinking of your intention, fold the paper in three toward you. Anoint it with the oil, then trace the symbol of Sagittarius (see Chapter 3) with your finger, envisioning the divine archer's arrow pointed toward truth and insight. Rub the ground anise over the paper clockwise in a spiral, visualizing divine guidance coming from the stars.
3. Holding the paper, say aloud:

   *"By the flame with which this paper burns,*
   *I divine the answer of my concern."*

4. Ask your question, set the paper aflame, and gently rest it in the dish.

5. Notice how the flames engulf the paper—does the fire flare quickly, or is it a slow burn? Does the fire stop halfway or immerse the paper within moments? Carefully watch the development and dance of the flame, as though it were telling a story, and from that, you will have your answer.

# *Higher Self Flame Meditation*

**Astrological Timing:** New Moon, Sagittarius New Moon, Thursday, Sunday

**Celestial Correspondences:** Jupiter, Sun, Sagittarius, Chiron

**Energies:** Higher Self, Insight, Spirituality, Clarity, Wisdom, Personal Truth

Shine a light on your spiritual center and access guidance beyond time and space with this spell to help you connect to your higher self. Your "higher self" is an aspect of yourself that exists beyond time and space (your personal galactic center, so to speak). It holds timeless wisdom to help guide you and inspire vision, hope, and perspective in times of need. Use Sagittarius's star power to help strengthen your connection to this part of yourself so that you can feel confident in your truth and become a beacon for the things you wish to manifest in your life.

## You Will Need:

White candle
¼ teaspoon olive oil
¼ teaspoon dried rosemary

¼ teaspoon ground anise or anise seed
1 star anise
Lapis lazuli

## Directions:

1. Anoint the candle with oil. On a small plate, mix rosemary and ground anise, drawing the Sagittarius symbol (see Chapter 3), then stir clockwise with your finger. Roll the candle in the rosemary and

anise toward you, envisioning calling a stronger connection with your higher self.

2. Light the candle. Turn off all the lights in the room, hold the anise star and look at the candle through the anise star. Gaze into the flame and visualize yourself breathing in the fire and flame, cleansing negative energy. Now imagine feeding the flame with your breath (lightly). Notice how you engage in an active relationship with this flame.

3. Breathe in the aroma of the star anise. Look at it through the light, as though it's a star, and take hold of your lapis.

4. Still gazing at the star anise with the candlelight behind it, imagine a similar bright white or golden flame above your head. Feel its warmth and radiance warming the top of your head, then your neck and shoulders. Let the flame slowly warm your whole aura and body so that you feel this glowing warmth and light within and around you.

5. Breathe in the cleansing aroma of the candle and really connect to this light—see what it feels like or if it has any wisdom for you. Allow any messages to come.

6. When done with your meditation, place the star anise and lapis by the base of the candle to charge. Let the candle burn out. Keep the star anise and lapis to meditate with whenever you need wisdom from your higher self.

## *Map-Based Pendulum Prophecy*

———— ✍ ————

**Astrological Timing:** Dawn, Wednesday, Thursday, Jupiter's Hour

**Celestial Correspondences:** Sagittarius, Moon, Jupiter, Mercury, Gemini

**Energies:** Knowledge, Education, Perspective, Education, Travel

Different places in the world have different energies, and you can glean important meaning and insight from various locations. Considering possible places to travel or learn more about? This map and pendulum divination spell will help you uncover what area has wisdom for you. With Sagittarius-aligned herbs to call down this travel-related sign, a pendulum (or a weight like a pendant on a string), and a map, you will divine a location to research (or maybe even visit!) to expand your mind and divine wisdom.

## You Will Need:

Map                                          Pendulum
½ teaspoon ground clove

## Directions:

1. Place your map in a quiet space where you can focus.
2. Sprinkle clove on the map in the symbol of Sagittarius (see Chapter 3), saying aloud:

   *"Sign of far travel, with all due speed,*
   *What place will have insight for me?"*

3. Hover your pendulum above the map. Move it gently across the longitude and latitude lines on the map, noting where it has distinct movement. Mark any place on the map where you notice a response, and use the combination of longitude and latitude markers to discern specific locations. Hover your pendulum there, and see how it moves to discern if this is the spot.
4. Look up information about that area—in an encyclopedia entry or recent news and articles, and try to interpret relevant or interesting information for yourself.

# *Archer's Mark Manifestation*

**Astrological Timing:** Thursday, Jupiter's Hour, New Moon in Sagittarius

**Celestial Correspondences:** Jupiter, Sagittarius

**Energies:** Opportunity, Expansion, Manifestation

Take aim and make your shot with this Archer's Mark Manifestation spell! With herbal ingredients aligned to Jupiter and Sagittarius, you will construct a target with which to aim your burning arrow of magick (your candle). In true Jupiter fashion, this spell will expand the realm of what you think is possible, letting your intentions manifest in new and exciting ways. Cast this celestial target spell when you're looking for opportunities to grow and expand yourself but you're not quite sure how to get there!

## You Will Need:

Orange or gold candle and candleholder

¼ teaspoon olive oil

1 teaspoon ground anise or anise seed

1 teaspoon ground clove

1 teaspoon ground nutmeg

Fireproof dish

1 star anise

## Directions:

1. Sit down in your sacred space and think about what you are aiming for. Think about the higher perspective of this goal. For example, if you were seeking a specific job with a particular company, a more general outcome might be a well-paying job that advances your career. Zooming out in this way allows for the universe to step in, and manifest the outcome that will be best for you in the long run.

2. Anoint the candle with oil, pulling oil toward you. On a small plate, mix ground anise, clove, and nutmeg, then roll candle through mixture. Set aside.

3. On your fireproof dish, create an outer ring with ground anise near the edge, thinking of the general energy of what you are manifesting. This will represent the spiritual energy coalescing and an outermost target.

4. Sprinkle a second circle inside that with ground clove. This will quicken the spiritual energies and represents your close second outcome.

5. Sprinkle the innermost circle with ground nutmeg. With nutmeg's energy of luck and manifestation, this inner ring will represent the bull's-eye of your spell—the higher goal of what you are aiming for. Place your candle in the very center, with the star anise by its side, representative of your goal hitting its mark.

6. Think of your intention and light the candle. Let it burn. When you are done, you can keep the star anise in the center and tend to this dish as a little altar, add decoration if you like, or pour all the herbs into a little bag to carry with you as a blessing until your desire manifests.

# *Ethereal Embers*

—————— ❧ ——————

**Astrological Timing:** Thursday, Jupiter's Hour, Sagittarius New Moon, New Moon

**Celestial Correspondences:** Sagittarius, Jupiter, Vesta, Chiron

**Energies:** Purification, Divination, Intention-Setting, Vibration-Raising

Sagittarius season brings the shift toward the new year and allows you to expand your mind, raise your energetic vibration, and reach for new heights. With these Sagittarius-aligned herbs for cleansing, healing, and divination, as well as spices for abundance, you will cleanse your energy field of any old vibrations and feed your inner fire with new intentions. Use the fire and resulting embers to bless goals or even for scrying! For best results, perform under the Sagittarius new moon around midnight.

## You Will Need:

Fireproof dish or cauldron

¼ teaspoon dried rosemary

¼ teaspoon dried sage

¼ teaspoon dried rose petals

¼ teaspoon ground nutmeg

¼ teaspoon ground clove

## Directions:

1. On the night of the Sagittarius new moon, set out the fireproof dish and your ingredients.
2. In your dish, mix together rosemary, sage, and rose petals. These Sagittarius season–aligned herbs will help invoke purification and healing and strengthen divination.
3. Thinking of your intention, light the herbs with fire. The flame will go out, but you will fan the embers toward you, producing a spicy, warming aroma. Breathe in its cleansing smoke. Visualize the embers and smoke cleansing your energy for the new year.
4. As these herbs burn, sprinkle nutmeg and clove above them for luck, money, and to raise spiritual vibrations. You may also wish to visualize feeding your own fire with your intentions as you do so, or ask a question and watch how the fire or smoke responds.
5. After feeding the flames, use the smoke to bless your aura and intentions.

# Wealth and Abundance Spell

———— ❧ ————

**Astrological Timing:** Thursday, Jupiter's/Venus's Hour, Friday

**Celestial Correspondences:** Jupiter, Sagittarius, Venus

**Energies:** Abundance, Expansion, Money, Opportunities, Manifestation

With the expansive, abundant power of this planet, you will exponentially multiply your finances day by day with this seven-day spell. Adding pennies to the spell each day represents adding new financial opportunities. Cast this spell when you'd like to manifest more money or grow something—whether it be a client base, your business network, or your savings.

## You Will Need:

Large green pillar candle
Toothpick
¼ teaspoon olive oil
¼ teaspoon ground clove

¼ teaspoon ground nutmeg
7 whole cloves
Fireproof dish
Bunch of pennies

## Directions:

1. Use the toothpick to engrave the candle with Jupiter's symbol (see Chapter 5). Dress the candle for abundance, anointing it with oil and sprinkling with ground clove and nutmeg.
2. Thinking of expansive abundance, push the points of the whole cloves into the candle (marking/separating the candle height-wise into seven or eight sections) so that the tips are in, but the rest sticks out. You may need to poke the wax first with a toothpick to create a hole for the cloves to more easily slide in.
3. Place the candle in the center of your fireproof dish and surround it with five pennies, forming a star around the candle.
4. Place your hands around the candle, thinking of abundance coming your way. Light the candle and let it burn until it reaches the first clove. Then extinguish the candle.
5. The next day, add another layer of pennies atop the first circle and light the candle again until you reach the following clove marker. Keep adding a new layer of pennies each time. When the candle is burnt out, keep the charged up pennies on you to attract abundance!

# *Cosmic Coffee Mix*

———— ✌ ————

**Astrological Timing:** Sunday, Thursday, Tuesday, New–Full Moons

**Celestial Correspondences:** Mars, Leo, Aries, Jupiter, Sagittarius, Sun

**Energies:** Excitement, Vigor, Luck, Money, Power, Attraction

Put some pep in your step with this bewitching coffee brew. With the energy-enhancing benefits of coffee, the excitable energy of Sagittarius, and the magnetic energy of Jupiter, this coffee mixture is sure to reignite your inner flame. You can also use it for divination—look at the grounds left over in your coffee cup! Craft and charge under powerful Sagittarius or Jupiter alignments (such as the Sagittarius new moon), and use for several days in the morning to continue reaping the benefits of these alignments.

## You Will Need:

¼ teaspoon ground anise
½ teaspoon ground clove
¼ teaspoon ground nutmeg
½ teaspoon dried rose petals
¼ teaspoon ground ginger
5 tablespoons ground coffee

6 ounces water
Maple syrup for sweetener,
    optional
Almond milk, optional
1 cinnamon stick

## Directions:

1. In a bowl, combine all ingredients except water, maple syrup, almond milk, and cinnamon stick, breathing in the aroma of each one.
2. Use your finger to draw the Sagittarius symbol (see Chapter 3), infusing the blend with the exciting energies of this star sign.
3. Brew 2 tablespoons of this mixture with 6 ounces of hot water. Store the rest in a jar to reuse later or to charge under a Sagittarius Moon, the Sun, or another favorable alignment.
4. Once brewed, sweeten to taste with maple syrup and almond milk. Stir clockwise with cinnamon stick, thinking of your intention. Then sip away and enjoy!

# Chapter 16

# CAPRICORN SEASON

**Capricorn Season:** December 22–January 19
**Best Day:** Saturday
**Best Time of Day:** Saturn's Hour, Midday–Afternoon

While Sagittarius raised your eyes to higher pursuits, Capricorn grounds you firmly back in reality, bringing your attention and awareness to accomplishments, focus, and determination.

This part-fish, part-goat sign has the determination of the mountain goat to climb the steepest peaks of accomplishment, plus the flexibility and ancient wisdom of deep-sea creatures to accomplish her goals. Ruled by Saturn, this season inspires you to reflect on the structure and efficiency of your goals and tasks—what is real, solid, and necessary, and what is not? Bringing your focus to tenth house matters of career and accomplishment, this seasonal star energy encourages you to reflect on your reputation and your greater goals in life. Using stones like fluorite and quartz for focus and clarity and spells for stability, protection, and success, Capricorn season will help you harness timeless, grounded wisdom as you manifest abundance in the material world and channel the cosmic energy of Capricorn to harness mastery and determination with any task!

# Quartz Point Meditation

―――――― ✐ ――――――

**Astrological Timing:** Saturday, Sunday, Tuesday, Saturn's/Mars's Hour, Capricorn New Moon

**Celestial Correspondences:** Capricorn, Earth, Aries, Mars, Saturn

**Energies:** Focus, Reflection, Clarity, Determination

In this spell, you will attune to the focusing power of Capricorn and a natural quartz crystal and reflect on this representation of cardinal earth. Through this meditation, you will uncover how to initiate energy through the earth element to cultivate perseverance and clarity on the personal goals you'd like to manifest on the physical plane. Use this meditation whenever you need to concentrate or ground yourself throughout Capricorn season as you work on achieving enduring goals.

## You Will Need:

Natural quartz point

## Directions:

1. If possible, go outside and lie down on the ground for this meditation. If not, lie down wherever you are comfortable.
2. As you lie down, breathe in deeply, feeling the weight of your body rest against the earth. Be conscious of its gravity.
3. When you feel calm, look at your quartz point. Notice all of its shapes and any formations or patterns you see within it. Notice how the point has facets, leading from the body of the crystal to a single point. These stones can take millions of years to form.
4. Reflect on how this quartz point can represent the stable aspect of the earth and how all this stone's energy terminates into one single point of focus.
5. Ponder that energy within yourself by asking these questions:
   - What do you wish to manifest in this lifetime on the physical plane?
   - What accomplishment does all your energy terminate in, like this stone terminates in a point?
   - How can you build a stable, enduring structure like this stone?
   - How can you focus your energy to further this goal?

6. When you are done pondering, hold the stone in your right hand. Reconnect to the gravitational pull of the earth and envision your single goal. Visualize moving energy from the earth you feel upon your back, through your body, and through the crystal's point, channeling that energy out into the world.

# Capricorn Energy Alignment

————— ✌ —————

**Astrological Timing:** Saturday, Saturn's Hour, Capricorn Moons

**Celestial Correspondences:** Capricorn, Taurus, Virgo, Saturn

**Energies:** Grounding, Power, Focus, Manifestation, Clarity, Clear Vision

Using stones that match Capricorn's capacity for crystal clear vision, motivation, and manifestation, this cosmic crystal grid will help clear the way for effective Capricorn-aligned spellwork. With quartz for clarity and magnification, fluorite for focus and discernment, pyrite for abundance, and bloodstone for endurance and vitality, this crystal grid layout is perfect for attuning your energy body to the focus and determination of this sign. Whether preparing for Capricorn season to manifest some powerful magick or harnessing the focus and stamina of this sign any time of year, this Capricorn Energy Alignment will help attune your energy to the frequencies of this sign for clarity, focus, perseverance, and determination.

## You Will Need:
Clear quartz                                   Pyrite
Fluorite                                       Bloodstone

## Directions:
1. If possible, perform this meditation outside on the ground, on a blanket or mat. Otherwise, find a comfortable spot inside.
2. Sit down on your mat and hold the stones in your hand, noticing their weight. Lie down and place each stone atop their corresponding energy center (see Chapter 6 for energy center placement information): clear quartz at the crown of your head, fluorite on the third eye, pyrite on the solar plexus, and bloodstone on the root.

3. As you lie down, keep noticing the weight of the stones on your body as they respond to the earth's gravity, similar to how you are resting upon the green earth. Visualize Capricorn's constellation shining upon the crystals from above, illuminating them. Allow your body to absorb this energy, staying conscious of the grounding earth with each breath.

4. When you feel that your energy centers have been recharged, you may end the meditation, bringing your attention back down to your body and arising.

# Money Manifestation Wand

—————— ✌ ——————

**Astrological Timing:** Jupiter's/Saturn's Hour, Thursday, Saturday, Sunday

**Celestial Correspondences:** Jupiter, Capricorn, Taurus

**Energies:** Money, Abundance, Manifestation

Like Capricorn, cinnamon is firm and stiff, but in water it becomes flexible. Cinnamon, the tightly wound-up tree bark from the *Cinnamomum* genus of trees, invokes the protective, abundant energy of trees and is often associated with spirituality and quick manifestation. In this spell, you will use this property of cinnamon to nestle money inside of it as metaphorical seed money. Use this spell to bring in more money, or you can make several wands to line the outside of a votive candleholder for all future money spells.

## You Will Need:

1 cinnamon stick

Cinnamon incense

Piece of paper and writing utensil

Dollar bill

String or ribbon

## Directions:

1. Place cinnamon stick in a mug. Notice how tightly wound the cinnamon stick is. It might resemble the spiral pattern of growth in a goat's horn—akin to Capricorn.

2. Pour hot water over the stick. Allow it to sit for about 20–30 minutes. If using a higher-grade culinary cinnamon stick, you

may need to repeat this step twice, as these tend to be firmer. The cinnamon stick will become flexible, allowing you to unravel it, or it may unravel on its own. As it unravels, think about material earth opening up to you (how the right ingredients can coax the toughest of things to open up).

3. While you wait, light incense and think about how much money you need to manifest or what you desire. Be sure to get specific. Write your affirmation on the paper.

4. Once the stick is unraveled, tightly roll the dollar bill and paper together. Pass it through the cinnamon smoke and say aloud:

*"Cinnamon, Capricorn,*
*Flexible and sturdy,*
*Yet determined as can be.*
*Manifest, quickly, this money for me."*

5. Remove the cinnamon stick from the water. You may need to unroll it, especially if using a finer-grade cinnamon stick. Place the bill and paper in the open cinnamon stick and roll the cinnamon stick up again. Use the string to tie around the center of the cinnamon stick, providing a sturdy, protective home for your money.

6. Drink the cinnamon tea you made, from having the cinnamon sit in hot water, as you visualize this abundance coming to you!

## *Saturn Sundial Spell*

**Astrological Timing:** Midday–Afternoon, Saturn's Hour, Saturday

**Celestial Correspondences:** Saturn, Capricorn, Taurus, Sun

**Energies:** Balance, Productivity, Efficiency, Time Management

In the modern world, it can be challenging to have a balanced and healthy relationship with time management. Honor the time and boundaries of Saturn in a healthy way with this sundial spell. In a nod to a more ancestral method of timekeeping, you will create your own spiritual sundial to help you connect to the power of Saturn, honor the harvest, and respect this time as a cosmic manifestation of your place with the cosmos. If you want your sundial to be accurate, you will have to look up instructions online. But this spell is perfect for creating a sundial you can use for intention and magick!

## You Will Need:

Piece of paper and writing utensil
1 stick
Twine

12 stones (see crystal grid alternative in the sidebar)

## Directions:

1. Go outside around noon. Think about Saturn, lord of time and structure, and his Roman namesake as lord of grain, agriculture, and time.
2. Now think of your intention, whether it be to better manage your time or have a healthier relationship with it. What form of balance and time works best for you in this season of your life? Write your intention on the paper and tie it around the stick with twine. Thrust the stick into the earth and position it so that it has the smallest shadow.
3. Divide the stones. You may wish to divide them by how you want to spend the hours of the day. For example, how many of those stones/hours do you want to devote to a hobby, or to a certain goal or task? You can even paint them different colors; distinguish what you want to devote your time to; or have each stone represent the houses, thus forming twelve sections of life that will support your central pillar.
4. Think of what each stone represents and nestle it in a place where each number would be on the clock. Reflect on each hour and how you wish to spend your time.
5. You can honor this sundial by setting intentions with it daily, placing sheaths of grain near it to represent abundance from the cycles of time and life and as an offering to Saturn, or turning it into an outdoor altar that you decorate for different times of the year.

### Crystal Grid Alternative
*You can replace the stones in this spell with favored crystals to represent each sign/house, and/or replace the stick with a crystal tower/obelisk or quartz point, thus turning the sundial into a crystal grid unique to your energy and goals!*

# Master(y) Key Spell

—————— ☙ ——————

**Astrological Timing:** Saturday, Saturn's Hour, Wednesday

**Celestial Correspondences:** Saturn, Chiron, Capricorn, Vesta, Virgo

**Energies:** Mastery, Wisdom, Perseverance, Knowledge

While the discipline of Saturn can seem daunting, once you learn the lessons of this strict planet, you can unlock mastery in any field and transform your greatest weaknesses into your greatest strengths. In this spell, you will decorate and bless a skeleton key to help you symbolically unlock doors to mastery in an area of your choice. Whether working to learn a new skill, start a new job or hobby, or ace a class, this master key will be just the celestial charm you need.

## You Will Need:

Cinnamon incense

Small green candle

Toothpick

Piece of paper and writing utensil

Decorative key (often called a skeleton key) with a long shaft

Wire or glue

Small quartz point

Brown, gold, and/or orange embroidery floss (or color of choice, as relevant to your intention)

## Directions:

1. Sit before your ingredients and light the incense to help set the mood. Use the toothpick to engrave Saturn's symbol (see Chapter 5) on your candle, and light it.
2. Write what you wish to master on the paper and roll it around the shaft of the key. Seal it with drippings from the candle.
3. Use the wire or glue to affix the quartz point to the tip of the key, a symbol for where you'll be directing your energy and focus.
4. Starting with the shaft, weave embroidery floss around the key in any way you like, visualizing mastery blessing all work that you do. You may wish to weave back to the shaft and create a tassel there.
5. When done, pass the key through the incense smoke and a safe distance above the candle flame, saying aloud:

*"With Saturn's Key, I harness mastery;*
*That every door should unlock for me."*

6. Place the key by the base of the candle to continue to receive blessings from its flame and the smoke, and let it burn out. Use the key as a charm to channel your energy.

# Vinegar Protection Spell

————— ↝ —————

**Astrological Timing:** Capricorn Full/New Moon, Saturday, Saturn's/ Mars's Hour, Tuesday

**Celestial Correspondences:** Capricorn, Saturn, Mars, Aries

**Energies:** Protection, Boundaries, Banishment, Limitations, Restriction

Banish negativity, extinguish bad habits, and craft better energetic boundaries with this protection spell. As the planet of boundaries, Saturn is an expert on restricting energy. Combined with efficient Capricorn, which has no problem tossing away what is no longer useful; protective black pepper and garlic; the strength of thyme; and the banishing qualities of vinegar, these celestial energies will help restrict what you let into your life. Craft this spell jar with a specific intention in mind (such as banishing a bad habit), or make one to shake anytime you need a dose of extra protection.

## You Will Need:

1 onion
Small glass jar with lid
3 peeled garlic cloves
¼ teaspoon black pepper
4–5 fresh thyme sprigs

Vinegar (enough to fill jar)
Sharpie
Small black candle
Salt

## Directions:

1. Think about what you are creating boundaries for in your life: better boundaries with friends or family members; protecting your energy or home; or addressing personal boundaries, such as stopping bad habits. With that in mind, slice the onion on a cutting board as

though you are cutting a boundary between you and those things. Slice the onion into several rings.

2. Slit the onion rings and spiral them along the inside of the jar, forming rings of protection, just like Saturn's!

3. Peel the garlic and place it in the jar, thinking about its Mars rulership, its scent, and its protective energy. Sprinkle in black pepper, then add thyme sprigs in the center for strength. Then pour in banishing vinegar.

4. Close the jar, and use the Sharpie to draw the sigil for Saturn (see Chapter 5) on it.

5. Secure the candle on top of the jar lid. Sprinkle salt around the candle, then burn it, ushering in protection.

6. Anytime you need extra protection or better boundaries, shake the jar or keep it by your bedside.

# *Beet Star Spell*

—— ✍ ——

**Astrological Timing:** Saturday, Midnight, Saturn's Hour, Capricorn New Moon

**Celestial Correspondences:** Capricorn, Aquarius, Saturn

**Energies:** Grounding, Passion, Sacrifice, Commitment

Capricorn knows a thing or two about commitment. Call down this star sign to help inspire fidelity, whether in a relationship or to a goal or purpose, with this Beet Star Spell. An ingredient associated with Saturn and Capricorn, beets are grounding and, because of their association with Aphrodite, can signify love and romance too. Sometimes used in witchcraft to replace the use of blood, beets are perfect Saturn symbols for grounding, passion, sacrifice, and commitment. Use this spell to usher forth grounded commitment for your passion, whether related to love or a personal aspiration.

## You Will Need:

1 beet
Knife or toothpick

¼ teaspoon olive oil for commitment or honey for romance
1 teaspoon ground cinnamon

## Directions:

1. Sit before your beet and think of what pattern or idea you wish to commit to. A symbol of fidelity, this taproot vegetable will help you plant new, enduring roots for something passionate in your life.

2. Use a knife or toothpick to engrave a few words or a symbol of what you want to bring into your life. Then engrave the symbols of Capricorn and Saturn (see Chapters 3 and 5) onto your beet.

3. Rub the beet with olive oil or honey. You may wish to say aloud as you do so:

*"Symbol of Saturn, and of Capricorn*
*The Stars from which dedication is born*
*To this passion, I am [or we are] sworn."*

4. Sprinkle the beet with cinnamon for quickening and manifestation, and hold it in your hands, thinking of your vision. Plant it outside right away, or perform the spell and plant the beet during a favorable Saturn or Capricorn transit, the Capricorn new moon, or around midnight on a Saturday.

# Chapter 17

# AQUARIUS SEASON

**Aquarius Season:** January 20–February 18
**Best Day:** Wednesday, Saturday
**Best Time of Day:** Mercury's Hour, Saturn's Hour,
Sunrise/Morning, Afternoon

Following strict, responsible, orderly Capricorn, Aquarius is the second zodiac sign after the New Year. And like the cocoon of winter within which this energy exists, Aquarius is a time of reinvention, metamorphosis, and breaking free of limitations.

Whereas Capricorn season is very grounded in reality, Aquarius (true to his air sign nature) is all about the mind, limitless ideas, and perspective. Ruled by Uranus, the planet of freedom, innovation, and sudden flashes of genius, Aquarius invites you to expand the boundaries of what is possible. This is a time to reexamine how you view yourself and review your eleventh house themes of the relationship circles you have. Aquarius is the rebel that allows you to break chains, change identities, and reinvent the way you think and see the world. He paves the road to new possibilities, sometimes in ways you never thought possible.

# Celestial Sound Meditation

————— ✤ —————

**Astrological Timing:** Aquarius Moons, Uranus Transits, Wednesday, Mercury's Hour

**Celestial Correspondences:** Aquarius, Gemini, Libra, Mercury

**Energies:** Cleansing, Awareness, Vision, Connection

Like a sudden thunderclap ringing through a valley, the vibration of sound can be a powerful way to get air moving—and with it, new ideas, insights, and innovations. A sign of rebellion and breaking free of confining boundaries, Aquarius season asks you to liberate yourself. In this meditation, you will connect with your environment and observe how sound can be used in your celestial spells.

## You Will Need:

Sound device, like a bell or rattle

## Directions:

1. Sit outside, if possible, to observe nature. Breathe deeply, looking around you, and notice how air interacts with everything around you. The breeze tickles your skin, weaves through trees and plants, and pushes around loose dirt. Breathe in, aware of how air connects you to all other life in this moment.
2. Shake or ring your sound device, then stop. Notice its sound and pitch. Ring it again, noticing the suddenness of the sound, like a crash of thunder rumbling through the air. Notice the quiet and stillness afterward. Ring it a few more times, then stop, noticing how the sound or vibration makes you feel.
3. Even as a fixed air sign, Aquarius inspires innovation and updates outdated modes of thinking and of life. Think about these questions:
   - What are ways you can innovate your life?
   - How do you interact with your relationships in your life—is it a time for a new community and sense of self?
   - In what ways are you limited?
   - Like the bell or sudden burst of thunder, how can you resonate powerful change and innovation in your life?

4. Ponder further themes of Aquarius, referring to Chapter 3 if desired. Take the insight gleaned from this meditation to help guide your Aquarius season spells.

## *Aquarius Energy Alignment*

**Astrological Timing:** Wednesday, Saturday, Saturn's/Mercury's Hour

**Celestial Correspondences:** Aquarius, Uranus

**Energies:** Wisdom, Insight, Vision, Freedom, the Mind

Aquarius season brings the chance to embrace your eccentricities and sense of individuality. Set the tone for Aquarius season and summon these cosmic energies into your life through this easy crystal self-healing session. By aligning corresponding Aquarius stones to key energy centers, you will call in a new level of wisdom and information to take with you into the rest of the spells in this chapter.

### You Will Need:

Clear quartz point

Aquamarine

Blue apatite

Feather, optional

### Directions:

1. At dawn or in the morning, go outside with your stones. Watching the growing light in the sky, visualize that same light of new information and your unique eccentricities lighting up within you.

2. With your stones in hand, visualize a beautiful dawn opening up in the sky within you, and light shining in new horizons, expanding your field of vision. Visualize a bird soaring through the sky toward this new expanse of land. Feel the beauty of this expansiveness, and breathe this vision into the stones. Leave the stones out to charge in the morning light and soak up the energy of a new day. You may wish to place a feather upon them for the spirit of air.

3. Retrieve the stones around midday and, when ready, lie down in your meditative space. Place the stones atop the corresponding energy centers (see Chapter 6 for placement information): clear quartz at the crown (the point of the quartz pointing down toward you),

aquamarine at the third eye, and blue apatite at the throat. Feel their energy opening up your energy centers, like the sun bursting forth on a new day, bringing in warming ideas and exciting expansiveness.

4. Lie there, absorbing the energy. Perhaps meditate on the vision of a bird drifting through the morning horizon, opening up new perspectives and ideas to you. You may repeat this meditation throughout Aquarius season to continuously align you to these energies.

# Smoke and Mirrors

**Astrological Timing:** New Moon, Aquarius New Moon, Favorable Uranus Transits, Mercury's Hour, Wednesday

**Celestial Correspondences:** Aquarius, Uranus, Pallas, Mercury

**Energies:** Insight, Problem-Solving, Purification, the Mind

Looking for answers or insight into what's ahead? Connect to Uranus, and channel your inner scry as you channel this planet's astral energy for sudden insight with this smoke-scrying spell. Using the expression of fixed air through smoke, you will discern symbols to find clarity. For added astral energy, perform this spell during Aquarius season, during favorable Uranus transits, on those rare days when you see Uranus in the sky, or when the Moon is in Aquarius.

## You Will Need:

Fireproof dish or cauldron
¼ teaspoon dried rosemary
¼ teaspoon ground anise or
   anise seed
¼ teaspoon dried lavender
¼ teaspoon dried peppermint
Mirror
Feather
Incense charcoal, optional

## Directions:

1. Gather all your ingredients and sit in your sacred space.
2. In the fireproof dish or cauldron, add your herbs. Place your mirror behind the dish so that you can look at it as the smoke rises. Take a handful of herbs between your palms and ask that these herbs provide clarity and insight on something that is plaguing your

mind. Lightly breathe your intention into them, then drop them back into the dish.

3. With the feather, mix herbs together, saying aloud:

*"Spirit of air, gust through, so that I may see a way through."*

4. Draw the sigil of Aquarius (see Chapter 3), then set the herbs aflame.

5. Fan the herbs with your intention in mind to invite the flames or embers to produce smoke. Look at the mirror across from you and soften your gaze, discerning what symbols you see or message you get. You may wish to use an incense charcoal, safely lighting it and placing it in your fireproof dish, and then placing the herbs upon it to produce a steady flow of smoke. Otherwise, you can relight the herbs anytime you wish to ask a new question. Discern any symbols that you may notice.

## Cosmic Cord Cutting

**Astrological Timing:** Sunday, Saturday, Saturn's/Mercury's Hour, Wednesday

**Celestial Correspondences:** Aquarius, Capricorn, Saturn, Uranus

**Energies:** Cleansing, Purification, Liberation

Fly free like an Aquarius and cut away old, limiting energy with this energy-cleansing spell. While Aquarius is a humanitarian sign, it loves freedom above all else and doesn't like to be boxed in by labels or false perceptions. It is time to abandon old ideas about yourself and the world— that are preventing you from progressing. With this cutting ties spell, you will cut the cord to that which no longer serves you and fly free to broader horizons. (For deep-rooted energy work, it is best to see an energy professional rather than do this on your own.)

### You Will Need:

White candle
1 small lemon wedge
⅛ teaspoon dried peppermint
⅛ teaspoon dried sage
⅛ teaspoon ground anise or anise
    seed

Fireproof dish
Yellow string long enough to wrap
    around candle and reach your
    solar plexus energy center
Selenite
Scissors

# Directions:

1. Anoint the candle with cleansing lemon juice and sprinkle with herbs. Set on fireproof dish.
2. Take the yellow twine in your hand and think about what you are cutting out of your life. Is it an old idea, a false perception, an old career path, or an organization you are no longer a part of?
3. Tie one end of the twine around the candle. Take the other end and, envisioning it as a cord of connection, bring it to your third (solar plexus) energy center. This is where you often form energetic cords to others that can dim your inner light.
4. Say aloud:

   *"The past is the past, and now, no longer lasts.*
   *With Aquarian liberty, I cut the cord and am free"*

5. Cut the cord with the scissors at the knot by the candle.
6. Light the candle and, thinking of your intention, hold the part of the twine that was "attached" to you to the flame, letting it catch fire. Drop it on the fireproof dish to let the string burn safely. Know that the fire will cleanse and release the energy. Alternatively, for extra fire safety, you can remove the string from the candle after cutting it, and throw both ends away.
7. Hold the selenite to your solar plexus energy center, letting the stone cleanse and protect this energy center from any further energetic debris. You may wish to lie down and absorb its energy as the candle burns.
8. Let the candle burn safely over the dish when it reaches the remaining knot of the string on the candle. When the candle is done burning, take the ashes of the string to a crossroads and let the wind disperse the ashes.

# Pallas Wisdom Charm

———— ✌ ————

**Astrological Timing:** Nighttime, Full Moon, Wednesday, Mercury's Hour

**Celestial Correspondences:** Pallas, Aquarius, Libra, Mercury, Uranus

**Energies:** Wisdom, Problem-Solving, Ideas

Pallas Athena's wisdom and sense of originality flow through Aquarius. Attune to this goddess of wisdom and her token symbol—the airborne owl—with this feather charm spell to help you gain wisdom and insight, and to see all sides of a situation. Like the owl's unique vision, which enables it to see at night, you will gain Pallas Athena's wisdom and have a bird's-eye view of your situation as you start on a new path.

## You Will Need:

1 dried rosemary sprig
Fireproof dish
Feather
Piece of paper and writing utensil

Ribbon
Aquamarine bead (or another bead of choice)
1 star anise

## Directions:

1. Think about what area you seek wisdom in. Are you traversing a new path and want a charm to help bless and guide your journey? Is there a specific situation you seek insight into?
2. Wave the rosemary sprig around your head, cleansing away old thoughts and ideas. Light it and set on the fireproof dish so that this herb of memory and the mind continues to burn and bless the space.
3. Take the feather in your hand. Close your eyes, breathing in the cleansing smoke, and think of Pallas Athena and her owl. Visualize an owl soaring through the night, having a perspective most don't. Ask for that wisdom—to be granted this clarity of sight, even through darkness, on whatever path you traverse.
4. Open your eyes and write your intention down on a small piece of paper. Say aloud:

   *"Pallas Athena, Asteroid of Wisdom, Goddess of Might.*
   *Her sacred owl, who through the dark takes flight.*

*Bless me with insight, that I might find my way through the darkest of nights."*

5. Wrap the paper around the base of the feather and tie the ribbon around it. You may wish to secure it with glue.
6. At the end of the ribbon, tie the aquamarine bead and the star anise.
7. Pass your charm through the rosemary smoke, blessing it with wisdom.
8. Keep your feather by you as you seek wisdom in this new endeavor, rubbing it against your third eye energy center or using it to dust away negative, limiting thoughts from your mind.

# *Sharing Your Message Spell*

─────── ❧ ───────

**Astrological Timing:** Dawn, Aquarius/Leo Full Moons, Mercury's Hour, Sunday, Wednesday

**Celestial Correspondences:** Aquarius, Uranus, Leo

**Energies:** Purpose, Originality, Renewal, Inspiration, New Beginnings

Through countless ancient cultures, the Aquarius constellation was seen as pouring the water of spirituality down to the earth to share with all humanity. With the Sun in Aquarius and your mind being opened to new possibilities, now is the time to question the path you are on or reorient toward a new one. What is your unique message that you share with humanity? With this cupbearer spell, you will channel the ambrosia of the gods and pour your own medicine to share with the world, whatever that message may be.

## You Will Need:

Pitcher with water
Special glass
Quartz crystal point

Water or favorite drink (maybe an aligned drink or tea from this book!)

## Directions:

1. Conduct your spell outside at dawn for best results (so you can capture the power of the sun rising and lighting up a new day).

2. Place your glass and pitcher in the sunlight. As the sun lights up the sky more and more, hold your quartz in your hand. Think about what message you wish to share with the world and how you will do that—whether through art, a career, or day-to-day life.

3. Watching the horizon, think about Ganymede spilling the ambrosia of the gods, sharing it with the earth. Feel his strength and rebellion, and pour the water into your glass and onto the surrounding earth.

4. Thinking of your intention, position the quartz point in the drink and draw a five-pointed star, visualizing the sunlight channeling through the stone and charging your drink. Stir clockwise, then either hold the stone or set it aside.

5. Watching the sun rise, sip the water, enjoying each drop as you visualize your new path. Think about this charged water intermingling with every cell in your body, restoring it and giving life with this new vision. You can keep the quartz point with you to help you remain focused and clear on your new path.

*Amplify This Spell*
*Combine this spell with the New Path Cleansing Footbath in Chapter 18 to help you bless your new path forward!*

## Inviting Genius Spell

———— ❧ ————

**Astrological Timing:** Mercury's Hour, Gemini/Aquarius Moons, Wednesday

**Celestial Correspondences:** Aquarius, Pallas, Uranus, Mercury

**Energies:** Cleansing, Insight, Ideas

Draw luck and sudden genius to your life with this Uranus-blessed bell charm. Using the power of sound to summon new ideas, you will clear away old energy and call the genius of Uranus into any situation. Use while working on important projects or before meditating to purify your energy field and invite new and exciting information into your mind. For best success, conduct this spell during a sudden storm to charge it up with Uranus's lightning genius.

## You Will Need:

Cinnamon incense, optional

Blue or white candle

¼ teaspoon almond or olive oil

¼ teaspoon dried rosemary

¼ teaspoon ground clove

Fireproof dish

Small bell charm

Sharpie

## Directions:

1. Sit before your altar in your sacred space. Light cinnamon incense, if desired, to heighten the spiritual energy in the room.
2. Anoint the candle with oil. On a small plate, mix together rosemary and most of the clove (reserve some clove for Step 5). Roll candle through mixture and set in fireproof dish.
3. Think of lightning amid the storm resulting from two clouds crashing together, the sudden, brilliant, and electrifying flash of light. With this visualization in mind, light your candle.
4. Ring your bell three times above your head, at the crown. Visualize insight coming through as light. Say aloud:

   *"With the ring of this bell times three,*
   *I call forth genius insight to me."*

5. Use the Sharpie to draw a lightning bolt atop the bell and place it by the candle. Rain remaining clove down upon it. Let it charge up as the candle burns down.
6. Refresh the power of the charm every time there is a storm, if desired, by repeating this spell.

## *Reap What You Sow Cleansing Spell*

**Astrological Timing:** Saturn's Hour, Saturday, Sunday, Waning Moon

**Celestial Correspondences:** Saturn, Scorpio, Vesta, Aquarius

**Energies:** Cleansing, Purification, Old Patterns

Throughout many ancient cultures, grains were a symbol of abundance and provided sustenance through the winter months, as they could be stored easily and safely. As seeds, these important symbols can represent both the past and the future. Using the symbol of grain to reflect on old patterns you wish to stop and fire to transmute them, this cleansing spell will help you work on changing patterns from the past and invite new abundance and blessings.

## You Will Need:

Small Mason jar or glass candleholder

Enough brown rice to support candle in mason jar, or 1 tablespoon if placing in candleholder

Fireproof dish

Small white candle

Lemon wedge

¼ teaspoon dried rosemary leaves

## Directions:

1. In jar or candleholder, pour some of the rice. The rice represent sustenance, as well as patterns of the past you inherit and learn from family. Think about what pattern you are cleansing, giving thanks as you release it. This rice will be used to support the candle, and might get burnt, hence the use of a fireproof dish (be sure to keep an eye on it!). Alternatively, you can support the candle with a candleholder and place the rice counterclockwise by the base.

2. Dress the candle by rubbing it with lemon and sprinkling with rosemary. Nestle candle within the grain in the candleholder. Placing your hands around the candle, visualize what old patterns you are putting to rest.

3. Light the candle, saying aloud:

   *"Grains of past, seeds of the future, the fruits of old harvests that lie in store; I transform old patterns that serve me no more."*

4. Let the candle burn down, and when you are done, throw the grains into an outdoor fire or toss in the trash.

## Chapter 18

# PISCES SEASON

**Pisces Season:** February 19–March 20
**Best Day:** Friday, Thursday
**Best Time of Day:** Venus's Hour, Jupiter's Hour

L
ike the sirens singing their ethereal song, ushering sailors to their shores, Pisces season calls you back to your spiritual center at the end of the journey through the water cycles of the zodiacal year.

In the watery cradle of Pisces, now is the time to explore your dreams, aspirations, fantasies, and the nightly reveries that come with sleep. Using the power of mutable water, you will dive deep to access spiritual information, heal old wounds, and dissolve fears to bring unity. Explore your twelfth house and undo your sense of self, or connect to the dreamy, psychic power of Neptune and channel cosmic information and inspiration. From using the power of flowers to inspire peace, to a Pisces potion to enhance your psychic dreams, and even a cleansing footbath to bless you as you walk a new path in life, you will use the power of water to invite spiritual connection and deep healing. Dive into Pisces season so that you can swim through the currents of life with ease.

## *Water's Depths Meditation*

**Astrological Timing:** New/Full Moon, Monday, Friday

**Celestial Correspondences:** Neptune, Moon, Pluto, Scorpio, Cancer

**Energies:** Healing, Subconscious, Awareness

Plunge into the Neptunian depths of your soul using the imagery and strength of the water lily, a flower associated with growth, calm, and happiness. This spell is helpful for connecting to your subconscious to uncover, access, understand, and heal past wounds. In this meditation, the image of a pond is used to connect to water, to symbolize your individual subconscious, as opposed to universal, collective unconscious. Allow the healing spirit of water to soothe your emotions and the dissolving capability of Neptune to help you disintegrate wounds that may be blocking you. Stones such as labradorite and lapis make good companions to hold in your hand for this spell.

## You Will Need:

Bowl of water
Image of water lily, optional
Neptune Deep Healing Oil (in
    this chapter) or another kind
    of psychic oil, optional

Labradorite and/or lapis lazuli,
    optional

## Directions:

1. Place the bowl of water before you and, if you like, the image of a water lily. At this time, you may wish to anoint your third eye with the Neptune Deep Healing Oil.
2. Hold the stone(s) if desired. Close your eyes and visualize a beautiful water lily floating upon the surface of the water. The water moves, but the lily simply floats, allowing the current to flow underneath without unseating its position. Soak in the beauty of this flower.
3. Imagine what its aroma might be or what the scenery around it might look like. The lily pads and wildlife represent matters on the surface that you may be aware of or may be in the back of your mind. Notice what kind of life and creatures come into your awareness in the scene, to note for future insight.
4. Return your focus to the lily and how it hovers gracefully, unbothered, in the water. Now visualize and follow its roots down through the water, with the water representing your subconscious.
5. As you follow the stem and roots down, notice what you encounter in the water. Once you get down to where the roots plunge into the bottom of the water, back into the earth, connect to your core emotional being here. Ask yourself these questions:
   • What is the root of what is bothering you in your life right now?

- What can the plant spirit of the water lily bring you?
- How, like the water lily, can you go with the flow yet remain rooted?

*Divine Answers from Water*
*Enhance the magick of this healing meditation by using the water to scry, like in the Moon Scrying Spell in Chapter 10.*

# Pisces Energy Alignment

——— ✑ ———

**Astrological Timing:** Pisces Moon, Neptune Transits

**Celestial Correspondences:** Neptune, Pisces, Cancer, Moon

**Energies:** Intuition, Wisdom, Healing

Pisces season brings us to the twelfth house, where you can disintegrate false ideas of yourself and be vulnerable. This is the time to work on opening your third eye and crown energy centers so that you can heighten your psychic connection for your celestial spellwork. You can also do this particular crystal healing layout to connect to your spirit guides and allies.

## You Will Need:

Aquamarine

Amethyst

Mother-of-pearl

Bowl of water

Salt

## Directions:

1. For extra energy, let your stones charge under moonlight if it is available at this time. This can help imbue your spellwork with extra energy.
2. When you are ready to do your meditation, lie down. Dip the stones in the bowl of water, then set them atop your third eye, crown, and heart energy centers (see Chapter 6 for placement information)—the aquamarine right between your brows, the amethyst on your crown, and the mother-of-pearl upon your heart. Place the bowl of water at your feet.
3. Take a few deep breaths deep into your belly, relaxing more and more with each one.

4. Visualize yourself drifting off to sea, the water currents moving through you. Imagine sunlight or starlight shining and lighting up the stones on your crown, heart, and third eye energy centers, channeling spiritual energy.

5. Rest here as long as you like. When you feel ready, arise and cleanse your hands and ankles with the water, grounding you back down to earth. Drop the salt into the water, visualizing cleansing away any lingering energetic blockages. Pour the water down the drain or outside to ground in the earth.

## New Path Cleansing Footbath

—— ✒ ——

**Astrological Timing:** Friday, Venus's Hour, Sunrise, Dark–New Moon

**Celestial Correspondences:** Neptune, Pisces, Chiron, Aquarius

**Energies:** Cleansing, Blessing

Cleanse away the old and bring in the new with this cleansing footbath. Oftentimes, your feet aren't given enough attention—but these vessels carry you forward on your path and hold up your body. On a spiritual level, they can also symbolize emergence into the world. With spiritual Pisces ruling the feet and helping you wash away old labels and ideas, this aligned footbath will help you cleanse yourself of the past and bless yourself with the future so that you may travel a new, magickal path!

### You Will Need:

1 tablespoon dried lavender
1 tablespoon dried jasmine
Basin for footbath

1 tablespoon Himalayan salt
¼ cup Epsom salt
3 star anise pods

### Directions:

1. Boil water as you gather your ingredients.
2. Place lavender and jasmine in a bowl, smelling their aroma as you do so. Breathe in their relaxing scent, reflecting on each herb's meaning (see Chapter 6).
3. Think of what you are cleansing away and the new path you wish to walk on. Put your hands over the herb mixture and visualize

the herbs glowing with your vision, until you feel an energetic resonance in your hands. Say aloud:

*"Neptune, god of the water, planet of deep healing and dissolving.*
*Bless these herbs to bring peace,*
*To cleanse away the old and bless the new."*

4. Use your finger to draw the sigil for Neptune (see Chapter 5) in the herbs, imagining his trident knocking down the old and ushering in cleansing waters to bless for the future.
5. Add boiling water to the herbs, allowing them to steep. When water has steeped and cooled a bit, pour over your feet in the basin, feeling the cleansing, warming energy on your feet. Stir in both salts, imagining them dissolving and cleansing old issues.
6. Sprinkle in any extra dried flowers for blessing, then drop in the star anise as a symbol of spiritual alignment, divinity, and destiny. Take time to wash your feet with care, letting them soak in the cleansing herbs.

# Celestial Dreams Tea

**Astrological Timing:** Full Moon, Neptune Transits, Sunset/Moonrise

**Celestial Correspondences:** Neptune, Pisces

**Energies:** Dreams, Peace, Psychic Powers

Enhance your psychic dreams and invite rest with this calming Celestial Dreams Tea. Ruled by water, potions are an excellent way to connect to Piscean energy. Given that Neptune's influence can be felt more strongly during Pisces season, this can be an excellent time to work on active dreamwork— whether it be dreaming up new aspirations, digesting the meaning of your day through the subconscious realm of your dreams, or inviting a peaceful psychic rest. So sip away, and let your mind wander to new waters!

## You Will Need:

1 chamomile tea bag or ½ tablespoon dried chamomile
¼ teaspoon dried lavender

½ teaspoon dried jasmine
1 star anise

## Directions:

1. Boil water. Gather herbs in a cup and reflect on your intention for this tea: Do you wish to invite peaceful rest? Perhaps induce and welcome psychic dreams? Or unravel the meaning of events of the day and invite healing through sleep?
2. Swirl the cup around so that the herbs dance a bit. Close your eyes and ask for clarity on your chosen subject.
3. Pour boiling water over herbs and let them sit, taking a moment to enjoy the aroma as it steeps. You may wish to add a cinnamon stick for a magickal stirring spoon and for some spice.
4. Sip peacefully. When the cup is empty, discern a meaning in the leftover tea, if desired.
5. Place the star anise under your pillow to help promote psychic sleep.

## Neptune Deep Healing Oil

**Astrological Timing:** Venus's Hour, Friday, Pisces Full Moon

**Celestial Correspondences:** Neptune, Pisces, Chiron

**Energies:** Healing, Intuition, Spirituality, Enchantment

Inspire enchantment, healing, and Piscean calm with this aromatic Neptune-inspired healing oil potion. Neptune invites you to plunge deep into the depth of your mind and its subconscious. A potion of its own, the aroma and magickal ingredients of this oil recipe will soothe your mind and enhance meditation to let your mind wander. Place in a diffuser or rub onto your third eye energy center before meditation or card readings or into your palms before healing. If you have trouble accessing any of the ingredients, you can swap essential oils for herbs, and vice versa—just be sure to account for scent balance and give the oil time to sit and infuse with the herbs.

## You Will Need:

Small bottle for oil
10 drops jasmine essential or
    absolute oil
7 drops lemon essential oil

5 drops lavender essential oil
Pinch ground anise
Pinch ground thyme
⅛ cup fractionated coconut oil

## Directions:

1. On the night of a full moon, place your bottle before you. Using a dropper, carefully place each essential oil into the bottle.
2. Breathe in the fragrance, making sure it matches a scent that will soothe, relax, and engage your third eye energy center.
3. Hold the bottle, visualizing the oil blessing you with the capacity to travel through realms for wisdom and healing.
4. Sprinkle in anise and thyme, then pour in coconut oil. Seal the bottle and swirl it in a clockwise motion, visualizing the healing, insightful energy of Pisces and Neptune. Place the oil out to charge under the full moon.

## Neptune Dissolving Spell

**Astrological Timing:** Pisces Full/Waning Moon, Neptune Transits

**Celestial Correspondences:** Neptune, Pisces, Chiron, Aquarius

**Energies:** Banishing, Healing, Renewal

Channel the power of water and Neptune's ability to dissolve boundaries with this special potion and spell. Whether you're looking to dissolve the root of old wounds, an old sense of self, or even a person from your life, the twelfth house provides the space to disintegrate what is no longer true to yourself so that you can be born spiritually anew in prep for the restart of the zodiacal year with Aries season. By the simple act of dissolving cleansing salt in water and returning it to its spiritual form, you can enact sympathetic magick and dissolve something in your life, thereby allowing such energy to be cycled into something new and better.

## You Will Need:

Bowl of water                          ½ lemon
Sea salt

## Directions:

1. Think about what you wish to dissolve in your life, whether it be old, outdated ideas about yourself, something you wish to heal from your life, or perhaps something someone said.

2. Fill the bowl with water.

3. Say what you wish to get rid of or dissolve by speaking it to the water. You can visualize the energy of that situation going down your arms and hands into the water, or you can speak and pray over the water. Alternatively, you can use a straw to blow through from your belly into the water. This vocal technique will help open your vocal cords to hone your voice as you breathe out that energy with power, deep into the cooling water.

4. Once you have gotten everything out of your system, sprinkle the salt in the shape of a pentacle (a five-pointed star inside a circle) into the water. Visualize the salt dissolving and neutralizing the energy.

5. For a final act of cleansing, squeeze the lemon into the water to cleanse away any extra energetic debris.

6. Dispose of the water through each of the drains in your house, symbolically sending the energy away from your space. Alternatively, you could place the water outside where the sun will slowly evaporate it, allowing it to return to the water cycle and be reborn, just like you!

### Try Sugar Instead
*If you wish to dissolve boundaries between yourself and another person, you can dissolve sugar (instead of salt) into a drink of choice to share to help them sweeten up to you! Alternatively, use the Healing Salt Mixture from Chapter 8 in place of sea salt for an extra magickal boost.*

# Flower Power Potion

—— ❧ ——

**Astrological Timing:** Venus's Hour, Friday, Full Moon

**Celestial Correspondences:** Pisces, Libra, Venus, Neptune

**Energies:** Ease, Unity, Harmony

Invoke oceanic ease and cool down situations with this floating candle spell. Using the power of Neptune to dissolve boundaries and the power of Pisces to go with the flow, no matter how crazy the tides of life are, this spell is designed to help bring ease and unity to any situation. Use this potion to bring people together or to help yourself thrive and survive through otherwise turbulent waters (like a party with some rowdy in-laws).

## You Will Need:

Piece of paper

Blue ink pen

½ teaspoon honey

Wide vase or decorative
    container

Flower food

1 floating candle per person
    involved

Flowers on stems

## Directions:

1. On your paper, write what your intention is. Are you bringing peace and unity to a situation? Are you seeking blessings during difficult times?

2. Fold the paper toward you with an inhale, breathing in the positive, soothing energy of Pisces. Dab your petition paper with a bit of honey. Place the paper down and your vase atop it.

3. Drop a dab of honey into the vase to symbolize healing all wounds. Pour in water, listening to the peaceful, cleansing sound of water rushing in. Sprinkle flower food into the vase and stir clockwise, visualizing all boundaries or qualms dissolving with Neptune's power.

4. Anoint the candle(s) with a dab of honey. Breathe your intention into it/them and place in the water.

5. Next, pinch the flower heads off their stems to represent how you are cutting away the stem of the problem. Breathe in their aroma as you place them in the water around the floating candle(s).

6. Place your hand above the potion, feeling the energy of the beautiful flowers, candle(s), and soothing water underneath. Close your eyes and visualize your intention. Say an affirmation aloud. Light the candle(s) and enjoy!

### Add Extra Harmony

*To heighten the harmonizing potential of this spell (especially when having guests over), combine with the Cosmic Harmony Diffuser Spell from Chapter 13, adding an additional layer of aesthetic magick to invite unity in your guests.*

# Pisces Moon Psychic Mist

———— ✍ ————

**Astrological Timing:** New–Full Moon, Monday, Favorable Neptune Transits, Pisces or Cancer Transits

**Celestial Correspondences:** Moon, Neptune, Pisces, Cancer

**Energies:** Spiritual Purification, Intuition, Peace

Infused with the power of the Moon, this mist is designed to help enhance your sense of psychic feeling. With the alluring, spiritual scent of jasmine to help open your psychic senses; and the peaceful, cleansing lunar energies of lemon and lavender, this spray will uplift and enhance your intuitive sense. Spray before meditating, sleeping, divination, or whenever you wish to enjoy this enchanting floral scent!

## You Will Need:

1 tablespoon vodka

1 vanilla bean

Jar with lid

5 drops lavender essential oil

5–7 drops jasmine essential oil

7 drops lemon essential oil

2 tablespoons purified water

Spray bottle or mister

Moonstone

## Directions:

1. At the new moon, infuse vodka with vanilla bean in a jar.
2. At the full moon, collect the infused vodka. Add lavender, jasmine, and lemon oils. Pour in water. Transfer to spray bottle.
3. Hold your moonstone and visualize the Moon's celestial light shining down upon you, opening your third eye. Drop moonstone into bottle and leave out to charge under the full moon.

# APPENDIX A:
# ELEMENTAL CORRESPONDENCES

## FIRE

**Signs:** Aries (Cardinal), Leo (Fixed), Sagittarius (Mutable)
**Planets:** Sun, Mars, Jupiter (Shared)
**Colors:** Fiery Tones—Red, Orange, Gold, Pink, Yellow
**Aspects of Life:** Identity/Sense of Self
**Themes:** Action, Creativity, Drive, Passion, Vitality, Willpower
**Crystals/Stones:** Bloodstone, Carnelian, Citrine, Garnet, Hematite, Orange Calcite, Peridot, Pyrite, Quartz, Ruby, Sunstone
**Ingredients:** Allspice, Basil, Bay Leaf, Black Pepper, Cinnamon, Clove, Coffee, Cumin, Dill, Fennel, Ginger, Lime, Nutmeg, Olive, Orange, Rosemary, Saffron, Vinegar, Walnut

## EARTH

**Signs:** Capricorn (Cardinal), Taurus (Fixed), Virgo (Mutable)
**Planets:** Saturn, Venus (Shared)
**Colors:** Earthy Tones—Black, Brown, Green, Dark Red
**Aspects of Life:** Physical/Material Reality
**Themes:** the Body, Nature, Stability, Structure, Wealth
**Crystals/Stones:** Chrysocolla, Emerald, Fluorite, Hematite, Peridot, Petrified Wood, Rutilated Quartz
**Ingredients:** Allspice, Beet, Clove, Jasmine, Maple, Olive, Sage, Salt, Wheat

## AIR

**Signs:** Libra (Cardinal), Aquarius (Fixed), Gemini (Mutable)
**Planets:** Mercury, Jupiter (Shared), Uranus
**Colors:** Light Tones of Blue, Gray, Yellow, Lavender, White
**Aspects of Life:** Communication/the Mind

**Themes:** Communication, Connection, Ideas, Reasoning, Thought, Travel
**Crystals/Stones:** Blue Lace Agate, Moldavite, Quartz
**Ingredients:** Almond, Anise, Caraway, Lavender, Marjoram, Nutmeg, Olive, Parsley, Peppermint, Sage, Thyme, Walnut

# WATER

**Signs:** Cancer (Cardinal), Scorpio (Fixed), Pisces (Mutable)
**Planets:** Moon, Neptune, Pluto, Venus (Shared)
**Colors:** Water/Ocean Tones—Blue/Indigo, Gray, Purple, Turquoise, White, Green
**Aspects of Life:** Feeling/Sensing and Intuition/Soul
**Themes:** Compassion, Emotion, Intuition, Renewal, Subconscious
**Crystals/Stones:** Amethyst, Aquamarine, Blue Lace Agate, Chrysocolla, Fluorite, Labradorite, Lapis Lazuli, Moonstone, Mother-of-Pearl, Quartz, Rose Quartz, Selenite
**Ingredients:** Anise, Apple, Blackberry, Cardamom, Coconut, Jasmine, Lemon, Olive, Poppy, Rose, Sugar, Thyme, Vanilla

# APPENDIX B:
# PLANETARY CORRESPONDENCES

In this section, you will uncover correspondences used throughout this book for each of the planets so that you can easily swap out ingredients as needed. As Neptune, Uranus, and Pluto were discovered later than the other planets, you will see notes about old rulers for these signs. If the intentions of the ingredients match or align in some way, you can use the ingredients of the planets that are considered their lower octave. For example, you can inspect Mars ingredients for Pluto intentions, as long as the intentions match, or investigate correspondences for Pluto's element of water. Also note that although the sun and moon are technically not planets, in astrology, they are referred to as such under the umbrella of planets and are treated so here. For a more thorough resource of correspondences, check out *Llewellyn's Complete Book of Correspondences* by Sandra Kynes and *Cunningham's Encyclopedia of Wicca in the Kitchen* and *Cunningham's Encyclopedia of Magical Herbs* by Scott Cunningham.

## SUN

**Element:** Fire
**Day:** Sunday
**Signs:** Leo
**Colors:** Yellow, Orange, Gold, Red
**Aspects of Life:** Consciousness, Purpose, Identity, Creative Expression
**Themes:** Beginnings, Blessings, Confidence, Leadership, Success
**Crystals/Stones:** Carnelian, Citrine, Orange Calcite, Peridot, Quartz, Ruby, Sunstone
**Ingredients:** Bay Leaf, Calendula/Pot Marigold, Cinnamon, Honey, Lime, Orange, Rosemary, Saffron, Walnut

## MOON

**Element:** Water
**Day:** Monday
**Signs:** Cancer
**Colors:** Silver, White, Blue

**Aspects of Life:** Emotions and the Soul, Nurturing
**Themes:** Intuition, Nurturing, Rebirth, Sensitivity, Subconscious Cycles, Wisdom
**Crystals/Stones:** Aquamarine, Moonstone, Mother-of-Pearl, Quartz, Selenite
**Ingredients:** Coconut, Egg, Jasmine, Lemon, Milk, Nutmeg, Rosemary, Saffron, Olive

# MERCURY

**Element:** Air
**Day:** Wednesday
**Signs:** Gemini, Virgo
**Colors:** Yellow, Blue, Orange, Gray, White
**Aspects of Life:** Communication, Thought, Learning
**Themes:** Change, Communication, Flexibility, Ideas, Information, Memory, Travel
**Crystals/Stones:** Blue Lace Agate, Carnelian, Citrine, Hematite, Peridot
**Ingredients:** Almond, Anise, Caraway, Dill, Fennel, Jasmine, Lavender, Marjoram, Olive, Parsley, Peppermint, Rosemary, Sage

# VENUS

**Element:** Earth
**Day:** Friday
**Signs:** Taurus, Libra
**Colors:** Pastel Hues: Light Blues, Green, Purples, Pink, Yellow, White
**Aspects of Life:** Attraction, What We Find Value in
**Themes:** Artistry, Beauty, Charm, Compassion, Connection, Emotions, Harmony, Love, Money, Pleasure, Relationships, Romance
**Crystals/Stones:** Calcite, Carnelian, Chrysocolla, Emerald, Lapis Lazuli, Lodestone, Malachite, Mother-of-Pearl, Peridot, Rose Quartz
**Ingredients:** Apple, Barley, Blackberry, Cardamom, Rose, Vanilla

# MARS

**Element:** Fire
**Day:** Tuesday

**Signs:** Aries, Scorpio (Old Ruler)
**Colors:** Deep Red Hues, Orange, Pink
**Aspects of Life:** Action, Force, Passion
**Themes:** Beginnings, Bravery/Courage, Determination, Power, Strength, Willpower
**Crystals/Stones:** Bloodstone, Citrine, Garnet, Hematite, Pyrite, Ruby
**Ingredients:** Agave, Allspice, Basil, Black Pepper, Coffee, Cumin, Ginger

## JUPITER

**Element:** Air, Fire
**Day:** Thursday
**Signs:** Sagittarius, Pisces (Old Ruler)
**Colors:** Blue, Purple, Turquoise, Sea Green
**Aspects of Life:** Expansion, Abundance, Growth
**Themes:** Authority, Blessings, Influence, Justice, Leadership, Luck, Opportunities, Optimism, Perspective, Power, Prosperity, Spirituality, Success, Wealth, Wisdom
**Crystals/Stones:** Amethyst, Emerald
**Ingredients:** Allspice, Anise, Clove, Maple, Jasmine, Sage

## SATURN

**Element:** Earth
**Day:** Saturday
**Signs:** Capricorn, Aquarius (Old Ruler)
**Colors:** Dark Hues, Black, Blues, Browns, Gray, Green
**Aspects of Life:** Responsibility, Boundaries, Limitations
**Themes:** Agriculture, Authority, Concentration, Discipline, Endurance, Knowledge, Responsibility, Stability, Strength, Structure
**Crystals/Stones:** Carnelian, Hematite
**Ingredients:** Beet, Vinegar

## NEPTUNE

**Element:** Water
**Day:** None (you could use Friday since Venus is considered the lower octave of Neptune)

**Signs:** Pisces
**Colors:** Sea Tones: Blue, Green, Purples
**Aspects of Life:** Collective Unconscious, Psychic Connection, Transcendence
**Themes:** Consciousness/Subconsciousness, Psychic Ability, Sensitivity, Spirituality, Unity
**Crystals/Stones:** Amethyst, Aquamarine, Fluorite, Labradorite, Lapis Lazuli, Mother-of-Pearl
**Ingredients:** Anise, Chamomile, Jasmine, Sage

# URANUS

**Element:** Air
**Day:** None (you could use Wednesday since Mercury is considered the lower octave of Uranus)
**Signs:** Aquarius
**Colors:** Indigo Blue, Bright Yellow
**Aspects of Life:** Revolution, Freedom, the Future
**Themes:** Change, Genius, Global Community, Hope, Illumination, Individuality, Liberation, Motivation, Premonition, Vision
**Crystals/Stones:** Labradorite, Quartz
**Ingredients:** Caraway, Clove, Rosemary, Sage

# PLUTO

**Element:** Water
**Day:** None (you could use Tuesday since Mars is considered the lower octave of Pluto)
**Signs:** Scorpio
**Colors:** Black, Brown, Deep Reds
**Aspects of Life:** Transformation, Endings, Rebirth
**Themes:** Change, Danger, Darkness, Death, Destruction, Justice, Karma, the Occult, Rebirth, Sexuality, Spirituality, Transformation, Wealth
**Crystals/Stones:** Amethyst, Garnet, Labradorite
**Ingredients:** Basil

# APPENDIX C:
# OTHER NOTABLE CELESTIAL BODIES

Asteroids are relatively newer discoveries, so information about them is still being uncovered, as are their correspondences. To find relevant correspondences, feel free to reference the astrological object's element and corresponding signs to get creative in swapping out ingredients. To uncover more information about these and other new, notable astrological bodies, check out *Astrology for Yourself* and *Asteroid Goddesses* by Demetra George and Douglas Bloch.

| Celestial Body | Associated Element | Corresponding Signs | Themes |
|---|---|---|---|
| Ceres (Dwarf Planet) | Earth | Cancer, Taurus, Virgo | Unconditional Love, Nurturing, Mother-Child Relationships, Fertility, Repeated Loss |
| Vesta (Asteroid) | Fire | Virgo, Scorpio | Discipline, Focus, Dedication, Self-Work |
| Juno (Asteroid) | Water | Libra, Scorpio | Meaningful Relationships, Commitment, Intimacy, Power Within Relationships |
| Pallas (Asteroid) | Air | Leo, Libra, Aquarius | Originality, Creative Wisdom, Artisans, Justice/Social Causes, Feminism, Sexual Identity |
| Chiron (Comet) | None | Virgo, Sagittarius | Healing from Wounds, Holistic Health, Wisdom |

# APPENDIX D: STAR SIGN CORRESPONDENCES

In this section, you will find correspondences for each sign, as used in this book. Old rulers (planetary rulers before the discovery of Neptune, Uranus, and Pluto) are noted for the relevant sign. Each sign also includes stones and herbs that match the energy of that sign. Most of these stones and ingredients were chosen with consideration for what is accessible and cost-effective. For example, diamond is one of the traditional birthstones for Aries, but while not an exact equivalent, clear quartz is a much more affordable and accessible option. Once you feel confident with the material in this book, you can check out more in-depth references on astrological correspondences. Look for *Llewellyn's Complete Book of Correspondences* by Sandra Kynes and *Cunningham's Encyclopedia of Wicca in the Kitchen* and *Cunningham's Encyclopedia of Magical Herbs* by Scott Cunningham.

## ARIES

**Aries Season:** March 21–April 19
**Celestial Bodies:** Mars
**House:** First House
**Element:** Cardinal Fire
**Colors:** Red, Orange, Yellow, White, Pink
**Themes:** Action, Courage, Initiating, Passion, Physicality, Vitality, Willpower
**Crystals/Stones:** Bloodstone, Carnelian, Citrine, Clear Quartz, Garnet, Pyrite, Ruby
**Ingredients:** Basil, Blackberry, Cinnamon, Clove, Ginger, Olive, Peppermint, Rosemary, Thyme

## TAURUS

**Taurus Season:** April 20–May 20
**Celestial Bodies:** Venus, Ceres
**House:** Second House
**Element:** Fixed Earth

**Colors:** Green Hues, Flowery Pastel Tones of Pinks, Yellows, Blues, Oranges, Reds
**Themes:** Abundance, Desire, Grounding, Pleasure, Stability, Wealth
**Crystals/Stones:** Chrysocolla, Emerald, Lapis Lazuli, Peridot, Pyrite, Rose Quartz, Ruby, Rutilated Quartz, Selenite
**Ingredients:** Apple, Blackberry, Cardamom, Rose, Sage, Thyme, Vanilla

# GEMINI

**Gemini Season:** May 21–June 20
**Celestial Bodies:** Mercury
**House:** Third House
**Element:** Mutable Air
**Colors:** Blues, White, Yellow, Violet, Turquoise
**Themes:** Adaptability, Communication, Connection, Ideas
**Crystals/Stones:** Aquamarine, Blue Apatite, Blue Lace Agate, Chrysocolla, Citrine, Clear Quartz, Fluorite, Orange Calcite
**Ingredients:** Almond, Anise, Bergamot, Caraway, Dill, Fennel, Marjoram, Parsley, Peppermint, Walnut

# CANCER

**Cancer Season:** June 21–July 22
**Celestial Bodies:** Moon, Ceres
**House:** Fourth House
**Element:** Cardinal Water
**Colors:** Silver, White, Light Blue, Sea Green/Turquoise, Pink
**Themes:** Emotions, Healing, Inner Awareness, Intuition, Nurture
**Crystals/Stones:** Amethyst, Chrysocolla, Citrine, Clear Quartz, Labradorite, Moonstone, Mother-of-Pearl, Rose Quartz, Ruby, Selenite
**Ingredients:** Apple, Calendula/Pot Marigold, Chamomile, Dill, Jasmine, Maple, Rose

# LEO

**Leo Season:** July 23–August 22
**Celestial Bodies:** Sun, Pallas
**House:** Fifth House

**Element:** Fixed Fire
**Colors:** Orange, Red, Yellow, Green, Gold
**Themes:** Creativity, Performing, Pride, Self-Expression, Strength
**Crystals/Stones:** Carnelian, Citrine, Garnet, Orange Calcite, Peridot, Ruby, Sunstone
**Ingredients:** Anise, Calendula/Pot Marigold, Chamomile, Cinnamon, Clove, Dill, Lavender, Nutmeg, Olive, Rosemary, Saffron, Walnut

# VIRGO

**Virgo Season:** August 23–September 22
**Celestial Bodies:** Mercury, Vesta, Ceres, Chiron
**House:** Sixth House
**Element:** Mutable Earth
**Colors:** Brown, Dark Blue, Dark Gray, Black, Green, Pink, Purple, Gold, Yellow
**Themes:** Community, Dedication, Details, Health, Practicality, Self-Sufficiency
**Crystals/Stones:** Amethyst, Aquamarine, Blue Apatite, Carnelian, Chrysocolla, Citrine, Peridot
**Ingredients:** Almond, Barley, Caraway, Celery, Dill, Fennel, Lavender, Maple, Oak, Parsley, Peppermint, Rosemary, Salt, Walnut

# LIBRA

**Libra Season:** September 23–October 22
**Celestial Bodies:** Venus, Juno
**House:** Seventh House
**Element:** Cardinal Air
**Colors:** Pink, Purple Hues, Blues, Black
**Themes:** Aesthetics, Art, Balance, Connection, Peace
**Crystals/Stones:** Amethyst, Aquamarine, Bloodstone, Citrine, Emerald, Lapis Lazuli, Rose Quartz
**Ingredients:** Apple, Barley, Cardamom, Maple, Marjoram, Rose, Sugar, Thyme, Vanilla, Wheat

# SCORPIO

**Scorpio Season:** October 23–November 21
**Celestial Bodies:** Pluto, Juno, Mars (Old Ruler)
**House:** Eighth House
**Element:** Fixed Water
**Colors:** Bold, Intense Colors: Red Tones, Orange, Gray, Black
**Themes:** Intimacy, Passion, Transformation, Truth
**Crystals/Stones:** Aquamarine, Bloodstone, Carnelian, Garnet, Labradorite, Ruby, Rutilated Quartz
**Ingredients:** Allspice, Basil, Blackberry, Black Pepper, Clove, Dill, Ginger, Peppermint, Saffron, Vanilla

# SAGITTARIUS

**Sagittarius Season:** November 22–December 21
**Celestial Bodies:** Jupiter, Chiron
**House:** Ninth House
**Element:** Mutable Fire
**Colors:** Red, Orange, Yellow, Gold, White, Purple, Blue
**Themes:** Beliefs, Optimism, Perspectives, Philosophies
**Crystals/Stones:** Amethyst, Blue Lace Agate, Citrine, Emerald, Garnet, Labradorite, Lapis Lazuli, Ruby
**Ingredients:** Anise, Clove, Coffee, Ginger, Maple, Nutmeg, Rose, Rosemary, Sage

# CAPRICORN

**Capricorn Season:** December 22–January 19
**Celestial Bodies:** Saturn
**House:** Tenth House
**Element:** Cardinal Earth
**Colors:** Earthy, Dark Tones: Black, Gray, Brown, Green, Deep Red
**Themes:** Achievement, Ambition, Perseverance, Practicality
**Crystals/Stones:** Bloodstone, Carnelian, Clear Quartz, Fluorite, Garnet, Hematite, Ruby
**Ingredients:** Barley, Beet, Cinnamon, Jasmine, Poppy, Thyme, Vinegar

# AQUARIUS

**Aquarius Season:** January 20–February 18
**Celestial Bodies:** Uranus, Pallas, Saturn (Old Ruler)
**House:** Eleventh House
**Element:** Fixed Air
**Colors:** Turquoise, Silver, Indigo, Purple, Blue, Yellow
**Themes:** Change, the Future, Genius, Innovation, Originality, Possibility
**Crystals/Stones:** Amethyst, Aquamarine, Clear Quartz, Fluorite, Garnet, Labradorite, Moldavite, Selenite
**Ingredients:** Anise, Apple, Lavender, Olive, Peppermint, Rosemary, Sage

# PISCES

**Pisces Season:** February 19–March 20
**Celestial Bodies:** Neptune, Jupiter (Old Ruler)
**House:** Twelfth House
**Element:** Mutable Water
**Colors:** Purple, Blue Tones: Blue, Aqua, Green, White
**Themes:** Mysticism, Peace, Psychic Ability, Spirituality, Understanding, Unity
**Crystals/Stones:** Amethyst, Aquamarine, Bloodstone, Blue Lace Agate, Fluorite, Labradorite, Moonstone, Mother-of-Pearl, Selenite
**Ingredients:** Anise, Clove, Jasmine, Lavender, Nutmeg

# APPENDIX E:
# HOUSE CORRESPONDENCES

## FIRST HOUSE

**Themes:** the Self, the Body
**Associations:** Aries, Mars, Cardinal Fire

## SECOND HOUSE

**Themes:** Wealth, Value, Your Relationship with Material Possessions
**Associations:** Taurus, Venus, Ceres, Fixed Earth

## THIRD HOUSE

**Themes:** Communication
**Associations:** Gemini, Mercury, Mutable Air

## FOURTH HOUSE

**Themes:** the Home
**Associations:** Cancer, Moon, Ceres, Cardinal Water

## FIFTH HOUSE

**Themes:** Pleasure, Hobbies/Creativity, Children
**Associations:** Leo, Sun, Pallas, Fixed Fire

## SIXTH HOUSE

**Themes:** Daily Routines, Service, Health, Work Habits
**Associations:** Virgo, Vesta, Mercury, Mutable Earth

# SEVENTH HOUSE

**Themes:** Partnerships, One-to-One Connections
**Associations:** Libra, Venus, Juno, Cardinal Air

# EIGHTH HOUSE

**Themes:** Death, Sex, Transformation
**Associations:** Scorpio, Pluto, Juno, Fixed Water

# NINTH HOUSE

**Themes:** Search for Meaning, Beliefs, Foreign Travel
**Associations:** Sagittarius, Jupiter, Chiron, Mutable Fire

# TENTH HOUSE

**Themes:** Vocation/Career, Societal Contributions/
Accomplishments, Authority
**Associations:** Capricorn, Saturn, Cardinal Earth

# ELEVENTH HOUSE

**Themes:** Groups, Friendships, Humanitarianism
**Associations:** Aquarius, Uranus, Pallas, Fixed Air

# TWELFTH HOUSE

**Themes:** Self-Undoing, Endings, New Beginnings
**Associations:** Pisces, Neptune, Mutable Water

# APPENDIX F:
# PLANETARY HOURS

The ancient founders of Western astrology dedicated not only each day of the week to a planet but also a planet to every hour, known as a planetary hour. Dividing the hours of daylight and darkness into twelve hours each, these early astrologers marked a pattern of the planets as the Sun, Venus, Mercury, the Moon, Saturn, Jupiter, and Mars, with the first hour after sunrise being ruled by the planetary ruler of the day. For example, "Sun"day, the first hour following sunrise, is ruled by the Sun. The hours follow the pattern after that. Of course, we know now that the only times there are equal days of light and darkness is at the equinoxes, so estimate this to the best of your ability. Additionally, Neptune, Uranus, and Pluto were not known at the time of these divisions, so use these planets' "lower octave": Venus's hour for Neptune, Mercury's hour for Uranus, and Mars's hour for Pluto.

| Estimated Hour Starting at Sunrise | Sun. | Mon. | Tues. | Wed. | Thurs. | Fri. | Sat. |
|---|---|---|---|---|---|---|---|
| 1 | Sun | Moon | Mars | Mercury | Jupiter | Venus | Saturn |
| 2 | Venus | Saturn | Sun | Moon | Mars | Mercury | Jupiter |
| 3 | Mercury | Jupiter | Venus | Saturn | Sun | Moon | Mars |
| 4 | Moon | Mars | Mercury | Jupiter | Venus | Saturn | Sun |
| 5 | Saturn | Sun | Moon | Mars | Mercury | Jupiter | Venus |
| 6 | Jupiter | Venus | Saturn | Sun | Moon | Mars | Mercury |
| 7 | Mars | Mercury | Jupiter | Venus | Saturn | Sun | Moon |
| 8 | Sun | Moon | Mars | Mercury | Jupiter | Venus | Saturn |
| 9 | Venus | Saturn | Sun | Moon | Mars | Mercury | Jupiter |
| 10 | Mercury | Jupiter | Venus | Saturn | Sun | Moon | Mars |
| 11 | Moon | Mars | Mercury | Jupiter | Venus | Saturn | Sun |
| 12 | Saturn | Sun | Moon | Mars | Mercury | Jupiter | Venus |

| Estimated Hour Starting at Sunset | Sun. | Mon. | Tues. | Wed. | Thurs. | Fri. | Sat. |
|---|---|---|---|---|---|---|---|
| 1 | Jupiter | Venus | Saturn | Sun | Moon | Mars | Mercury |
| 2 | Mars | Mercury | Jupiter | Venus | Saturn | Sun | Moon |
| 3 | Sun | Moon | Mars | Mercury | Jupiter | Venus | Saturn |
| 4 | Venus | Saturn | Sun | Moon | Mars | Mercury | Jupiter |
| 5 | Mercury | Jupiter | Venus | Saturn | Sun | Moon | Mars |
| 6 | Moon | Mars | Mercury | Jupiter | Venus | Saturn | Sun |
| 7 | Saturn | Sun | Moon | Mars | Mercury | Jupiter | Venus |
| 8 | Jupiter | Venus | Saturn | Sun | Moon | Mars | Mercury |
| 9 | Mars | Mercury | Jupiter | Venus | Saturn | Sun | Moon |
| 10 | Sun | Moon | Mars | Mercury | Jupiter | Venus | Saturn |
| 11 | Venus | Saturn | Sun | Moon | Mars | Mercury | Jupiter |
| 12 | Mercury | Jupiter | Venus | Saturn | Sun | Moon | Mars |

# BIBLIOGRAPHY

Bobrick, Benson. *The Fated Sky: Astrology in History.* New York: Simon & Schuster, 2005. Kindle.

Cunningham, Scott. *Cunningham's Encyclopedia of Magical Herbs.* Woodbury, MN: Llewellyn, 1985.

————. *Cunningham's Encyclopedia of Wicca in the Kitchen.* Woodbury, MN: Llewellyn, 1990.

George, Demetra, and Douglas Bloch. *Asteroid Goddesses: The Mythology, Psychology, and Astrology of the Re-Emerging Feminine.* Lake Worth, FL: Ibis, 2003.

————. *Astrology for Yourself: How to Understand and Interpret Your Own Birth Chart.* Lake Worth, FL: Ibis, 2006.

Gerber, Richard. *Vibrational Medicine.* 3d ed. Rochester, VT: Bear, 2001.

Hadas, Julia Halina. *Moon, Magic, Mixology.* Avon: MA: Adams Media, 2021.

Hall, Judy. *Judy Hall's Crystal Zodiac.* London, UK: Octopus, 2017.

Kynes, Sandra. *Llewellyn's Complete Book of Correspondences: A Comprehensive & Cross-Referenced Resource for Pagans & Wiccans.* Woodbury, MN: Llewellyn, 2013.

McCarthy, Juliana, and Alejandro Cardenas. *The Stars Within You: A Modern Guide to Astrology.* Boulder, CO: Roost, 2018.

Morrison, Dorothy. *Everyday Sun Magic: Spells & Rituals for Radiant Living.* Woodbury, MN: Llewellyn, 2005.

Zolar. *The History of Astrology.* New York: Arco, 1972.

# INDEX

Note: Page numbers in **bold** indicate main discussions and magick associations.

*The Modern Witchcraft Book of Astrology*